IMPROVE YOUR ODDS

THE

FOUR PILLARS

OF BUSINESS SUCCESS

Alan Yong

Alan Yong

Table of Contents

Acknowledgements

Over the course of my time on this Earth, I have discovered that there are only a few things in life that I am really passionate about. Chief among those things are gardening, cooking, and business. My love for the soil led me to spend seven years helping to build Smokeys Daylily gardens into one of the largest daylily growers in the world. I'd also long dreamed of writing a cookbook so that my grandchildren might one day be able to recreate many of grandpa's dishes that they so loved in their childhood years. That has yet to happen, largely because I am mindful of the tremendous commitment in time and effort that such an endeavor would entail.

That third passion is the one that brings us to these pages today. My forty years of business experience have been filled with intermittent suggestions from others that I write a book like this. And it is probably something that I should have done before now, but – just as with my earlier plan to write a cookbook – I recognized that I would need to make a substantial commitment if I was to produce the sort of business book that could actually be of service to entrepreneurs.

Oddly enough (and as so often happens with these things), it was my involvement in another business endeavor that lit a fire under me to finally get to work on this project. It started about a year after I founded DNotes – a Bitcoin alternative digital currency, in an industry that is perhaps best known for its lack of central control and sound leadership. I had convinced the DNotes team that the best strategy for us to be successful on a long-term basis was to manage DNotes as a business without actually controlling it as one.

My belief was that this approach would enable DNotes to maintain the vital characteristic of remaining decentralized. At the same time, we focused on developing our centralized ecosystem while providing leadership guidance to our community and DNotes. I ended up utilizing every bit of my business experience and leadership skills and built a couple of awesome online communities that eventually became instrumental in making the writing of this book possible.

Alan Yong

This has been an amazing experience of teamwork and collaboration in a global setting. I am most grateful to the DNotes and CryptoMoms communities for their encouragement and support. I am particularly indebted to Theodore (Joe) Hauenstein and Kevin DeLucenay for their endless support and encouragement. Joe, in particular, has made significant contributions to make the publishing of this book possible. I am most grateful to the DCEBrief's team led by Ken Chase, along with Cindy Williamson, Marc Fortenberry, Chris Cooper, and Timothy Goggin; providing me with great research and editing support. Timothy has been most helpful in narrating the DNotes story with editing help from Fernanda Powers, who also contributed to the writing of the Smokeys Gardens' story. Additionally, I like to express my thanks and appreciation to Robert, Brandon, Mark, Nele, and many others who assisted in different ways to make the publishing of this book a success.

I am most grateful to everyone who has generously supported my Kickstarter campaign for the launching of this book project. I trust that it will go a long way to help this book realize its goal of being a helpful resource for small business owners and those who are thinking about starting new businesses.

Above all, I am deeply indebted to my family - and most especially my dear wife Lucy for her love, encouragement, and support to see me through.

I am eternally grateful to all who have taught me well, including George Williams College, and Northern Illinois University where I earned my MBA over forty years ago.

This book is dedicated to small business owners worldwide. May you all find the success you seek, and see all your dreams come true.

With best wishes and kind regards,

Alan Yong

Introduction

As we continue to strive for a better life, at times in frustration and a feeling of helplessness, let us agree on one simple truth: where you are right now matters far less than where you are going from here. There is little that can be done to regain missed opportunities or retroactively correct the mistakes made in the past.

However, with an awareness of our shortcomings, willingness, and commitment to change, we can learn from history and the mistakes of the past. We can also gain deep knowledge and wisdom from others who have gone down the same path and beyond. This book honors those who have already achieved everything that they desire in life and in business, but is specifically written for those whose aspirations remain just beyond their grasp.

I do not believe that long term business success is an accident or the result of good fortune. If you have already achieved great success, then you and your employees must have done many things right. I deeply respect you for your accomplishment.

However, for those who have yet to achieve their objectives, including anyone whose business still has room for dramatic improvement, this book should prove thoughtful, insightful, and helpful. This is a book written specifically for startups, small business owners and their management teams (companies ranging in size from new startups to 500 employees), and can provide them with the help and guidance they need to gain the success for which they strive. If that sounds like you - if you're passionate about what you are doing and desire nothing more than to obtain the type of business mastery that will help you be the true architect of your company's success, then read on.

Furthermore, since employees are one of the key pillars of business success, this book is also written with them in mind. They will find helpful information, meaningful insights, and inspiration; all of which can help them to become better employees with a deeper understanding and appreciation of what it will take for the business to succeed. As a result, they will have ample opportunities to contribute to the success of the business, thereby, making it easier for them to align themselves with the company's missions, goals, and objectives. Ultimately, this will help employees enjoy greater success in their career.

Additionally, I have made a persuasive case to replace the much disliked traditional "Employee Performance Review" with "Mutual Goals Review" that is significantly more rewarding and collaborative in promoting employees' career advancement than the subjective grading of employee weaknesses. It serves the mutual interest of both the company and the employees with a unified purpose of fulfilling the company's goals, missions, and the ultimate vision.

I want you to take a moment and envision yourself either designing or redesigning your company. As you do so, imagine that you are creating a complete and functioning system with a multitude of subsystems and component parts. Now imagine that this system you're creating is somehow disordered to the point where some of those components are not working properly, causing those subsystems to fail to work in harmony with one another. Sounds like a disaster waiting to happen, doesn't it? Unfortunately, that lack of harmony and disordered component parts is a common feature of many new business enterprises. All too often, even the most energetic entrepreneurs fail to give enough attention to the finer details of the company's design before they launch their business ventures.

In order for that imagined system to operate as it should every component has to work as designed, in unison with every other component, each fulfilling its essential role within the various subsystems that make up the whole of your operation. They must be unified in purpose, efficient, and capable of performing at optimal levels on a consistent basis. When you have a company that can achieve those standards, then you have a company that can achieve almost any goal.

Ideally, your goal is to create the type of company that is almost impossible for your competitors to fully replicate. The thing is, though, that you cannot do that all by yourself. Yes, it all has to start with you, but at some point you will have to begin to rely on a team to help you achieve your vision. Ultimately, that team will end up being one of the most important factors in determining just how successful your new enterprise will be.

While it is clearly important for any team to strive for the ultimate success of a business venture, there are far too many instances where even the best team fails to follow through on the company's vision. Entrepreneurs routinely start out with great visions and expectations and then find that everything seems to unravel on them within just a few short years, if not earlier.

The question is why? Why do even the most visionary entrepreneurs often find their best and brightest ideas failing to gain traction in the marketplace? In some unfortunate cases, successful and established companies took a sudden turn for the worst, and failed. Why do so many businesses fail so early? More importantly, what steps can you take now to ensure that you're not just another one of those statistics? This book's purpose is to answer that question and many more, while helping you develop a new way of approaching your own quest for business success.

If there is one fact that is crystal clear, it is that your vision will be central to everything you do from this point forward. To succeed, you must start with a clear and coherent vision for your business, and you must be passionate about it. That vision, however, is not your mission. It is instead the ultimate goal that guides the strategic decision-making that you employ to reach your objectives.

Do you have that vision yet? It's fine if you don't yet have that perfect clarity, as long as you know that you're not fully there. Problems occur when people think that they have a vision, but later find out that they began without any real sense of the bigger picture. Too often, they discover much too late that what they had were short-term objectives and a sense of a mission, but no overriding vision to help them get to where they needed to be to achieve their ultimate goals. In other words, many entrepreneurs simply start out focusing on the wrong elements of the success equation, and then end up wondering why their plans fail.

Start with your vision, and that will provide the destination that you are ultimately trying to reach. From there, you work on establishing initial objectives and goals that you want to achieve. Then you develop the winning strategies that can offer you the best opportunity to reach those goals. Subsequently, you learn to master the art of flawless execution of your winning strategies. Notice, if you will that none of the team members we mentioned earlier are even a consideration at this point in the process. There's a good reason for that: you have to create the vision, mission, and short-term goals for your company before you even think about recruiting help. Those elements have to be firmly in your mind - or better yet, documented so that you have something to which you hold yourself accountable before you ever make that first critical hire.

Only when you are done establishing your vision, mission, goals, and strategies can you actually begin to build a team. At that point, you have to find the type of competent people you believe to be most likely to buy into your business philosophy and mindset. You need people who are capable of being inspired by your exceptional leadership style and strategic vision, as that is the only way to ensure that they are in turn capable of helping you to create the type of business culture that your enterprise needs for success. That culture should motivate everyone in the company to consistently deliver their highest level of commitment and performance, and thereby contribute to the efforts to reach your business goals. Once you reach that point, you will have created a system that basically channels the mindset of its leader even when your attention is elsewhere. You will have designed a system for effectively cloning yourself.

The key, though, is to ensure that the "you" that you're cloning is the best "you" it can be! This book is designed to help you find that best part of you, so that you can begin to build a team with the type of unified vision and purpose needed to achieve true success.

Improve Your Odds

In many ways, a lot of new entrepreneurs take the same approach to business startups that they would take in a casino. Many just assume that the inherent risk associated with starting a new company makes such a venture little better than gambling. That belief is often strengthened when they take note of the statistically high rate of new business failures.

The fact is, though, that there are some key differences between business ownership and a few hours spent in a casino. In the gambling world, the outcomes are truly random and thus outside of your control. And while there are certainly games where you at least have some input into how you choose to play a certain hand or wheel, the fact is that all of the primary components of each game are designed to be beyond your ability to influence. It means that any betting victories you may have are entirely the result of chance. That's why we refer to gamblers who win as having been "lucky."

Gambling is a fickle thing, though. For every person who sees Lady Luck smiles their way when they hit the jackpot, there are an untold number of players who lose everything they have. And while professional gamblers can certainly develop elaborate strategies and spread their play out over a larger number of games in an attempt to create more favorable odds by taking advantage of the laws of probability, in the end they remain as vulnerable to the whims of chance as any amateur first-time player. Even the best gamblers can go bankrupt if they experience a long enough series of losses.

Business is only a gamble to the extent that life itself is a gamble. After all, no one can control every outcome in life, and the same is true in the business world as well; unpredictability is one of life's surest constants. Still, there are clear differences between an activity like gambling that is almost entirely random in nature, and something like business ownership that has no greater randomness to it than most other areas of life. More to the point, in business there are ways to effectively manage and exercise a large measure of control over the odds you face each day. That is, if you have aspirations of achieving something more than mediocrity. On the other hand, if you create a new startup without a clear plan for taking your rightful place among the top thirty percent in your industry, then you really are engaged in a huge gamble and should consider yourself lucky if you manage to remain in business for even five years.

Unfortunately, that is the reality for the vast majority of new entrepreneurs. Most never make it. In fact, the odds are so stacked against the unprepared new business owner, and the outcomes are so incredibly uncertain, that it is actually easy to understand why so many people consider the launch of any new business enterprise as little more than a gamble - and a rather large one at that. That's also one of the reasons why it is often so difficult to convince others to bet on your great ideas and business concepts. The risks are high, and the potential for loss in such an investment is simply too great for most people to bear.

Just consider the data. While estimates vary, the consensus seems to be that somewhere between 67% to 80% of all new businesses fail within the first 10 years, though the exact numbers are often dependent on the industries involved and other factors in the economy during any given time period. My own studies and observations have revealed that approximately 60% of all new enterprises fail within the first five years, with a minimum of 70% failing before the end of their first decade of existence. Then there's the fact that many businesses that manage to make it past that first decade do so in a state of intermittent profitability, never achieving either success or stability.

If that sounds like a steep mountain to climb, then you're obviously paying attention. Still, there are reasons why all of those businesses fail, and there are methods and strategies that you can use to help you avoid many of the pitfalls that serve to trap the lion's share of would-be entrepreneurs. Regardless of whether you are considering the launch of a startup, a restart, or a start-over, you cannot allow yourself to be deterred by the odds. You should, however, recognize how daunting they are, and do all that you can to ensure that you're prepared to overcome them.

Let's be clear: I'm talking about reversing the odds so that they are actually in your favor! Better yet, my goal is to help you become the engineer of your own success so that you can reduce as much uncertainty as possible and stack the odds in your favor. And what would that mean for your chance of business success?

Well, if we can agree that at least seventy percent of all businesses currently fail within ten years, reversing those odds would mean that your business would have a seventy percent chance of success. And I'm not talking about the kind of success where you just keep the doors open and manage to scrape by week after week. It's my mission to show you how you can increase your odds of realizing the type of success that will have competing among the upper echelons of your chosen industry.

It can be done, and in the following pages of this book I will explain exactly how you can accomplish this seemingly impossible feat.

Just consider what it would mean to you to know that your business has a 70% chance of achieving true success:

1. That increased chance of survival will make it easier for you to obtain seed money from investors.

2. If you know that the odds of success are in your favor, you will feel less guilty about receiving investments from friends and family members who might otherwise be placing their college funds or retirement accounts at risk.

3. The knowledge that you've done all you can do to stack the odds of success in your favor can serve to motivate you and unleash the true power of your business passion.

Before you make up your mind about whether or not this is even possible, remember the words of Henry Ford:

"Whether you think you can or you think you can't. You're right"

I would only add to that one thing: if you want your new company to be the best in class, then you've come to the right place. This is the book for you. Of course, if you think that being best in class does not matter, then it does not matter.

Quest for the Best

No company ever becomes the best in class by accident. You have to position your business to achieve that status, and that is a mission of such size and scope that you simply cannot accomplish it without implementing winning strategies. All of this represents the type of serious commitment that will require the utmost focus, discipline, patience, persistence, tenacity, and leadership skills if you are to be successful. And yes, those are the principles and traits that Jim Collins identified in his book "Good to Great." He found them all in abundance among level 5 leaders, and referred to this philosophy of duality as the Stockdale Paradox - a reference to the late Vice Admiral James Stockdale's coping strategy during his imprisonment in a POW camp during the Vietnam War.

Stockdale had described the mental state that it took to survive the camps as one that recognized the importance of acknowledging your current challenges while still maintaining the focus, discipline, patience, persistence, and tenacity needed to maintain faith in your own vision for success.

That is the essential trait of leadership that is all too often lacking in the business world today. It is a principle that recognizes that leaders choose to accept the blunt and brutal facts of their reality, but never lose sight of their belief that the right team and strategy, skillfully executed, can ensure that they prevail when all is said and done.

In business, many fail to meet their goals because they never build the type of foundation that provides them with the complete package they need for success. The ability and discipline to focus on all of the things that matter, along with the passion to excel in every single department, function, and business activity, is absolutely critical for ensuring that you have the optimum opportunity for business success. You cannot afford to let yourself be blindsided by overconfidence due to a misguided faith in your ability to excel in just one or two skill sets - or hope that superiority in those areas will somehow mask your mediocrity in every other area.

It doesn't really matter if you believe that you have tried your best, or that you have worked hard to do your part. When others on your team fail to bring their skill sets to bear in a way that helps you to excel in every area of your business, then you leave yourself open to failure. One or two areas of competency are not enough to succeed; the true measure of your competitive superiority can only be found in the total of all of your scores.

Everything is interrelated. It might seem as though poor performance in one area of your business is isolated to that function, but that is simply not the case. Poor performance in one aspect of your business degrades performance everywhere else. It means that when you are weak in certain areas of your company's operations, your scores are not only lower in those areas but they impact the scores of other areas as well. Ultimately, that causes your overall business performance score to suffer.

Remember, your business is a complete system. Every subsystem within your company either helps or harms every other subsystem. All of those components or subsystems have an impact on the output and performance of every business function and the business as a whole. When there is weakness in any area, the business is weaker than it should be. Components that fail to perform at peak levels tend to bring down the performance of other components, and the overall impact is magnified in proportion to the total number of interdependent parts at work within the system. Moreover, the more complex the system is, the more impact each individual component has on the entirety of the company.

Complexity increases interdependence, and magnifies the impact any given component has, whether for good or ill. When components operate at peak performance, greater productivity and positive benefits can be enjoyed. When there are weaknesses, the exact opposite is true.

It can sometimes be hard to envision just how important it is to deliver a complete package, but there is an example that can offer some illumination on the subject. Just think about your favorite talent show or sports competition where winners are determined by a panel of judges, with the total scores from eight different criteria used to make that decision. A competitor who scores 10 out of 10 in two categories, but who has mediocre scores of 7 of 10 in the other six categories will ultimately lose out to the competitor who manages to score 8 of 10 across all eight categories.

And so it is with the world of business. Being the best in class in every category is always a winning strategy whenever it is tried. To be the best in class, you have to realize that everything matters, though there are always a few that matter a lot more than others. The most important of them all are the four pillars of business success; you, your great ideas, your employees, and your customers. Focus on them to improve your odds of business success.

Chapter 1 - Be Equal to or Better than the Competition

Few people ever stop to consider what being in business really means. Very often, new entrepreneurs make the mistake of launching their companies without ever considering what they're really up against. Make no mistake: unless you are the inventor of a completely new and revolutionary product that is uniquely unlike anything the world has ever seen, you will have competition. Unless your service is so groundbreaking that it provides consumers with solutions to problems they probably didn't even know they had, you will have competition. The fact is that there are very few exceptions to this one fundamental truth about business: for most entrepreneurs, the task at hand is to figure out how to compete for your share of a market that is already being serviced by the competition's offerings.

There are relatively few examples of innovative ideas that are truly revolutionary in nature. Yes, there are innovations that periodically alter the landscape of some segment of the consumer marketplace, but those dynamic and revolutionary business changes are not as common as many might think. For the vast majority of new entrepreneurs, business is about entering a market that is already being served by others. And that means most new business owners are men and women who believe that they can compete against those established companies.

Unfortunately, it can be a costly mistake to launch a new business based only on the assumption that "you can do it too." All too often, that assumption leads entrepreneurs to start companies with the goal of simply being in business. If you believe that you can achieve success simply by going through the motions, chances are that you will struggle to achieve your goals. That rule applies whether you are starting a new business or adding new products and services. If you are in business just to be in business, then you probably won't be in business long.

To be successful, you have to have a compelling reason for your actions. When you're launching your own startup company, you need to at least have confidence in your ability to match the best in your industry. Without that underlying core belief, you might as well continue to work for someone else, because you will likely never achieve the type of success you need if you are to remain in business for any length of time.

Alan Yong

Of course, to reasonably believe that you can compete with the best, you first have to believe that you've positioned your company in a way that provides it with the best chance for fulfilling your vision. You have to earnestly believe that your strategic plans provide you with the position you need to obtain that often-elusive competitive edge. And even then your well-planned strategies could fail if you do not have the right foundation on which to build. So, start with a basic inventory to determine whether you've positioned yourself for success. Remember: without a firm foundation, nothing you build will ever last.

Gut-Check Time:

Any entrepreneur who expects to achieve success with a new startup had better be prepared to do a little self-evaluation before he or she begins. Every new business' foundation is only as strong as its founder, so you have to be sure that you and everyone in your life are fully prepared for the quest for success. That determination can be more easily made by answering two basic questions:

1. Do you have the requisite passion and tenacity you will need to actually make your business a success?

There's a reason this question is first, because if you cannot honestly answer it in the affirmative then none of the remaining questions matter. Search your heart and assess your reasons for launching your company. If those reasons amount to nothing more than simply creating your own job to fill an income vacuum, then you have chosen the wrong path. A lack of passion for your chosen business will inevitably end in disaster.

The fact is that history is littered with the remains of small businesses that were doomed by their owners' lack of passion. If you think about it, chances are that you know or have known a small business owner who lacked passion for his chosen business. I've seen many entrepreneurs go through the motions without any real love for their companies. Many have struggled for years, waiting for everything to turn around of its own accord. Some have even gone so far as to press their own family members to join them in an attempt to make things work but often with no better result.

If you want to avoid that dreary outcome, then be sure that you have the passion you need. You have to love what you do, and wake up every day excited at the prospect of meeting the day's challenges. That enthusiasm can fuel the desire you need to maintain true passion for your company over time. Without it, your chances for success are severely handicapped before you even begin.

2. Do you have the support you will need to endure the rough times?

Are you married, or in a committed relationship? If so, then be sure to obtain your partner's pledge of support before you even begin your business venture. That means discussing the pros and cons of your company launch before you ever fully commit to bringing it to life. The reality is that you both need to be ready for whatever comes - good or bad - and prepared to work through the tough times. The last thing that you need when you suffer a setback at work is to have added trouble manifest at home. If your spouse or partner has any doubts or misgivings about business ownership, be sure to resolve those issues right away.

This is absolutely critical. There is virtually no chance that you will go through each day without experiencing some level of difficulty, and when work gets rough your home is the only refuge you will have when you need to rejuvenate and reorganize for another day. You must be able to leave your troubles at work if you expect to survive business ownership for the long-term. If your spouse cannot fully commit to your endeavor, then you are going to come home to a whole other set of business-related problems.

Face it: even if he or she is not a formal partner in your company, your spouse is a de facto business partner just by virtue of your home relationship. Can you rely on that partner to help to keep the home a place of peace and tranquility that provides you with the atmosphere you need to ensure that your batteries are fully recharged before you venture out each day in search of a better life for your family? If not, then that is an issue you should address before you launch your business.

The thing to remember is that you have almost no chance of being better than the competition if your life is so unbalanced that you cannot even find the peace and comfort you need when you come home at the end of your day. There are few if any exceptions to this simple rule. The best planning in the world will do little to change things if you lack a strong support system, and even your best efforts will still leave you feeling as though you end each day with more problems than you had when it began.

Spousal support is therefore one of the most critical elements of business success. It is part of the foundation on which you will build your entire business structure. As a result, it is among the first things you must secure before you begin. Think of it like a video game, if you will: you do not get to move on to level two until you have successfully completed level one.

Your Mindset Matters

Mindset is the key that will help you to unlock the door to success. To be the best in class, you have to have a mindset that says that you must be equal to or better than your competition. And, as I noted earlier, if you believe that you cannot be at least equal to your rivals, you are right. With that mindset, you will never be able to match them, since you will have already set yourself up to accept something less than the best. That lack of faith in your own ability to succeed will almost invariably shape your destiny in a way that ends with your failure.

Remember, from a statistical standpoint, you are more likely to fail than succeed anyway. Is that acceptable to you? If so, then just recognize that your business success is being left to little more than the whims of fate. The odds are against you, and will remain so for as long as your mindset tells you that you can never be the equal of your competition. It is only when you fundamentally alter that mindset and start to commit to being nothing short of the best that you can finally begin to turn those odds in your favor.

For most entrepreneurs, the focus is always on that end result. That leads to a great deal of discouragement when setbacks occur, since those goals can end up looking as though they're moving even further out of reach. That's the problem with having a mindset that sees only the ultimate goal: it causes you to get frustrated when the goal is so distant that your daily efforts seem to move you no closer to success. Success might be your final and ultimate goal, but the wise man recognizes that it is not typically something that can be realized overnight.

The proper mindset for success recognizes that victories can arrive on a daily basis. When you refocus your mind to emphasize that which you can do today rather than that which still lies out of reach, you can achieve tremendous progress. And while some daily victories might be more meaningful than others, they can all have bearing on your ultimate quest for success if they continue to move you in the right direction. Even on those days when you seem to miss the target altogether, just aiming in the right direction can be enough. Once that mindset begins to be established, the only thing that can keep you from eventual success is your own unwillingness to continue to fight. As long as you do not give up prematurely, your skills will continue to be honed, and your ability to garner larger and larger victories will only grow over time.

There's a reason why so much of this first chapter begins with an emphasis on you and your state of mind. You need to have a mindset that is both consistent and sustainable if you are to succeed. In fact, mindset is the main difference between success and failure in business, because it is an essential part of the foundation on which you will build. Mindset directly impacts your goals, your expectations, your strategies, and your actions. By the time you are finished with this chapter, you should have an understanding of what it takes to be a champion for your business. You will better understand why you as the owner and leader of your business team must be the first true believer in your own commitment and ability to be at least the equal of your business rivals. And once you truly believe that you can be their equal, you must begin to believe that you can be their better – only then, you can build a business that is truly the best in class.

Business mirrors sports in so many ways. Obviously, there are some differences as well, such as the fact that you as the owner are both the coach of your team and its star player. But, like any sports team, your company team wants to win. You want to be the champion in your league. To win that championship, however, everyone on your team - the coach, the star player, the supporting cast, and even the water boy - all have to be willing to push themselves to their limits. They have to share a belief that they can remain together in their effort to win, irrespective of setbacks, lost games, or even perceived bad calls during the game.

Just as it is in sports, mindset in business is a belief system that governs your unique skill sets and knowledge base. That is not to say that it is all about knowing more than everyone around you, or being the most highly skilled in your field, however. It is about exploiting your maximum knowledge and skill sets to achieve the very best outcome. The mindset reflected in a total, unyielding, and unwavering commitment and dedication to hard work, as you strive to master that which you need to master, and execute every task to the best of your ability - accepting nothing less than your personal best.

Because it is a belief system, mindset can seem almost religious in nature. Like many religious faiths, it can be contagious and have a direct impact on your organization's culture. When they are strongly-held and conveyed in a powerful and consistent manner, beliefs can spread throughout any environment, and enact dramatic changes that move people, organizations, and entire societies. That is why it is so critically important that you begin with the right mindset - because it is your beliefs that will help to shape your team, your business systems, and your entire company.

As the leader, it falls on you to set the company direction, serve as an inspiration, and motivate everyone in your company with whom you interact. It is your words, deeds, and beliefs that will influence the people on your team over time. It is vital that you recognize the impact that you have, since there is a cascade effect at work throughout the company. Each person that you influence will then influence others throughout the business enterprise. Over time, that cascading dissemination of your beliefs becomes your organization's culture.

Think about that. The very fact that your vision, beliefs, and actions can create a company-wide culture should give you pause. You are, for good or ill, the source of your company's life essence. What you are, it will become. You drive change and set the tone for your organization's accomplishments. You blaze the trail that your team members then work to turn into a navigable highway. That makes it critically important that you know where you are leading everyone before you ever take that first step - lest you be forced to start over down a different path later. And you don't want to have to start again, since that can have crippling, unproductive effects on your business, allowing your rivals the time they need to either outpace you in the marketplace, or catch up to you if you were already in the lead.

So guard your words and give heed to your own actions. Always remember just how powerful the mindset of a leader can be. Throughout history, great leaders have capitalized on their own mindsets to sway the opinions and beliefs of thousands and even millions of their followers. Within your own organization, it is you who is that great leader. To use that awesome responsibility and power to maximum effect, you have to know exactly where you want your team to go, and then make sure that your mindset is properly conditioned to get them there.

Being Best in Class

Where mindset is concerned, one thing is seemingly unalterable: most people in the world are followers. They do what they see others do, because it is in their nature to stay within their comfort zones. That causes them to take the convenient routes mapped out by those who have come before them, remaining within the confines of the well-traveled and safe roads that everyone else traverses. That is the safe route and the choice of almost every man and woman in the past. It is the choice most people make today, and will almost assuredly be the preferred option for the vast majority of people in the future. There is a powerful argument to be made for taking that safe route.

Being a follower means never taking the type of risks that could have any serious impact on your life. To be sure, that lack of risk severely curtails the possibility of large rewards, but it also diminishes the chances of large losses too. For most people, it is enough that they have the opportunity to exist in a state of relative safety somewhere in the mediocre middle of life, shielded from the dramatic extremes of true success and abject failure. They are willing to trade dreams of something bigger for the promise of some small sense of security.

The very fact that you dream of building your own business is a powerful sign that you are someone more than one of the several billion people who are content to be followers. You have that leadership spark within you, and envision something more than a sheltered life filled with only small risks and equally small rewards. You dream bigger than that, and have courage to match those aspirations. Still, taking that leap outside of your comfort zone does not necessarily mean that you have to reinvent the proverbial wheel.

That is correct; you don't have to reinvent that wheel to find success in the marketplace. All you have to do is make it a little bit better, a little more adaptable to different terrain and weather conditions, or add some other improvement that differentiates it from the competition. Think about it this way: if you just want to match your competition then you have to do what it takes to be their equal. That means doing exactly what they are doing, or as close to it as you can get. But if you want to be better than your rivals, then you need to offer something more. Sometimes that means minor improvements over their products or services; other times it means doing something radically better than anyone else in your field.

Now, none of this is to suggest that you have to be a market leader right away. It can be perfectly fine to travel down an existing highway that is already well-traveled by others in the marketplace. For many new entrepreneurs, that initial journey down a well-traveled road can provide the time needed to gain critical experience and expertise that can be utilized later as you look to carve out your own path as a trailblazer. The time will come when you will have to be ready to blaze your own trail. That is, after all, the only way to move away from the competition and actually rise above them, as you develop the competitive edge you need to differentiate yourself and ultimately dominate within your niche market.

To get there, you have to learn to focus your resources on things that offer you the best return. The best option is to emphasize areas of improvement that your competition will find difficult to replicate, and direct your efforts to making those areas your chief selling points. That puts you on the path to offering everything that your rivals offer, but in a new and improved way.

Eight Areas Where You Can Strive to Be Best in Class

1. Be More in Tune with Your Customers.

If you want to be the best in class, work to gain a better understanding of your customers. Discover what they really care about, and develop strategies for keeping pace with those sentiments as they change and evolve over time. Often times, even the top businesses can get into a rut when it comes to maintaining a solid understanding of how their customers think. Companies both large and small can easily fall into the trap of assuming that attitudes, wants, and needs remain static over time. Nothing could be further from the truth!

In fact, customer attitudes change for a variety of reasons, and with greater frequency than most people realize. Changing economic conditions, evolving technologies, new service models, and subtle cultural shifts can all cause a company's market to gradually abandon it over time. However, if you can learn how to engage your target market in a way that helps you to keep pace with those customers' needs, and do it better than your rivals, then you will have gained the type of competitive advantage that can help you to become the best in class and remain there on a long-term basis.

2. Focus on Customer Service.

This can be considered a corollary of the first suggestion, since it flows naturally from the idea of getting in tune with those customers. Many new entrepreneurs fail to grasp that customer retention is both easier and less expensive than customer acquisition. That simple axiom is all you need to know to understand that the surest way to success is to recognize that nothing good will ever happen to you if you don't learn how to keep the customers you have.

Now, it is important to recognize that your current customers are somebody else's target audience. Each of your rivals covets those customers, and will be focused on drawing them away from you, so you have to have a strategy that services your existing clientele in a way that builds trust and loyalty to your brand. You have to be best in class at customer retention to avoid spending all your time and effort chasing new customers to replace those you lose to your competition. You need only do the math: if each new customer you gain is merely replacing one that you've lost due to inferior customer service, can you really expect to grow your company?

Develop processes for engaging those existing clients and becoming truly responsive to what they say they need. That may end up including loyalty programs or better credit terms for long-term customers. It may include a new willingness to add the products or services they say they want. It may even require that you consider loyalty discounts or other benefits. Or it may just require a subtle change in the way your team communicates with each customer. The point is that you cannot be the best in class if you lose customers as fast as you acquire them.

3. Differentiate.

Differentiation has long been critical for business success, but there is a new school of thought that actually places such a strong emphasis on differentiating yourself from your competitors that it essentially suggests that companies not even focus on being better than their competition. That approach asserts that being different is more important than being better. It basically disavows the idea of competition by suggesting that entrepreneurs focus exclusively on separating themselves from comparison with rivals. Rather than competing with other companies directly, you simply focus on communicating the things that make you different than everyone else. While I would not go that far in my praise of differentiation, there should be no doubt about its importance in the quest to be best in class.

Differentiation is about more than simply being different than your rivals. It is about communicating those differences. As the marketplace grows ever more crowded, with online-only stores and service outlets rising in competition with brick and mortar enterprises, being able to effectively communicate those differences is more important than ever before. Think about a product or service you regularly use, and then think about the businesses you know that provide those offerings. Chances are that the main thing separating those companies in your mind is the effectiveness of their communication.

The best companies are able to communicate their advantages in a way that truly differentiates them from everyone else in their market niche. They are keenly interested in and aware of how others perceive them. To rise to the top of your field, you have to adopt that same mindset and focus on those customer perceptions. Your customers - both existing and prospective - have to see how you differ from the competition. That provides them with the unique selling proposition that explains why your company is special and worthy of their business.

4. Focus on Better Branding.

Being best in class requires careful attention to everything, because everything truly does matter. Nowhere is that more true than in how you brand your company, because that goes right to the heart of what customers think and feel when they see your logo or hear your company name. Even if you do everything else better than your competition, chances are that you will be unlikely to garner any real traction in the marketplace if your branding is weak. Your brand should be in line with your unique selling proposition so that you create that indelible impression in the minds of each and every customer who encounters your message.

That means finding the right message, the right images, and the right level of consistent image promotion necessary for building a company image that fully complements your desire to be the best in class. From your storefront to your website, consistent, quality content is an absolute must. If you have already started the branding process, evaluate it now. Consider the things you need to achieve with your messaging, and look for any weaknesses in your current approach. Evaluate everything, including your signs, printed materials, online presence, packaging, and more. Nothing should be off limits, including your company name.

If you have or plan to have a brick and mortar operation, then give special attention to how the store looks. A well-kept storefront is essential for conveying a professional image. It also helps both customers and employees to feel more at home, and can even increase employee happiness and productivity. Something as seemingly minor as how your team answers the phone can help or harm your company image.

Trust is a key consideration in many products and services; such as financial services. Consequently, if that is the business you are in, building a trusted brand is invaluable. In other cases, value, reliability, and great customer services are valuable to have in what your company is best known for.

5. *Invest in Public Relations.*

Public Relation is an extension of your branding and marketing strategies. Many small business owners do not exploit the power of good public relations because of the wrong assumption that this important function is limited to companies with big budget that can hire expensive PR firms. It certainly helps to have the connection of PR firms and their expertise, but much positive work can be done with a relatively small budget.

However, it is essential to ensure that you must have a product or a service that is worth promoting. Furthermore, if you do not have your house in order it is a losing proposition to just throw money at PR. When you have a well-oiled machine across your entire organization with a great product or service coupled with great customer support, good PR work is invaluable.

Alan Yong

PR is a campaign to promote your company and products in the best of light. It focuses on sharing your success story with your targeted audience by building awareness, credibility, interest, and respect for your company. When done effectively, it has the power to influence and shape the industry, building a trusted brand for your products. Using clear and consistent messages, as you share your story with passion and conviction, you rally your fan base to support and share your cause.

With credibility and substance, supported with deep knowledge of your trade or industry, you can build a large following as a thought leader and be frequently quoted as an authority. This in turn, will create a demand to include you as a speaker in industry exhibitions along with press interviews.

Good PR takes dedicated and sustained efforts to get your messages out to your target audience through the use of multiple mediums, including frequent press releases, blogs, speaking engagements, participation in trade exhibitions, and social media campaign. It is best to have a strategic plan well laid out on a yearly basis. In many ways, good PR is a great tool to promote the concept of "pull marketing" when people want to know more about you and want to buy your products based on the awareness, credibility, and trust you have built for your brand. Along with a commitment to great customer satisfaction this is a far more effective approach to customer acquisition, retention, and referral, as opposed to the "push marketing" approach of hard sales.

6. *Be Better at Identifying Trends to Target New Markets.*

A big part of your mindset has to be future-oriented. While there always seems to be more than enough in the present to occupy any entrepreneur's mind, sustainable growth can only come when you develop an attitude that is always forward-looking. Give heed to not only what is happening in the here and now, but to the changes that are currently shaping the what-will-be. Today's evolving trends give us clues about what tomorrow's reality will look like, and the entrepreneur who learns to identify these trends will always have an advantage when it comes to meeting the needs of tomorrow's customers.

That ability to see new markets before they fully develop can help to ensure that your business will be well-poised to serve its existing market on a long-term basis, and will also give you early opportunity to advance into new markets as they emerge. That alone can help to ensure that you remain a cut above the competition, especially if they end up being caught flat-footed due to a lack of foresight.

7. *Identify Complementary Products and Services.*

Do not get complacent with your products and service offerings. One of the biggest mistakes any company can make is to become so self-satisfied that complacency sets in. That can lead to stagnation, especially when your customers' tastes or needs change. We live in an age of ever-increasing expectations, with more people than ever before demanding more and more from the businesses they frequent. Can you be agile enough to recognize the need for adapting to changing circumstances? If not, then it would be a good idea to develop that agility now.

This hearkens back to that need to develop solid engagement with your customer base so that you have a proper understanding of those customers' wants and needs at all time. That can help to drive the development of new products and services by providing you with the consistent, reliable market research you need to minimize risk. It also enables you to add new offerings that complement what you already do.

A good example of this occurred as a result of the Internet's increased popularity. As their customers became more reliant on having anytime access to wireless capabilities, many restaurants, bars, and other shops began to offer free wireless service to their patrons. Today, there are many places where a drinking establishment would find itself at a competitive disadvantage if it failed to offer free Wi-Fi. With the right strategy and tools in place, you can be that type of trailblazer, and identify those complementary services and products before your competition even realizes that their customers' needs have changed.

8. *Be the Best Employer.*

Alan Yong

A lot of employers talk about the happiness of their employees, but too few actually give it anything more than lip service. For many business owners, the relationship between company, management, and the employee team is reduced to nothing more than a wage agreement. Oh sure, there may be internal campaigns to generate a sense of teamwork and self-actualization, but when you talk to many of those employees outside of the workplace you'll quickly discover that much of that employee-centric talk is just that: talk.

If there has been one major sea change in the employment scene over the last few generations, it has been the weakening of the bond between companies and those that they employ. Much has been said and written about how employees lack loyalty to the companies that employ them, but this has been a two-way street. Companies across the spectrum of the marketplace all too often see their own employees as just another commodity to be acquired or disposed of as needed. Large scale firings have been common for decades now, as large and mid-size companies alike simply cut their labor forces whenever their profits look to be lower than they had forecast. That's not a recipe for loyalty; that's the recipe for an "every man for himself" mentality.

Consumers today almost routinely express the belief that large companies simply do not care about their customers. Those companies have a culture that sends precisely the wrong signals to the people who they rely on to buy goods and services. If you have ever had occasion to contact one of those companies - whether it's a power company, bank, or large retailer, then you've almost certainly experienced that disinterest firsthand. In too many instances, customer service issues are met with a slow response, an uncaring attitude, or an outright refusal to help. The employees often seem to care not a whit whether the company retains your business or not.

That employee attitude has an origination point, of course: the corporate culture. In almost every instance, when an employee fails to demonstrate that he cares about the company's customers it is because that employee believes that the company does not care for him. In a perfect world, of course, every employee would simply do his or her job without respect to such things. But this is not a perfect world. People have feelings that are influenced by their beliefs, and when your employees think that you view them as nothing more than cogs in your company machine, they are likely to reflect that lack of care in their interactions with your customers.

To prevent that, you have to be the best in class when it comes to being an outstanding employer. Does that mean that you have to pay your employees more than they can receive elsewhere? Not necessarily. Obviously, if you want to retain skilled and highly motivated personnel, you need to ensure that they are receiving competitive wages. But if you think that the size of the paycheck is all that matters, then think again.

Today's employees are more likely to demonstrate loyalty to both you and your customers when you show that you can provide a competitive wage and the right kind of working environment. That environment should be one in which professional and career development is stressed, real efforts are made to demonstrate your appreciation for everyone on the team, and every effort is made to provide the kind of benefits that people actually need: flexible scheduling, an employer who actually values the members of his or her team, and an atmosphere that promotes positive engagement on every level.

It might seem like a small thing, but that is simply not the case. It takes a lot of work to develop strong relationships with your team members, but that work is well worth the effort if it produces a culture that values all aspects of the company. When you can show that you value your team, they will in turn value your business, and its customers. And those customers will notice.

Know Yourself; Know Your Rivals

Sun Tzu recognized the power of knowledge when he noted, "If you know your enemy and you know yourself you need not fear the results of a hundred battles." Though your competitors are not actual enemies in that Art of War way, they are rivals, and thus the principle laid out in those wise words is as important in business as it would be if you and those rivals were facing one another on the field of battle. We fear those things we do not know, just as we fear those things about ourselves that cause us to be filled with doubt. Knowledge has a way of eliminating fear.

Alan Yong

The fact is that the path to being equal to or better than all your rivals is a road that must be paved with bricks of knowledge. You must be intimately familiar with your competition, and identify their strengths, their weaknesses, and the threat that they pose to your dreams. You must gain the ability to objectively compare and contrast their strengths and weaknesses with your own, so that you can discover your opportunity for gaining an advantage. This is the war that you must fight, and it need not evoke fear if you work to gain the right level of knowledge about both yourself and your rivals.

If that sounds simplistic, rest assured it is not. The fact is that this is an area of competition where almost every small and mid-size business fails. If you doubt that, then try this experiment the next time you see two small businesses in the same local area. Go into one of them and ask the owner or manager what he or she really knows about that competitor. Ask about things like price differences, special offerings, or service terms. You will be shocked to discover that in most instances, the people who run either of those businesses knows almost nothing about the other.

As scary as that thought might be, it is even scarier when you consider how differently sports teams approach issues of competition. Take a football team, for example. If team A has a weekend game scheduled against team B, one of the first things the coach and staff do is to obtain as much game footage of the opponent as they can possibly find. They scour that footage to study and review exactly how that team plays on both sides of the ball. They examine the quarterback's cadence, his throwing rhythm, how he hands the ball off to his running backs, and how he calls audibles at the line. They review the routes the receivers run, offensive line blocking schemes, and every other aspect of the offense they can think of. And then they take the same approach as they study their opponent's defense.

And you know what? While team A is busy studying team B's game footage in preparation for the big game, the latter is just as busy studying the former's game films. That is just one indication of just how much value the average football team places on gaining knowledge about its opponents. Yes, that's right: sports teams spend a great deal of time gaining knowledge about their rivals before they meet them on the field of battle. Coaches study game film. Players study game film. And then they develop strategies to counter - or try to counter - the opponent tendencies that they identify.

34

It is actually more than a little worrisome to realize that unpaid college athletes spend that much time learning about their opponents, while the average business owner spends almost no time studying his own rivals. At the same time, however, that presents an enormous opportunity for you and your goal of becoming the best in class. If you are willing to commit to "studying the game film," then you can gain the type of knowledge that most of your eventual competitors will never even attempt to discover.

To truly know yourself and your competitors, you have to commit to being an expert on your industry. You must work to become deeply informed about its current state, future expectations, and looming challenges. You need to identify the problems that your industry is trying to resolve, and learn everything you can about your competitors' solutions. That is the only way to ensure that you are presenting better solutions in a better way. Does that sound like hard work? You are correct, it is.

To accomplish this goal, you have to be completely invested in your dream. It requires extensive knowledge, steadfast dedication, and decisive action. It will require that you use all of your faculties to develop the deep level of knowledge needed to create one or more strategies that can enable you to win the battle you are undertaking. And remember you cannot develop the right strategy for victory if you are ignorant of your competition, your industry, or your own company.

You have to work to find a way to position yourself to do that which others either will not or cannot do. If it helps, think of all of this as a game. Why do football teams study film to develop strategies? Is it so that they can identify what the other team does well and then go out and play to that opponent's strengths? Or do they instead try to identify that other team's weaknesses so that they can exploit them? Obviously, it is the latter.

In our game, the marketplace is our field of battle and we study our opponents in order to determine what we can do that they cannot - or a better or more compelling way to do even those things that they already do. To accomplish that feat, you have to change the rules of the game, and you do that by ensuring that you know more about them than they are willing to discover about themselves. It is that knowledge that will enable you to do things that they simply cannot or will not do. And, as you repeat that process of research, identification, and strategy development over time, your efforts will enable you to reach new heights and truly be better than your competition. With continued success, you accumulate the resources and capabilities your competitors can only dream of having. Hence, one of your best means of gaining the competitive edge is to do things others will not do, so that one day you will be in the position to do the things others can not do.

Chapter 2 - The Four Pillars

As we have discussed, everything in your business is interrelated. Consequently, every system within your company impacts and is impacted by every other system. Still, there are some critical components within any business that rise to a higher level of importance. With the exception of one-man enterprises, there are four components in every business that are so important that they need special consideration: you, your great business idea, your employees, and your customers. Together we call them the Four Pillars of Business Success. If you drop the ball in any of these four areas, you will significantly diminish your odds of achieving business success.

The importance of your role simply cannot be overstated. You are the coach, star player, and the creator of your business story. It is your vision that has to serve as inspiration for everyone in the company. Because you play such a critical role, you'll find that much of this book's focus will time and again circle back around to you. Your business, for better or worse, will end up being a reflection of you.

Your great idea is the reason your company exists. It encompasses the full range of products and services that you offer to your customers, and plays a large role in just how successful your company will ultimately end up being. When you have great ideas, you'll have great products and services. And when there is a demand for those products and services, and you have a great organization to help you meet that demand, you can experience tremendous success. Of course, even the best organization can achieve nothing without great products, services, and customer demand. Without viable ideas, you're virtually guaranteed to fail.

Employees are the main engine of business success, and the most complex component of the four. Obviously, whenever human interaction enters the equation, things can get complicated in a hurry. Moreover, these are the members of the team that you have to lead to achieve positive results for your company. Since you cannot do everything yourself, your team must be an extension of their leader to ensure that everything is done properly. As a result of their important role in the overall business process, multiple chapters of this book are devoted to Employees.

Last, but certainly not least, are the customers. Without fail, customers are the fuel that powers the growth of any company and make success possible. Unless your company is their only option - or they can otherwise live without the products and services that you offer, then your customers are all people who have chosen to make the conscious decision to give you their business. They will be choosing your products and services over all of your various competitors.

Customers make that choice based on their positive interactions with everyone and everything in your organization, and will make a different choice when those interactions are negative. In every instance, their patronage of your business is entirely voluntary, and subject to change at will. As a result, it is vital to appreciate just how important customer loyalty actually is, place a premium on customer retention, and actively work to ensure that you never take them for granted. Your fundamental mission and purpose to be in business is to successfully satisfy the customer's want for the product or service purchased.

First Pillar of Business Success: You

The most effective entrepreneurs never get tired of thinking about their business, its future, its customers, and its employees. They are never tired of examining the various components that make up the business, because they understand how important it is that everything functions properly. They know that a truly functional system has to have every subsystem functioning properly too. In short, they understand that whole "vision" thing.

When it comes to achieving business success, your vision is everything. But what does that mean exactly? A lot of times, books like this tend to talk about concepts like vision without ever examining it in detail. All too often, readers like you can reach the end of a book that talks about vision and be left with only the most nebulous grasp of what the word actually means within the business context. Before we proceed any further, let's take a moment to delve into what we are actually discussing when we address the issue of "vision."

That Whole "Vision" Thing...

Based on a revised quote from George Bernard Shaw, John F. Kennedy expressed his vision best when he said, *"Some men see things as they are and say why. I dream things that never were and say why not."*

Your vision is all about the future, sometimes involving things that have never been done. It is basically a mental image of your business as you see it existing somewhere in the future. That image is constructed in accordance with your actual goals and dreams, and is usually a reflection of not only how you see the world but of the place you envision your company occupying within that world. It answers the most fundamental question of all:

"Where is my business actually going?"

Now, if that sounds like the type of lofty question that requires a great deal of thought, you're right. Entrepreneurs don't generally stumble upon their business visions by accident. This is the type of future-centric imagining that actually requires active consideration and deep thought. You have to think about these things to create the type of concrete mental image that can serve as a destination worthy of the trip. For while your business vision has little to say about the strategic path you take to reach your ultimate destination, it says everything about what that destination actually is.

Your business vision can be inspired by a wide range of important company-specific concerns. For example, your company reputation as an employer and service provider can help to solidify your vision. Your financial objectives are an important consideration as well, as you want to ensure that your vision is broad enough to provide adequate income for you, your family, and your employees. Your desired rate of business growth, market sustainability, and even your own passion for the enterprise are all factors that come into play.

Naturally, your overall inspiration for going into business for yourself must be considered as well. As an entrepreneur, you have to have a reason for doing what you do. To be a successful entrepreneur, you are grounded by the principles and values you find important. All of those factors can help to create the vision that you need to ensure that your company is always moving in the right direction.

Ultimately, what you need to create is a mental image of precisely what your company would look like in its most ideal form. Imagine your company in its most perfect possible form, fulfilling its mission to the best of your expectations. When you can envision that reality, you have your vision in hand.

Your business vision is not a roadmap for success. It is a destination. Think of it this way: your values come first, and help to determine the type of business you want to create. Values are defining features of any company, and serve as a manual that can help to guide how everyone within an organization interacts at every level. Your values help to define how you view your employees, your customers, and your business mission. They serve as guidance to instruct your employees in their dealings with one another, with vendors, and with your customers. They are the glue that binds together the various components that make up your business culture. Still, your values should not be confused with vision. Values are reasons why you do the things you do to make that vision a reality.

With those values, you create and implement strategies. The strategies you use are the real roadmap, and help to determine the path you navigate on your way to realizing your vision. Strategies are the how-to tactical plans that can change over time as new information appears, new challenges arise, and customer needs and wants change. Roadmaps are like that, after all; there are times when unexpected construction and detours can force you to slightly modify your course for a time. At the end of the day, however, you have your destination in sight and can rely on your map to get you there as long as you continue in the right direction.

Vision is something else entirely. Your values are your reason for why you do things as you do. They are constant, and generally unyielding. Strategy is the map that offers the most viable path to ensuring that you reach your objective. It is flexible, and subject to modification when necessary. Strategy is about devising the best plan and tactic to best accomplish your mission and objective. Your success or failure is dependent on your execution of the strategic plan. Your vision, on the other hand, is the destination that you are trying to reach.

Why Vision Matters

The fact is that companies are complex organisms. If your business were alive, it would be comprised of a seemingly endless array of cells that must all be working optimally if the organism is to remain in sound health and capable of normal function. Defective cells create systemic weaknesses that can cause one system after another to fail. There are cascading effects that bleed from one area of the business organism to the next, creating disorder and dysfunction as they go. Left to run its course, that sort of disorder ultimately leads to a weaker company that falls short not just in the areas of original dysfunction, but across a wide spectrum of subsystems and systems.

Effective leadership is the best weapon against such disharmony. That means having the right business vision, and the type of infectious passion for your company and its mission that can help you to assemble and lead the team that can make that vision a reality. Because it serves as your ideal goal, that vision should be at the center of all your strategic thinking. Before you can have a workable business plan, viable strategic roadmaps, or buy-in from present or future team members, you have to have a vision.

A powerful and well-conceived vision can serve as the best inspiration for your employees as you work to shape them into copies of yourself. A great vision inspires the type of employee buy-in necessary for ensuring that your business values and company culture permeate your organization at every level. With the right level of buy-in, and the proper advancement of your core values and culture, you can rest assured that your vision is affecting every area of your company. You will have created an entity that has the type of single-minded purpose it needs to relentlessly pursue your objectives. Best of all that unity of purpose will provide the sense of direction your employees need to guide them along the right path even when you are not around.

Vision also matters because we have all seen examples of its absence. If you think about it for a moment or two, chances are you can rattle off a short list of small businesses you've encountered that seemed to lack any discernible direction. Businesses like that often start off with no real impact, gain no headway, and eventually settle into a restful state of mediocrity - if they're fortunate enough to survive at all, that is.

The fact that you have taken the time to get this far into this book is clear evidence that you expect something more from your own efforts. That's half the battle won already...

Second Pillar of Business Success: Your Great Idea/s

"Capital isn't that important in business. Experience isn't that important. You can get both of these things. What is important is ideas." - Harvey S. Firestone

For those outside the world of the entrepreneur, the marketplace often appears to be little more than a cluttered realm of colorful and varied products, useful and questionable services, and carefully-tailored messages hawking every offer under the sun. At its core, however, it is even simpler than that. The marketplace is nothing more than an ecosystem of competing ideas. If you hope to succeed as an entrepreneur, then you need to recognize the importance of your own ideas.

At its simplest, business is about selling the power of your own ideas. Those ideas can manifest as products, services, or both, but your success only comes when you convince a sufficient number of customers to trust your ideas more than they trust those of your competitors. Before you can do that, however, you have to actually have ideas and a willingness to take them to market. But what makes an idea a good business idea? How can you be sure that the idea you have is something that you can actually convince others to buy?

Business ideas - whether in the form of services or products - must be able to meet unserved or underserved customer needs and wants. When your products and services have a ready-made responsive audience, then you have an idea around which you can construct a potentially successful business. Innovation can be a great starting point, and the best ideas are always innovative, but innovation alone gets you nowhere. You can invent the most wonderful product in the world and still achieve nothing if you never manage to meet a single customer want or need. But with a responsive audience of consumers, your ideas can achieve almost anything.

The best business ideas should always offer a unique selling proposition as well. If your product or service is something that is somehow different than everything offered by your competitors, then you have something that customers can only get from you. That doesn't mean that you strive to be different just for the sake of being unique, but when you can truly say that your idea is different in a way that makes your customers lives better, then you know that you have the right idea to power your success.

Your idea should also be applicable to a market that offers potential revenue growth. The economy is like a living organism, and like most living things it often experiences injuries and illness in different areas of its "body." If your idea targets a market that is currently in a state of downturn, then it can be difficult to leverage the odds of success in your favor. The most promising ideas are, as you might expect, those that put your company firmly within a market niche that offers growth potential.

Great ideas can encompass everything from truly disruptive technologies to new business systems and services that offer customers an opportunity to eliminate middle men. Even products that offer only slight benefit improvements can provide an outlet for success, since they improve customers' lives. That's important to remember; given that truly groundbreaking innovation is such a rare thing in history.

Naturally, the real key to any great idea lies in the amount of passion you are able to harness in support of your effort to bring it to market. Without real passion for your ideas, your ideas will lack the type of sustainability needed for success. With passion, however, you can ensure that you remain committed to your ideas over time, and provide yourself the best chance for achieving your dreams of success.

Third Pillar of Business Success: Your Employees

Among all your business assets, the employees rank as the most valuable. That statement seems like such a no-brainer that you might even be wondering why I bothered to include it. Well, there's a good reason for mentioning it here, and it has to do with how few companies actually seem to believe that their employees matter. Make no mistake; the vast majority of companies that have mission or company value statements include some variation of that theme. If those companies actually believed those words, their actions would reflect those beliefs.

But do they?

Over the last several decades, there has been a well-documented decrease in the loyalty between employer and employee. Whether it is in manufacturing, retail, or the service industries, many employers have seemed to move to a model where employees are viewed as just another commodity that can be disposed of or replaced with minimal impact on the bottom line. Far too many companies have taken the productivity gains that a competent, experienced, and dedicated labor force can offer, and traded them for short-term increases in profitability achieved only from reductions in labor costs. That is not a roadmap for sustainable success.

The fact is that your employees are your company's most important asset. When you want to build a best in class business, you have to be able to trust that every aspect of your company is being operated as effectively as if you were doing the work yourself. And since you cannot simultaneously do everything yourself, you have to rely on your team to handle much of the work. How can you do that with a staff that is underappreciated, undervalued, and considered little more than a disposable asset? The simple answer is that you cannot.

Your employees impact every aspect of your business. They affect - whether for good or for ill - everything from your sales success to your overall profitability. They can impact your company image, enhance or poison your business culture, and enrich or diminish every system that helps your business function in a state of harmony. When your employees are properly trained, managed, and empowered to achieve the results you need, your entire company will be stronger.

Have you ever encountered a business with surly employees or one in which the employees lack motivation or interest in their jobs? Of course, you have. The world is filled with companies both large and small that have employees who seem wholly disinterested in effective customer care. For many customers who encounter such employees, that experience with the company is often the last. That is perhaps the most important indicator of just how much damage employees can do when business culture fails to provide them with the vision and value-driven environment needed to ensure that each member of the team properly represents the company's interests.

Employees are so valuable to your business success that much of your focus and energy should be directed toward locating, hiring, and empowering the best hires that you can find. That means finding the best employees that are available. Your hiring process should be intense, and designed to find only those people who can be molded to comport with your business vision. That means something more than just hiring the people with the most impressive educational or employment resume. It means actually working to identify potential hires who could literally be you if called upon to do so.

Once you find each employee, the real work begins. You must be committed to training, and imprinting your own vision on each member of the team. Every one of your team members must be trained to treat your company vision as their own, and positioned within your organization in a way that makes maximum use of their unique skills and capabilities. If you can find your employees' passions and learn to match them to the tasks and systems that allow them their best opportunity to channel those passions into results for your company, then you will go a long way toward providing them with the motivation they need to perform at peak efficiency.

Of course, your work is not done even then, since proper positioning of a great hire is just part of the process. Over time, you need to value your employees enough to help them increase their own value. Just as the coach of a sports team works tirelessly to help each player improve his or her skill set, so too does a good business leader strive to help his team members enhance their own business skills. Do everything you can to ensure that they have the latest industry knowledge at their fingertips, and provide the training they need to keep them at the top of their profession.

Employees are, without a doubt, your most important asset. In fact, they're so important to your overall success that we'll take an even more detailed look at them in Chapters 9 and 10.

Fourth Pillar of Business Success: Your Customers

Customers are vital for any business organization, and no company can survive without them. While it is not uncommon for an aspiring entrepreneur to cite the desire to "be his own boss" as a primary motivating factor for starting his own business, the fact is that entrepreneurs have bosses too: every single customer who provides the revenue every business needs to succeed. Even when you are properly positioned to lead your company, have a great business idea, and the best employees you can find, success will remain elusive if you cannot find the customers your business needs to power its growth.

When you recognize this fact, you will put yourself in a perfect position to focus your company's efforts on properly servicing your target market. Remember, regardless of anything else you might think about your company, its whole reason for being is to fulfill your customers' needs and wants. You can only achieve your company goals by successfully satisfying that singular purpose. Without that, nothing else that you do will even begin to matter.

Where customers are concerned, they can typically be classified at one of four basic levels: one-time buyers, occasional customers, those who frequent your business, and those who not only use your services but advocate on your behalf. To maximize customer relationships, you have to be focused on ensuring that your service is superior to anything else that these customers can encounter in the marketplace. That is the most effective way to not only encourage each customer to become a more regular consumer of your goods and services, but to even entice some to actively promote your company.

In essence, you want to ensure that the one-time buyer is so satisfied with your offerings that he or she returns in the future. When you can satisfy your occasional customers, you can encourage many of them to become regulars. And once they are regularly buying from you, their continued satisfaction can turn them into advocates - and, despite what some clever marketers might believe, positive word-of-mouth remains one of the most powerful and effective ways to get your marketing message out to a broader audience.

To maximize your customer relationships, it is important to identify them and get to know who they are and why they are buying from you. That entails gathering as much customer detail as you can, including information about what they buy from you, how often they purchase, and even certain demographic facts. Information such as customer occupation, interests, and expressed needs can provide valuable insight into which customers offer the best opportunity for long-term customer loyalty.

More importantly, that type of research can help you to remain on top of any changes in your customers' needs, so that you can be proactive in meeting them. Remember too that today's customers want more than to just have their needs met; they have certain expectations about how those needs should be fulfilled as well. Different customers often have different expectations when it comes to things like customer service, and those expectations can vary among demographic populations and can even differ from location to location.

Much has been written about the importance of customer retention, and by now most entrepreneurs are well aware of the benefits that they can enjoy by focusing a great deal of effort on retaining the customers they already have. After all, it costs far more to acquire new customers than it does to ensure that your current customer base remains satisfied. That often means introducing rewards programs for your best customers, or simply focusing your efforts on enhancing their customer experience to ensure that they continue to be amazed with your company's results.

It is also critical that you focus on the point at which your employees actively interact with your customers. Some estimates suggest that two-thirds of customers who abandon a business do so as the result of negative interaction with employees. You can avoid that by recognizing the importance of both your employees and your customers, and working to ensure that your team members understand their roles and know how to personify your company culture. That often involves emphasis on cross-training to reduce the likelihood of unforeseen mistakes, and active support for teamwork so that your employees all work together to make every customer interaction as positive as possible.

There is a powerful correlation between brand loyalty and positive customer experiences that can lead to better customer retention and increased revenue growth. If you want to achieve true business success, you will have to learn to focus like a laser on those customer interactions to ensure that you leave no stone unturned in your efforts to maximize the benefits this critical business component offers.

Chapter 3 - A System Approach – Designing Your Company

Anyone who has ever had to build something from scratch understands that a systematic approach to construction is essential if you want your creation to endure. This is true regardless of whether you're building a home, raising a barn, or creating your own business. Sound construction simply isn't something that happens by accident. And yet time and time again, aspiring entrepreneurs rush to launch new companies, without ever engaging in the careful planning needed to ensure that they are launching something that can last.

Take the average business plan, for instance. There is no disputing the importance of a comprehensive business plan when it comes to the development of a new business. When you have a truly detailed and realistic plan in front of you, it can force you to actually think through all of the key issues that will help to determine your success or failure. With a plan, you are forced to examine your own strengths, weaknesses, opportunities, and threats (SWOT). Sadly, however, that type of deep analysis is typically inspired only by truly sound business plans.

The fact is that far too many business plans are little more than a waste of time. Many include projections that are far too optimistic, and other expectations that have little to no chance of ever being realized. In many instances, entrepreneurs develop business plans that are more fiction than fact and that seem to be designed to accomplish but one thing: fooling lenders. And those are just the best-case scenario; many of these wild, unrealistic plans are actually examples of novice entrepreneurs fooling even themselves.

Does that sound harsh? Perhaps it is. Then again, I am speaking from experience here, as I have been guilty of this type of overly optimistic planning at different times in the past. Yes, over the course of my forty-year history as an entrepreneur, I have on occasion allowed myself to become so enamored with my good ideas that I ended up expecting better results than reality could provide. Yes, I have found myself saying things like "Sure, 5% market share with a 30% gross profit in three years sounds reasonable - and an annual growth rate of 50% is surely achievable." Like you, I'm human - and susceptible to the same irrational exuberance to which all humans sometimes succumb.

I tell you that so that you can more fully understand this: many of my early business plan projections failed to materialize. Back then, I had yet to learn one of the most fundamental lessons any entrepreneur can learn: there is a difference between projecting success and actually planning and positioning yourself to succeed. As New York Yankee legend Yogi Berra once noted, "If you don't know where you are going, you'll end up someplace else."

Of course, even the best and most comprehensive business plans are ultimately no guarantee of success. A business plan provides no assurance that your company will survive, much less succeed. However, it is still one of the many essential components you must have to improve your chances of being successful. For while a business plan can never assure you of success, the lack of one can all but guarantee your failure. That old saying about how "people don't plan to fail; they fail to plan" is as true today as it has ever been. You must differentiate yourself. You must plan to succeed.

Before you even craft your business plan, I'd like you to consider everything from a different vantage point than that to which you might be accustomed. Too often, new entrepreneurs fail to understand the true nature of the business environment. I want you to think about your business as the open system that it truly is, with all of its many internal systems and components continuously interacting with not only one another but with the outside world as well. At different times, it will face challenges from both external and internal threats, and in many instances these threats will be outside of the system's complete control. If you think that you're going to be able to create an enterprise that is somehow immune to obstacles, think again.

Now, why do I ask you to envision your own business in this way? It's simple: too many entrepreneurs launch their companies with Utopian dreams that quickly turn to frustration and disillusionment when those first challenges appear. Because they failed to understand how chaotic and unpredictable the business environment and economic marketplace can be, their plans quickly evaporated as soon as trouble appeared. To avoid that, I want you to understand what you are dealing with before you ever sit down to draft your comprehensive business plan. That will help you to understand how your customers and the marketplace will judge what you do, and provide you with greater insight into why it is so important that you score high in every business category if you want to be better than your competition.

The fact is that the right business plan can successfully project your enterprise as being among the best in class, and that can give you the opportunity to state your case in the marketplace of ideas. If you are unable to get that opportunity, then your business idea will join the thousands of other great ideas that are discarded and left for dead each and every year.

Why the System Approach Matters

To understand why the system approach matters, it can be helpful to understand the difference between closed and open systems. For a good example of a closed system, just consider a high-precision wrist watch. That watch is considered a closed system because its effectiveness is not dependent on its environment or any outside interactions. A well-engineered timepiece, even with its many moving parts (subsystems, if you will) can be relied upon to provide you with the same results every time you glance at it. The time you see will always be either consistently correct, or consistently incorrect. There is no variation in performance based on how you feel from day to day, or due to the influence of external factors. That ability to consistently function without respect to any outside influence is a hallmark of closed systems.

Now consider your business. Unlike that watch, your company is an open system. It is dynamic in nature, and is constantly interacting with other systems and subsystems - including those outside of its own. These interactions occur in both formal and informal ways, and can deeply affect every aspect of the enterprise. As a result, almost every aspect of your company can be impacted by factors both inside and outside of the business, and this impact can cause variances in everything from overall productivity to how you are perceived in the marketplace.

It is important to think of your enterprise as a whole system that is made up of people, resources, culture, structure, processes, and much, much more. All of these various elements must be organized in a way that enables them to work together to fulfill a well-defined mission. This cooperation must be facilitated so that your company can accomplish certain goals and objectives, using the organization's available resources and established processes. Because the company is an open system, however, these organized efforts have no guarantee of success. Internal or external factors can cause even the best efforts to fall short of your mark - especially when you've failed to plan and execute properly.

Successful integration of all of these disparate parts can only be achieved with the right planning, and with the right strategies and implementation. This is where system thinking comes into play, because it can make the difference between success and failure when trouble rears its ugly head. Issues will occur, but your continued success will depend on how you address each new complication. Your basic choices can usually be boiled down to two options: viewing each problem as an isolated challenge to be dealt with in just that one area of the business, or taking the system approach to problem solving.

System thinking requires that you examine each problem within the context of the overall system. It is a common sense approach that recognizes that all of the components and subsystems in your organization are interrelated and interdependent. When something goes wrong in one part of the company, that problem can have ripple effects that negatively impact other areas of the business as well. With a system approach to problems, you can prevent most of those unintended consequences, and avoid the system-wide damage that might otherwise spread through your company.

In essence, the system approach offers you an opportunity to deal with each new problem in a way that ensures that the integrity of the whole organization is maintained. System thinking is thus an enormously powerful tool to help you fine-tune your entire system, maintain equilibrium among all of the various components and sub-systems within the company, and consistently position yourself to outperform your rivals. As you might expect, a chaotic system that is constantly enduring unresolved problems - or problems that are only partially resolved - cannot help but be less productive than a system that is well-ordered and built for system-wide problem resolution. The latter will almost always have a clearer mission, and a better understanding of its goals and objectives.

What is the Systems Approach?

Put simply, the system approach of organization and management involves a somewhat new and radical way of looking at your business culture. It seeks new insight and solutions by changing the way problems are approached and recognizing that the broader system can be strengthened when all of your employees are encouraged to cooperate and to learn from one another. For a better understanding of this, just consider your own body, and try to relate your own human systems to those within your company.

Your body contains a large number of internal systems, including your nervous system, circulatory system, digestive system, adrenal system, and so on. Each of these systems has its own range of tasks and functions to perform, and each is somewhat autonomous in how it achieves those objectives. Your blood flows through your circulatory system as the various components of that system work in harmony with one another. Your respiratory system provides you with the oxygen you need. The mitochondrial factories in your cells convert nutrients into the ATP your body prefers to use as its primary energy source, facilitating the power you need to make it through each day.

Your company could be viewed in much the same way. If you provide products then chances are that you have production systems to go along with your marketing, sales, customer service, and management systems. If you provide services, then you have dedicated personnel performing those tasks, even as other team members fulfill the remaining roles in your organization. Each of those areas of the company has its role to play. On the surface, these different areas of responsibility often appear to be fragmented, and operate with little to no information sharing between departments.

But consider again how that works within your own body. While your circulatory system might seem to fulfill most of its roles without relying on other systems, is that really the case? Far from being completely independent, the system responsibility for moving blood throughout your body is itself dependent on other systems. It relies upon your respiratory system to provide it will the oxygen it then delivers to other areas of the body. It relies upon your digestive system for the consumed nutrients that it carries to your cells. At the same time, it also impacts all of those other systems as well.

When one system in your body suffers disruption, that failure has a cascading effect on other systems. When the circulatory system fails, it can negatively impact the digestive system. Each of those systems can disrupt the adrenal system. Your adrenals can disrupt the production of energy, and lead to exhaustion. Your respiratory system can ... well, you get the idea.

The bottom line is that failure in any of your body's systems can result in failures in other areas of the body. And when any of those areas are disrupted, the effect on your overall health can be catastrophic. Much of human illness, disease, and misery can be directly tied to minor failures in one or more of the body's systems. More importantly for our purposes, it must be noted that your health can be adversely affected not only by failures in one or more of the body's systems, but also by a failure of those systems to work together in unison. Disharmony can create systemic problems that disrupt your entire body!

The same is true with your company. The systems within your company - all of those different people, departments, and processes - must not only be effective within their own sphere of responsibility, but must also be effective in their interactions with every other area of the operation. This is critically important, since the failure of any element within a system can disrupt that system, and when one system becomes dysfunctional it can be difficult to isolate the problem before it spreads to other systems and the whole organization.

Think of the system approach as applied to the human body in this way: when a system within your body fails, it is important that the physician take into account the whole body before attempting any treatment regimen. Without an understanding of how one system can impact another, any course of treatment could have unintended consequences that damage other systems or harm the entire body. By understanding how these various systems interact with and impact one another, medical decisions can be made in a more holistic way that avoids those unforeseen problems.

The same approach should be used in business. When problems arise with one employee, an entire department, or even a particular process, a systems approach to solving the issue will take into account the interdependent nature of all of the disparate elements involved. This can lead to problem resolution strategies that do not just address the immediate concern, but actually work to enhance the health and effectiveness of the entire organization.

Alan Yong

Applying the System Approach to Your Company Design

When you are designing your company, you want to do it in such a way that promotes a positive atmosphere that facilitates productivity, mutual respect, and engagement at every level of the organization. You want to build it so that everyone's contributions to the success of the organization are appreciated by not only you, but by every member of the team. If that sounds like standard fare that everyone else is probably already doing, think again.

In most small businesses, entrepreneurs build their companies with the intent of fulfilling specific missions related to meeting customer needs. Things like product production, marketing, sales, and customer service are all distinct concerns that are addressed as though they existed in isolation from one another. Problem resolution is often neglected entirely, and business culture seldom, if ever, receives the direct attention it needs. In other words, your average small business starts with the intent of meeting a specific customer need, and sort of develops on its own into whatever it ultimately becomes. That is why so many entrepreneurs operate their enterprise for two, three, or five years without any notion that they have a problem, and then wake up one day to realize that the business they thought they were creating had grown into something they no longer recognized as theirs.

In many instances, this type of venture failed to consider much beyond those direct operational concerns required for keeping his or her business afloat. Things like brand, values, vision, mission, and culture were afterthoughts during the creation of the company, and thus never carefully defined by the business owner. Unfortunately, when those fundamental concerns are never addressed in a proactive way, bad things can and do happen. If there is one simple truth in business creation that no one should ever ignore, it is this: your business will have a culture. It will take on a mission, demonstrate values, and express some semblance of vision. How it does so will ultimately help to determine how your brand is perceived by your customers and the broader public.

Now, those things can be directly designed and shaped by you, or they can happen on their own. Which of those two options is more likely to produce the type of results you want for your business?

The reality is that you absolutely must work to define your company's brand, values, vision, mission, and culture, and not leave it to others in your company, or the marketplace itself. If you fail to address these things, you will soon find that others will define you - and that is rarely a good thing. This is not something that you can simply leave to fate, or even entrust to your employees or customers. It is instead something that you must work diligently to direct on your own, utilizing consistent and clear messaging to carefully define your new business.

At each step of the process, you must consider how your plans will help to define your company in an effective and sustainable way. Your vision must be clear, the mission should be properly conveyed, and your company culture must be properly rooted and nourished in accordance with your defined values. That culture should be designed in a way that encourages like-minded people to succeed in their contributions to the team, secure in the knowledge that they are part of something that is larger than them. To be sure, there will always be employees that simply do enough to get by, as well as those who can never really manage to fit in with your carefully-crafted group dynamic. Your job is to minimize those hires, while searching for new team members who are willing to share your overall business philosophy and adopt your company culture.

When successful these efforts will help to define your brand as well, and convey to the marketplace precisely the message you seek to deliver. Like everything else in business, positive branding almost never happens by accident. The best way to achieve it is with a system approach that seeks to incorporate all of the seemingly disparate aspects of your company and forge them into a united and effective whole organism.

The Broader System View

Of course, your competitors are in much the same situation. Each of them might be organized in subtly different ways than their rivals, but every single one of them is a unique whole system. Together, they collectively make up the body of your industry, which is in turn a system. And that industry - along with various associations, non-governmental entities, and consumers - makes up the broader system that we know as the private sector economy. Your business is but one system within an industry that is itself a system in that economy. Once you begin to adopt a system-based approach to your thinking, you quickly realize that pretty much everything is just a system within a system.

This is important to realize too, since most businesses ultimately derive their revenue from either within their own industry or from beyond. That revenue is vital fuel that powers your business, and will ultimately determine whether or not you are able to enjoy the success you need to remain in operation. That makes it vitally important that you position yourself within the broader economic system in a way that enables you to compete within your industry for that share of the market you need to not only maintain your business but grow over time. To achieve that market share, of course, you have to be well-positioned to efficiently deliver the goods and services that will provide you with the revenue you need.

There is a reason why I want you to recognize the existence of all of these different systems, and gain insight into how they all interact with and ultimately impact one another. The fact is that this interrelation between systems is a large part of the reason why you are never going to be as successful as you want to be if you allow yourself to just concentrate on being great in a few areas of your company. Most businesses that survive for more than a few years can lay claim to being great at something. Sometimes they can even claim to be great at two "somethings." The ones that are recognized as being the best in class, however, are the ones that are recognized as better than their peers across the entire spectrum of service and product categories.

Once you start recognizing these systems, and then realize their importance within the contest to be the best in class, the systems within your own company take on an entirely new level of importance. Within each group in your business, there will be many different tasks and routines on which your team will be judged and measured. Each of those smaller tasks may make up only a small portion of the overall category, but your team's effectiveness in that area contributes to the final score. The combined value of your perceived scores in all of the different categories determines whether or not you are perceived as being in that upper echelon of excellence within your industry.

So, how do you go about achieving that state of excellence? How do you align your business values with your vision, mission, and culture in such a way that you can best position yourself to become the best in class, and then sustain that position over time? It starts with your business design.

To achieve that level of across-the-board excellence, you have to ensure that your company has the leadership it needs to provide and execute the innovative, strategic vision you need for success. That vision must be clearly and consistently communicated to every member of your team, at every level of your organization. More than that, however, you must also realize that there is more to leading than just managing. Managers might get things done, but leaders inspire others to not only get things done but become leaders themselves. A leader in isolation is never enough for success, no matter how great he or she might be.

Your goal should be to ensure that every system and subsystem in your organization has the management it needs to foster your values and culture, but you cannot rest there. You must strive to ensure that your managers can transcend their managerial responsibilities and find ways to become leaders. Regardless of whether you choose a more centralized or decentralized path to achieving this result, it is something that must be done to ensure that you are able to rely on your team to work within and enhance the business you have designed.

It means that you have to master the art of coaching and inspiration. You must develop a skill set that allows you to communicate by both word and deed in a way that inspires your team members to share your broader vision and goals. At the same time, you have to be able to know how to coach and teach others so that they have access to your mindset and broader business philosophy, and then encourage them to pass that knowledge along to others within your organization.

As they do so, your inspiration will become contagious throughout the company. Your vision will become the vision of each and every team member in the organization, and your company culture will firmly take root as the values and mindset you've conveyed are planted like seeds in a field. With continual nourishment, those seeds will develop and grow until they eventually sprout and flourish, creating the company culture that you envisioned when your business first launched.

In essence, this approach to design begins with you, and ends with the creation of an entire team and organization that reflects your values and mindset - in much the same way that the planets in the solar system reflect the light of the Sun. When done properly, you will achieve the goal of multiplying yourself and extending the reach of your leadership. That will in turn expand your sphere of influence beyond only those with whom you have major interaction each day, and allow you to impact even those employees you may not regularly see. Because you will be creating a team of like-minded, vision and goal-sharing individuals, your organization will have the capability of achieving the type of exceptional results that others will only be able to wish they could enjoy.

Such an approach is long past overdue in the marketplace. While the experts tell us that perhaps thirty percent of all new companies somehow manage to remain in business for more than ten years, it would be a stretch to suggest that their survival equates to true success. Far too many of these surviving businesses find themselves in a constant state of chaos, and struggle just to stay afloat and make each payroll. There are surprisingly few companies that actually come even remotely close to achieving the type of success that their owners imagined on the day they launched their startups.

On the other hand, there are companies out there that consistently outperform their peers in the industry. For these companies, success has come from proven management and business practices, consistently applied over time. To succeed in your business venture, you must understand these practices and apply them in your own organization. I am passionately committed to sharing them with you, so that you can avoid the fate experienced by far too many of our fellow entrepreneurs.

Remember, everything matters - but certain things are significantly more important than others. While everything can have an impact on your success, there remain some things that are more impactful than others. The ability to relentlessly prioritize and focus on the most crucial areas is a major contributor to great business success. This book will focus on the four main pillars of business success. The spotlight will be shining on you, your employees, your great ideas, and your customers. Outshine yourself, throughout your organization, in each and every one of these areas and you will see great success in your endeavors.

To achieve that which you desire, you have to be able to recognize these more critical factors, and work to emphasize them within your own company. You must promote excellence in attention to detail, and ensure that every member of your team shares that focus. That will free you up to maintain your own focus on the larger key business philosophies and practices that must be attended to if you are to achieve that high best in class score that you seek.

Everything starts with you as the leader of your company and this is true regardless of whether you already have a detailed plan written in stone or just a simple vision jotted down on a restaurant napkin. As long as you have that vision and a commitment to learning how to provide the leadership needed to bring it to fruition, we can develop the winning strategies you need for success. We can create the plan you need to implement those strategies flawlessly, while ensuring that your company is well-position to gather new strength with each and every move.

In the end, you are not merely building a company. Anyone can do that. Instead, you are creating a culture that is built around your chosen business practices, your deeply-held philosophies, and your own unique mindset. It doesn't really matter whether your company is offering products or services; using your available resources in the most efficient manner possible is always one of the most important considerations you must make. Your challenge then is to strive for greatness in every important category of business covering:

1. Leadership and Management

2. Strategy

3. Execution

4. Structure and Process

5. Delegation

6. Employees

7. Mutual Goals Review

8. Products

9. Customers

As we delve deeper into each of these issues, and others as well, I want you to keep in mind the importance of ensuring that your company has been designed with the system approach in mind. In every category of your business, and in each task that you undertake, the potential for problems will always exist. A properly-designed company that has incorporated this system approach within its very culture will always be able to rise to each new challenge, address issues in a way that maintains harmony, and come out of the process stronger than when the problem first appeared.

Chapter 4 - Leadership and Management

If you ask business owners whether or not they consider themselves leaders, there is a good chance that almost all of them will answer in the affirmative. Entrepreneurs almost universally think of themselves in those terms, and there would seem to be good cause to justify those beliefs. After all, it takes a certain kind of person to take ownership of his own destiny and fearlessly confront the challenges involved in starting a new business. Unfortunately, however, the fact that you are brave enough to undertake that level of risk does not necessarily mean that you are a leader.

The fact is that most of the small businesses in operation today lack true leaders. In almost every instance, they are launched and operated by people who can best be described as managers. And among those small businesses that have failed, almost none had the type of leadership they needed to survive and flourish. In my opinion, this general lack of leadership in small business is one of the primary reasons that the rate of business failure is so abysmally high.

Too many of today's small business owners are followers. Rather than blazing trails, they all too often adopt the "me too" mantra that is so prevalent in failed enterprises. That mindset is the one that has you believing that you can do what others are doing, provided that you are just willing to invest the hard work and time needed to meet your goals. The "me too" attitude also presumes that a certain amount of luck is involved in any successful business enterprise, and that hard work will somehow magically make that luck work on your behalf.

Here's the thing, though: good luck is undependable, and no amount of hard work can ever force it to manifest and work in your favor. Worse, the reality is that the odds are actually stacked against you in that regard. If history proves anything in business, it proves that enterprises seldom succeed based on luck. In most instances, bad luck, hardships, and unexpected challenges seem to be far more common. With few exceptions, starting a new business always costs more, takes longer, and has more problems than anticipated. Great leadership throughout your entire organization will help you to minimize that and improve your odds of succeeding.

Also note that my earlier estimate that some 70% of business enterprises fail within the first decade is actually one of the more conservative assessments out there today. Researchers and published reports actually mention that number at the low end of their estimates, and operate from the assumption that 70% or more of all new businesses fail not within the first ten years - but within the first five. Were luck really a factor, one would think that at least some portion of that failed group would have seen at least enough good fortune to scrape by for a few more years.

To better highlight the real underlying problem in many of these failures, just consider what the average business owner brings to the table. In almost every instance where someone launches a new company, that entrepreneur has a certain level of competency in his or her field. That competence may include an in-depth expertise covering a preferred range of products, or unique skills that enable the company to provide quality services to customers. Being an expert in certain products or services, however, does not make one a leader. The average electrician is an expert in his profession, but that expertise does not necessarily translate to business leadership.

So, what is the end result when the most well-meaning entrepreneurs launch companies based solely on their own product and service expertise and a belief that they can achieve success by working hard and catching a little good luck here and there? If they lack the requisite leadership and management skills needed to keep their businesses on the right path, do they really have a chance at meeting their goals? A simple look at the numbers suggests that they do not.

No matter your level of expertise and commitment to hard work, there is virtually no chance of avoiding failure if you lack the critical skills necessary for success. History is littered with the remains of failed enterprises that never enjoyed the leadership and management talent required to know how to hire the right people, train them, and engage them in a committed endeavor to achieve a common objective. Without those key components for success, those businesses stumbled, struggled for survival, and ultimately failed.

Leaders versus Managers

"Management is doing things right; leadership is doing the right things." - Peter F. Drucker

If there is one thing I want you to take away from this chapter, it is this: there is a difference between being a leader and being a manager. Far too many people simply use those words as though they are interchangeable. They are not. Virtually all small businesses can lay claim to being managed; very few can honestly be described as being effectively led. The distinction between these two things is not merely a matter of semantics, but is actually something that goes right to the heart of understanding why your role is so important in the effort to be the best in class.

The difference between leaders and managers can be easily misunderstood, especially by those who have never had the opportunity to serve in either role. That factor, along with the fact that there are so few true leaders in the world today, tends to sow confusion in many entrepreneurs' minds. In reality, however, distinguishing between a leader and a manager is really simpler than it sounds.

Perhaps the easiest and most basic way to understand the difference is to recognize how people relate to each. Managers, by definition, have people that they are responsible for managing. Consequently, they have people who work under their direction. Leaders, on the other hand, have people they are responsible for inspiring. As a result, leaders have people that look to them for vision, direction, and values. These people thus follow their leaders.

But there is more to it than that. The differences can run far deeper, and take on a much broader importance within any organization. For example:

Leaders must be able to persuade people, both by word and example. That enables them to create followers among their employee base, as those workers are forged into a unified team with a shared commitment to achieving the mission. Managers, however, are tasked with communicating those persuasive ideas in a way that directs how they are implemented. Managing is less about winning followers than it is about coordinating employee efforts to complete assigned tasks.

Leaders have to be focused on the larger issues - the big picture, so to speak. They are responsible for creating a vision that can be communicated to everyone on the team, and ultimately each leader has to take responsibility for how well that goal is met. Managers adopt that vision and direct the team as it is implemented at every level of the organization.

Even in the area of exercising power, the differences could not be more evident. Managers are tasked with using power. They wield that power as they issue the commands necessary to ensure that everything within the company operates as designed. Through the exercise of this power, managers are able to react to changes as they occur, meet challenges, and maintain harmony and cohesion.

Leaders have a different relationship to power. While they could exercise power in the same blunt manner as the manager is obligated to do, most leaders tend to focus their attention on enhancing the power within others. Thus, the competent leader is one who empowers his managers and team members, since he knows that such empowerment can lead to improvements in every area of his company. Through this empowering of others, the leader creates the change the company needs for increased success.

As some have pointed out, management is all about learning how to motivate people to do what the company needs them to do to achieve its goals. Leadership goes a step further and motivates those people to actually want to do those things. That power to inspire flows directly from the difference between how leaders and managers typically look at the business. Managers are focused on the present, and on the nuts and bolts of the company machine that ensure that it runs properly. Leaders are future-focused, see the bigger picture, and emphasize the value of people over tasks and projects. A manager's job is to effectively communicate those things that need to be done. The leader is the one communicating where the company is actually going; inspiring, coaching, and empowering others to participate and contribute towards the accomplishment of the company's missions, goals, and objectives.

So we see that, though leadership and management can and should go hand in hand if your business is to succeed, they are certainly not the same thing. Even the best managers are often lacking in sound leadership skills, and some of the best leaders in history have been horribly ineffective managers. That fact has helped to keep the seemingly eternal debate about whether leaders are born or made as lively as it has ever been. For my part, I hold fast to the belief that almost everyone can hone their leadership skills. More than that, I believe that the development of those skills in each member of your team should be a primary team goal within your company, since the promotion of leadership skills enhances system-wide teamwork and strengthens the cohesion every company needs to fulfill its mission.

Because everything is interrelated, your company can enjoy greater inspiration at every level when mutual dependence, mutual cooperation, and mutual benefits are emphasized by all. The development of leadership skills throughout the enterprise can only serve to enhance those benefits, enabling everyone on the team to think, communicate, and execute the company's plan just as their leader would.

Why Leadership Matters

"People buy into the leader before they buy into the vision." - John C. Maxwell

It is easy to become so focused on maintaining operations and coordinating a team that you forget why leadership matters. Of course, part of the problem is that so few of us are ever afforded the opportunity to develop the type of leadership skills we need when we launch our own companies. Whether it is in early childhood, the formative school years, or most forms of employment, life often seems to demand that we conform to established roles and simply play our part in the larger drama that is life. Even in things like organized sports, there are few true leadership roles available, and most members of any given team are expected to follow the coach, team manager, or other recognized leader.

Professional life is almost always a continuation of that established pattern of following the leader. Where there is opportunity for taking on a leadership role, the competition is usually intense. Often times, existing relationships can influence the outcome of that competition, and those who actually demonstrate a talent for leading are not always given the opportunity they need to demonstrate their abilities.

In fact, a recent survey conducted by Gallup examined the state of leadership within the United States, and confirmed that there appears to be a growing crisis. That report, titled State of the American Manager, noted that just slightly more than one-third of the survey's 2500 respondents confirmed that they enjoyed serious engagement with their job. While that survey focused on management, it is easy to see the dangers that can result from that type of trend.

That lack of engagement is indicative of a failure of leadership within those companies, since managers receive their inspiration for job engagement from those who they view as leaders. If no one is leading, then there is no vision, no direction, and no overall sense of unity of purpose. As a consequence of such environment, those managers will flounder, and when managers disengage due to lack of leadership, that has an impact on every level of the organization. The employees those managers supervise are equally susceptible to losing their sense of purpose, and that disengagement can quickly spread throughout the entire organization.

On a broader scale, the impact of this lack of leadership may be felt for generations to come, since it is not only today's leadership that is being stifled but tomorrow's as well. For if there are not enough leaders today to foster those leadership skills in today's managers and younger employees, how can we expect that there will be an adequate supply of true leaders to meet the challenges of the future?

Leaders have to possess clear vision. This is not a gift that comes with birth, mind you, but a talent that must be developed over time and cultivated like a garden. Managers are expected to act and react. True leaders spend more time thinking than they do engaging. Without that time for thought and consideration, you cannot develop the vision you need to possess, and will be left with no clear mission or direction to impart to others.

At the same time, one of the central components of leadership is the character of the person who is tasked with leading others. Most people are unwilling to commit to following the lead of someone who they view as having a weak or poor character. The best leaders are those who demonstrate in both public and private the values that they proclaim to others. It is those people who always seem to rise above the crowd and earn the esteem, respect, and even devotion of the people they lead.

Of course, the true test of leadership is typically manifested during times of crisis. In business, unexpected times of crisis are almost a fact of life, and most followers never really appreciate what type of leader they have until they see how he or she reacts to the various setbacks and obstacles that come along.

Naturally, honesty and integrity matter as well, but that extends far beyond simply being a man or woman of your word. While it is important that you strive to be honest in your dealings with every person with whom you come into contact, it is even more vital that you learn to be honest with yourself. Know what you believe, make your positions on values clear to one and all, and then live by them. Remember, those values are the guiding principles of your vision, and the only way you will ever be able to sell that vision to others is if your own commitment to its underlying values is manifestly firm and evident to everyone.

Great leaders learn to promote cooperative teamwork, and do so by inspiring positive communication. They proudly express the values of mutual dependence, and strive to affirm the positive contributions made by every member of their team. Their appreciation is palpably sincere. They spend their time proactively thinking about and developing the solutions they need to overcome challenging problems and strategies for turning those problems into opportunities. They also share an uncanny capacity for understanding the types of contributions that they can offer to the resolution of these problems, and at the same time work to inspire everyone else on the team to contribute, follow, and support their vision.

Why Management Matters

While leaders are charged with planning, inspiring, risk-taking, and motivating others, managers play a dramatically different role within any successful organization. As a leader, you cannot always be everywhere that you might need to be. It means that at some point, you will have no option other than to rely upon your team and its managers to get things done. Besides, if you spent all your time engaged in every small decision made on a daily basis, you would have no time left for the broader thinking, planning, and strategy development your enterprise will need to succeed.

So, what makes a manager so important to any business? Just consider that Gallup survey again. It found that nearly two-thirds of the American managers consider themselves disengaged from their own roles within their companies, and that fact can only be viewed as an indictment of the nation's approach to the managerial process. And while it might be tempting to blame that dearth of managerial commitment on the ineffectiveness of the marketplace's leaders, that perhaps oversimplifies the dilemma we face.

Moreover, the statistics cited in that survey should be viewed as cautionary rather than unchangeable. If we know that some seven out of ten businesses typically fail within their first five years, and then add to that the knowledge that more than six in ten managers claim to lack the necessary engagement with their jobs, one thing should be abundantly clear: those two facts probably have some relation to one another.

In fact, it is reasonable to surmise that a widespread lack of engagement on the part of managers is having some negative effect on business survival rates. That makes sense, since we know that few business owners have the time to personally ensure that everyone on their team is adequately committed to the company vision and mission. And they certainly don't have the time needed to oversee every team member's work throughout each day. Without their managers, those leaders often have no intermediary level of leadership through which to communicate their ideals and mission to the entire organization.

No wonder so many companies suffer mission drift, fail to respond properly to crisis situations, and ultimately fail to survive.

The managerial role may differ from the leadership role in many ways, but it is every bit as vital to an organization's health and long-term chances for survival and success. Not only are managers directly responsible for conveying the company's mission to the employees by properly directing and overseeing their activities, but they are also on the front lines and typically have the most frequent contact with every member of the team.

That last part is important to keep in mind, since that regular interaction makes your managers an important fulcrum for employee success within the company. Managers have an important role to play in everything from employee recruitment to training, inspiration, and retention of team members. Of course, that also means that your managers play a critical role in ensuring customer satisfaction at every level of the business process.

By some estimates, effective management can enhance engagement of your team members by upwards of sixty percent. That translates into each and every employee being more committed to process, product, and customer service, which in turn enhances customer satisfaction and loyalty to your company. Often times, we tend to talk about employee productivity as though it were something that existed within a vacuum. The truth of the matter is that work productivity is largely dependent upon the quality of your enterprise's managerial capabilities!

Managers are the ones who execute the leader's vision. As a result of that awesome responsibility, managers have to be able to translate sound strategic visions into effective roadmaps that their team can follow to achieve the company's broader mission. As part of that translation process, they have to develop the standards, operating techniques, and work rules needed to maximize productivity and maintain the desired level of quality at every step of the process.

Personal skills are a necessity, because your managers are first and foremost your primary source of interaction with most employees. It is the manager who will most often direct the daily efforts of the team as they strive to fulfill your vision and mission. It is the manager who will be responsible for channeling the company's available resources to fuel those efforts, while assessing what additional resources may be needed at any given time.

Managers thus have specific job descriptions that are often defined by processes designed to meet certain objectives within specified periods of time. Their job entails planning, organizing, assigning, and monitoring employees in a way that delivers maximum productivity and efficiency with the least amount of cost. They are charged with ensuring that the company delivers on its promised goods and services in a way that fulfills its sales claims. Throughout it all they must ensure that these things are accomplished while meeting specified timelines, standards, unit cost requirements, and profit projections.

Theirs is more than an ethereal mission. They have a job that needs to be done, and the success of that job is determined by the actual results that they are able to produce. A failure to meet those result expectations can place their jobs at risk. As a result, it is common for managers to fall into a pattern of exercising their power to control their team, so that they are able to deliver the immediate results demanded by the projected bottom line. This can be an extremely short-term outlook, and is typically confined to whatever department any given manager controls. So focused is the manager on the results his team produces that concerns about other areas of the company are often given little consideration - since he typically views his job success as being defined only by the success of his immediate circle of authority and power.

Managers can certainly learn to inspire, coach, motivate, and even lead, but that remains a somewhat rare phenomenon. It tends to exist only within those companies that actively promote such an environment and culture. More often than not, managerial units descend into a state of semi-autonomy as they fail to receive the guidance they need from the leadership at the top of the company. As a consequent, authoritarian managers tend to exceed their delegated authority and start managing by fear and intimidation. On the other hand, risk-averse managers become lackadaisical in their duties and end up adopting attitudes more in alignment with their subordinates than with the broader interests of the company.

The ultimate goal then has to be the creation of a culture that fosters leadership within every level of the organization, to ensure that no area of the company is ever left rudderless. Managers are indispensable assets responsible for much of what makes the company what it is. Their role as organizer, overseer, and standard-bearer is simply too important to be left to the whims of chance.

Most importantly, it will be your manager who is charged with listening and communicating to the members of your team. Sure, you may address them on a frequent basis, but there will be many times when your other duties leave you unavailable for dealing with personnel issues, conflict resolution, and even many customer service questions. At those times, your manager has to have the personality and communication skills needed to ensure that employees and customers are properly cared for. Remember, most employees don't quit because you have a bad company. They typically quit because they are poorly managed.

Naturally, effective managers do more than just convey orders from on high or issue directives for employees to follow. The really great managers are able to assume accountability for their team, work to understand the attitudes and feelings of everyone they oversee, and consistently demonstrate a willingness to help out other team members when needed. They train. They teach. They listen. And, at the end of the day, they strive to make everyone around them better. And one more thing... they also lead by showing instead of telling.

To be sure, the manager's function is not the same as the leader's function, but there is no denying that good managers demonstrate some semblance of leadership. As a matter of fact, managers whose effectiveness extends no further than successful oversight and control over the people and departments in their charge actually do their companies a disservice. The best managers elevate the leadership qualities of those who serve under them. And even though the manager's perceived role is as the center of a circle of power that he uses to channel the team's efforts toward success that does not mean that he cannot also create a circle of influence of the sort that typically coalesces around effective leaders. In an ideal world, your managers will also be capable of fulfilling leadership roles as well.

Being A Leader and Manager

Small business owners seldom have the luxury of choosing one role or another. As an entrepreneur, you will most likely find that it is necessary for you to wear both hats. For most entrepreneurs, that often proves to be a serious problem, especially when you consider the fact that so few people truly know how to lead. To be brutally candid, the reality is that few people even know how to effectively manage. It is a wonder then that anyone ever manages to accomplish both at the same time!

To be successful with a small business - and especially a new startup that will probably have to exercise resource restraint in its early days, you as the owner will most likely have to serve as both a leader and a manager. Even if you have the resources to hire a manager right away, the very newness of your enterprise should motivate you to take a more involved role in much of the company's early operations. You probably already expect to wear multiple hats in the early days of your startup, and these two will be among the most frequently donned.

You will need to be both a great leader and a great manager if you want to be the best in class. When you are effective in both roles, you will be able to engage in a more masterful imposition of your business vision, and facilitate that vision's implementation throughout every layer of your company. Success in those areas will breed success elsewhere, and help you to build the strong, focused enterprise you need for success, powered by a culture that truly represents your values and strategic vision.

This has to become part of your strategic goals. When you are able to incorporate this mindset to a point where it becomes an integral part of your business culture, then it will provide you with the foundation you need to ensure that it is promoted throughout every layer of the company. From your managers and office personnel to your production and service people, everyone will ultimately be impacted by your efforts in this area. Part of that effort should include a committed attempt to foster creativity and leadership skills in every member of your team.

Granted, you will soon discover that not everyone is capable of being a leader. Moreover, not everyone who has the capability to lead actually has the desire to do so. Still, the only way to identify potential leaders within your organization is to cultivate leadership and actively determine who has the requisite skills and willingness to take on that role. At the end of the day, you will have a better understanding of where to direct your energies as you strive to develop competent leadership throughout the company.

Recognize too that there is another benefit to a committed approach to extolling and developing leadership qualities in your team members. When you can inspire those who follow you to not only appreciate great leadership skills but also strive to develop them in themselves, you will find that they become even better followers too. Whereas they might now follow you out of a shared belief in your vision or simple blind loyalty, the simple act of enhancing their own leadership capabilities will expand their understanding of you as a leader. They will suddenly enjoy new insight into why you do the things that you do, and can then have even more confidence in your vision and mission.

All of this will make them even more prepared to lead or follow, as they gain new understanding of their own importance within the larger system that you are building. Instead of just viewing themselves as mere cogs in a machine that they scarcely understand, they will realize that they have integral roles to play in the fulfillment of the company's objectives. As a follower, this is important because when that understanding is conveyed through word and deed to other team members, the mindset of that shared commitment to a goal cannot help but seep into other areas of the company as well. By helping to spread that mindset, even your followers can fulfill a leadership role by spreading your mindset to others.

The development of this understanding among your leaders is something that can help to ensure that the system you are building can withstand almost any structural disruption. Once you start creating layer after layer of committed leaders - and even committed followers who enjoy some level of leadership ability - you will find that every leadership component within your organization is fully capable of replacing itself. That means that when employees leave, get promoted, or simply miss work due to illness, there is always someone fully capable of ensuring that everything continues to run as it should. Why? That's simple: because you will have built leadership values directly into your company culture.

The question is this: how do you actually achieve that goal? We have established the benefits that you can provide your company by ensuring that you develop a culture that values leadership, but what steps can you take to effectively create that culture. Everything begins with the values you emphasize and your ability to communicate your vision.

Building a Leadership Culture

Like everything else good in business, a culture that values leadership ability does not simply appear out of thin air. It takes conscious effort on everyone's part to ensure that such a culture gets developed from the ground up. That need for universal buy-in, however, does not change one simple fact: everything has to start with you. As the leader, you set the tone for the types of values your company will exemplify. If you value good leadership, and foster leadership skills for all of your team members at every level of your organization, your employees will adopt that mindset as well.

Thus it is imperative that you be effective in communicating your vision. If there is one common complaint most managers make on a regular basis, it is that there is no one within their organization actively encouraging their development. And when managers don't feel as though their leaders place an emphasis on learning and developing new skill sets, they tend to view their jobs as dead ends that offer little to no real opportunity. And where there is no perception of opportunity, there is no real engagement of the sort that can help to foster the proper mindset your company needs for success.

Your role, therefore, is to ensure that every employee, from managers on down, fully comprehend your vision. They have to learn to see their opportunities through your eyes, and can only do so when you are fully committed to helping them better understand your plan for their development. With the right level of attention, you can help each team member better understand the organization's goals and their roles in achieving the mission.

As you work to develop this appreciation for leadership, focus on helping your team members better understand that your company emphasizes learning. It is a virtual certainty that your team will be comprised of a diverse group of people with equally diverse backgrounds. Encourage those more experienced employees to take on mentor roles with your more novice workers. Be sure, of course, that those seasoned workers are already in tune with your vision, lest they lead others astray. Once you start developing this system for passing on your vision and culture from one set of employees to the next, you will find that there is very little that your team cannot accomplish.

Finally, learn how to help employees develop the skills they need to truly shine in your employ. Part of that process entails encouraging them to focus their efforts on those things they consider strengths. Yes, that goes against some of the more common beliefs about training employees to strengthen their weak areas, but think about it for a moment. If you were asked to focus on your weaknesses each and every day, how enthused would you be about your job? Chances are you would be routinely discouraged and wondering why you were hired in the first place.

By emphasizing strengths, and encouraging each employee to strive to exercise those strengths on a daily basis, you enable every member of your team to feel productive and successful each and every day. That stimulates the type of engagement you need to ensure that the team is all on the same page and committed to success. Though it is tempting to want to help your employees gain new strengths, it is important to remember that none of them were hired for their weaknesses. They were hired for their strengths. Put them in situations where they can use those strengths and excel, and you will soon find that you have a happier and more productive team on your hands.

All of this contributes to the development of a company culture that cheers on your employees as they find success each day. When managers feel empowered and appreciated, and enjoy the opportunity for career development, they remain aligned with your company vision and are better able to successfully carry out their mission. When employees understand that mission and know that their company wants them to take on leadership roles in their own particular areas of strength, they are motivated to grow and achieve more than they ever thought possible. With a leadership culture in place, your company will be ideally positioned to meet almost any challenge.

Blending the Roles

Your task as an entrepreneur is to learn to blend the roles of the manager and leader as you try to wear both hats simultaneously. Obviously, there are certain aspects of each that are not necessarily open to that type of blending, but many of the most important characteristics of a true leader and effective manager can in fact be reconciled in one person. To successfully fulfill both roles, you need to be able to seamlessly slip from one hat to the next without losing focus or perspective.

Once you have your mindset firmly entrenched within your company culture, you can then focus on other leadership and management skills that will provide your enterprise with an even stronger foundation. To accomplish that, you need to envision your role as the perfect synthesis of manager and leader, and not get caught up in an overly focused emphasis on the broad generalized differences between those two functions. Just as you want your managers to be something more than number-crunchers or personnel directors, you too have to craft your role in such a way that you surpass the generalized perception of leadership as nothing more than inspiration and vision. You can do both in a seamless way, provided that you understand what you are trying to achieve.

Often times, it is easy to equate leadership with only those big picture areas of the business. As an entrepreneur, however, your true leadership power comes not from what you do, but from who you are. At the end of the day, your employees do not just want leaders with big visions and a standoffish approach to the company. They want a leader who seems worthy of following. They want a leader with the character traits they most commonly associate with leadership. There are several worthy of mention here:

1. Passion. Followers are more likely to commit their time and energy to following leaders who are capable of demonstrating real passion for their enterprises. If you can convey your own passion for the company vision, mission, strategy, and culture, you will not only find that others will follow you but that they will come to adopt that passion as their own.

2. Far-sightedness. This is part of that "vision" thing that confounds so many entrepreneurs. It is one thing to have a clearly defined vision for your business. It is quite another thing entirely to demonstrate to your employees that you actually have some level of foresight when it comes to your own business. Can you envision the challenges that your company might face a year from now? Three years from now? Five years into the future? If you understand your industry and company well enough to adequately forecast both the potential good and possible bad events that might occur in the short and long-term, your employees will have greater confidence in your ability to lead.

3. Wisdom. No, this is not the type of wisdom that comes only from a lifetime of experiences, but rather the wisdom that recognizes the things that are truly important in life. Wisdom informs character in ways that most people never really grasp until late in life, but you need not wait for your latter days to develop the type of wisdom your employees need to see within you.

4. Trustworthiness. Your word must be your bond. There are few things the average person detests more than suffering under a leader whose word has no more value than a hyperbolic barroom tale. Honesty should already be one of your personal and professional core values - especially if you expect to foster a spirit of honesty in your company culture. To that honesty you must also add integrity and dependability, so that every member of your team knows that he or she has a leader who can always be counted upon to follow through on his word.

5. Generosity. That one might give you pause, since it would at first glance suggest that you be the sort of person who freely gives of his material possessions. I am talking about a generosity of spirit that transcends the material. Leaders do not look for credit; they seek out reasons to give credit to others. If you want to be an effective leader, develop within yourself that generosity of spirit that will drive you to ceaselessly look for the positive within those around you, praise it when you find it, and encourage it where it is found to be lacking.

Developing these qualities within yourself (and kudos to you if you already possess them all in abundance) requires self-reflection and the ability to not only learn new things about your own character, but to faithfully exhibit those characteristics on a daily basis. You have to be able to first envision yourself in that leadership role, and understand how it is that you lead, before you can expect others to follow you in anything more than the most superficial of ways.

Thus, your role as a leader is focused on who you are, what you think, and how you express those ideas to those around you. Your role as a manager, on the other hand, goes beyond who you are. It extends to those things that you do, for management is about more than being - it is about doing. Leadership is active due to a leader's ability to project his ideas to others. Management is active from a more skill-based perspective. The process of becoming a better manager is thus dependent upon your ability to improve in those specific skill-based areas of the business, and demonstrating those skills each and every day.

When you lead, your emphasis is on consistently improving your ability to communicate and exemplify the virtues, values, and vision that you want to make a part of your company. When you manage, your focus has to be on consistently enhancing your interactions with team members, your ability to organize the members of your team, and the motivational skills you will need to ensure that every team member is committed to contributing all that he or she can to the cause.

Both roles require that you listen and properly control your own thoughts, words, and emotions. They also both entail a willingness to bear responsibility and accountability for all that happens within the organization. Executed properly, they complement one another in ways that many entrepreneurs never fully learn to grasp. More importantly, they provide you with a level of empowerment that can help to ensure that you construct and maintain the type of business enterprise you envisioned when you first committed to launching your company.

By focusing on your personnel management abilities even as you continually think about and refine the characteristics that cause people to want to follow you, you will fulfill your roles in a way that can empower you to accomplish virtually anything you choose. Entrepreneurs who learn how to successfully blend these roles quickly discover that the combined power of leadership and management can be the cornerstone for truly long-lasting success in the marketplace.

Remember, great leaders and great managers have many differences - but they share many things in common as well. When you lead, do so by example and strive to inspire everyone around you to be motivated to follow. Allow your positivity to serve as a catalyst for the creation of the productive environment you envision, and avoid destructive habits and conduct that could inhibit the growth of that positive culture. Become the type of great leader who understands the boundless potential offered by an environment in which everybody wins, and work toward the type of unified system-wide synergy that is most beneficial to everyone over the long-term.

And remember this as well: you simply cannot do it alone. You have to multiply yourself.

Chapter 5 - Strategy

"I believe that people make their own luck by great preparation and good strategy."
- Jack Canfield

****

Business is often compared to other human endeavors that involve teams working in unison to achieve large objectives. One of the most common of these comparisons highlights the similarities between business activity and organized sports - and with good reason! There are many aspects of business operation that can also be identified in successful sporting endeavors. Great leadership, effective teamwork, and sound planning and execution are all critical components of success in both the business and sporting world. There is one distinct area in which they differ, however, and that involves the necessity of adhering to established rules.

In team sports, the rules of competition are set in concrete, agreed upon by all of the participating teams, and designed to protect players and ensure the integrity of the game. If a team violates those rules in even a slight way, there are umpires and referees there to enforce penalties against the offending competitor. These penalties are not just designed to enforce fairness or equilibrium, but actually work to punish the violators.

Thus, an offensive holding call in football does not just result in the offense being forced to give up any positive gains they might have netted on the play; they are also assessed a yardage penalty that sets them back an additional ten yards. A quarterback who is called for intentionally grounding the ball - usually to avoid being sacked for a loss, of course, not only causes his team to suffer a ten-yard penalty, but also causes the loss of that down. Different types of penalties are assessed for a whole host of infractions that violate the rules, and range from minor yardage setbacks for the smallest violations to player ejections for physical altercations during game play.

Without these rules and penalties, organized sporting competitions would be little more than playground brawls, determined more by the outright ruthlessness of the teams involved than by anything remotely resembling strategy, skill, teamwork, and effective execution. The end result would be constant confusion, and neither the players nor the spectators would ever really be able to follow the action with any sense of understanding.

Unlike sports, business has a different approach to rules. Of course, there are laws that must be followed - statutes and regulations ostensibly put in place to ensure that the marketplace is fair to all participants. I am not talking about actual laws, however. Rather, I am talking about those often unspoken rules of business that are often assumed to be as inviolable as any statutory requirement. These rules are often based more on tradition than anything else, and are generally accepted by most entrepreneurs as being something that you bend or break at your own peril.

Reality is a pesky thing, though, and it has a way of proving even the strongest assumptions wrong. The truth is that business provides you all sorts of avenues for not only bending those commonly-recognized rules, but breaking them altogether. You can choose to ignore conventional wisdom and play by an entirely different set of rules than those adhered to by your competitors.

The benefits of doing so are obvious. After all, if you simply do what everyone else is doing, you will be sacrificing one of the clearest advantages any new business can garner: the ability to move the goalpost of consumer expectations and completely alter the playing field. When you refuse to abide by those rules your rivals have either consciously or unintentionally established, you create a competitive advantage for your company that can enable you to go beyond the call of duty and do things that none of your competitors would dream of attempting.

When you set about to change the rules, you will find that you can be uniquely equipped to position your company in a way that enables you to enjoy overwhelming competitive advantages, even as you remain beneath your rivals' radar. That requires you to think outside the box and find the best way to differentiate your products and services from everybody else's - either right off the bat when you launch your company or later if you feel that a strategic reset is in order. You have to think of ways that you can create these types of competitive advantages, regardless of whether someone else might consider your changing of the rules "unfair." Remember; apart from legally-binding statutes and regulations, there are no rules that bind you when it comes to marketplace competition. Once you recognize that fact, you will have taken the first step to creating a winning strategy.

Why Does Strategy Matter?

I understand why so many entrepreneurs launch their first business without a solid strategy in place. Many of them assume that their vision - along with their ability to provide solid products and services - is their strategy. Unfortunately, there is more to it than that. Vision is critical, since it tells you where you want to go. And products and services are essential because they provide the fuel that powers your trip. Your strategy, however, determines just how you plan to get to your destination. It is not just a road map of the sort you would use to navigate from California to Maine, but a logistic plan that details the how and why of every twist and turn you plan on taking along the way.

The size of your company is all but irrelevant when it comes to the need for a strategy. You might be a startup or small company. You might even be a mid-sized firm. It doesn't matter for our purposes. The fact is that if you have a big, bold idea for your business, then your battle plan begins with strategy. Remember, wars are not won in the first moments of battle. If they were, no strategy would be needed, since you could simply hurl your ideas and resources at the enemy with wild abandon, knowing that victory or defeat was something beyond your control. In business, as in war, detailed strategies are essential for creating the conditions necessary for eventual success.

We live in a hyper-connected world in which global collaboration is rapidly becoming the norm for those who position themselves at the cutting edge of new technology. For those entrepreneurs, new opportunities for success are emerging on a daily basis. The marketplace is shifting on a worldwide scale, and old paradigms and rules are continually being proven ineffective by those business leaders with the courage and foresight to move beyond conventional wisdom and embrace disruptive ideas.

For example, consider the impact of FinTech (Financial Technology) on today's marketplace. In the span of only a few short years, FinTech innovation has emerged as a truly disruptive force in a number of previously-static segments of the economy. Traditional banking and financial service entities once existed within a bubble that seemed utterly impervious to outside forces. No matter how innovative any new technology or market idea had been, the finance sector simply absorbed it and carried on as it had always done. That led many people - including insiders within the finance industry - to assume that the power of the banks and their control over the affairs of the marketplace was so absolute that it could never be challenged, much less overcome.

Today, you have only to pick up a newspaper or read online banking news to see just how wrong those assumptions were. Thanks to digital currency and the blockchain technology that empowers it; those financial entities are being forced to seriously think about their approach to business for the first time in anyone's memory. And this is not just the type of strategic consideration that can be resolved by adopting technology and adapting it to conform to their historical business practices. These new technologies are actively challenging financial firms in a way that cannot be addressed with minor changes to banking systems. Enduring success for the incumbents facing such a paradigm shift is most dependent on how well they can strategically reposition themselves.

Many in the banking industry already take it as an article of faith that the blockchain's disruptive potential is something that they have to embrace rather than ignore or attempt to co-opt. Although it has taken the banking industry sometime to recognize the challenges, they acted with multiple strategic moves once they became convinced that digital currency and FinTech will become quite disruptive to their industry. Strategic moves can be deployed in different ways such as calculated tactics to slow down the competitors with overwhelming patent filings and PR campaign to degrade the value of the disruptive technologies. Additionally, they can exploit their financial strengths to quickly acquire strategic partnerships, gaining instant participation in highly selected areas that give them the most advantages.

There is little wonder why so many entrepreneurs are now betting on the assumption that it is only a matter of time before digital currencies supplant national fiat currencies. Gaining network effects by the day, Bitcoin and well positioned digital currencies could become more widespread and widely used vehicles for economic transactions.

Obviously, digital currency and distributed ledger technology is just one example of how new technologies and ideas can disrupt the marketplace. If that is your passion, then the point is to learn everything that you can about it and work to position your business to exploit new trends and developments in the broader economy. If your passion involves something else, then learn about that. The thing to remember is that you cannot simply jump into any area of economic activity and expect to succeed.

You have to think strategically and develop your strategy in a way that enhances your ability to enjoy success. This is true regardless of where you are in the business development process. Whether launching a new company, expanding an existing enterprise, or developing and introducing a new line of products and services, the importance of creating a strategic plan simply cannot be overstated.

It is true that business management is not a pure science. If it were, then you would probably see more scientists running businesses. Because it is not pure science, there are many business terms that end up meaning different things to different people. The term "strategy" is an example of how meanings can vary. Obviously, a strategy is - at its simplest - a plan. Many in the business world, however, refer to such plans as a "strategic plan," as if to emphasize the meaning and eliminate any possibility for confusion. There is a good reason for that.

For most people, an ordinary plan often fails to contain the type of detail and analysis that you see in any effective strategy. You could, after all, make plans to go to the movie this weekend. That sort of plan is little more than a statement of intent; regardless of how committed you might be to the idea. In like manner, a business owner can make plans to enjoy a ten percent increase in profits in the next fiscal year. Without details and a carefully-crafted road map for achieving that increase, however, those plans are nothing more than goals. Obviously, strategy is much more than just a plan.

At this level of business thinking, a strategy involves a higher-level form of planning that describes and incorporates specific tactics that will be used to achieve identifiable goals. Take our earlier example of that hypothetical trip from California to Maine. The trip is a plan, but your strategy would include everything from specific details such as when and where you stop for rest, the costs involved in getting from point A to point B to point C and so on, and logistical concerns such as fuel, food, lodging, etc. Your business strategy takes a similar approach to identifying everything from tactics to resource needs within the context of an organized plan of action that will take you from business launch to success along a carefully-considered path.

Unfortunately, that is simply not how most strategic plans are managed. Even in instances where entrepreneurs take the time to develop such strategies, the sad fact is that few actually follow through on those efforts. In far too many instances, business owners spend days and weeks developing highly-detailed strategic road maps, only to abandon those strategies within a relatively short period of time. For most entrepreneurs, the enjoyable part is the creation of the plan, as they bask in the excitement that accompanies the launch of any new enterprise. Later, when that excitement has faded and the reality of day-to-day operations sinks in, those same owners simply get caught up in the action and fail to follow through. In fact, a Conference Board survey found that "60% of strategies are not successfully implemented."http://www.amanet.org/training/articles/what-is-strategy-execution.aspx

Strategy across All Levels of Your Business

While different people have different opinions when it comes to defining the meaning of strategy, I want you to think about the concept in a more comprehensive, all-encompassing manner. Your strategy is a plan that, when utilized on a long-term basis - can guide your business through its development for years to come. To do that, however, you have to develop the type of plan that is forward-thinking. Business strategy has to be about more than just getting through tomorrow with your customer base intact. It has to involve more than next month's planned product roll-out. And it cannot be just an overall plan to take your business to a certain destination.

A truly effective strategy is one that enables you to channel all of your company resources, expertise, and organizational skills in a way that creates competitive advantages at every level of your enterprise, with a consistent focus on achieving future goals.

If you think that one singular strategy can accomplish that objective, think again. Strategic development becomes more complex as your business grows, and an overriding company-level strategy will always have deficiencies that can prevent your enterprise from achieving the type of success you envision. Even if everyone in the company can somehow remain wholeheartedly committed to following a broad company strategy to the letter, it is still more likely than not that you will be disappointed by the results.

To understand why this is true, consider the systems approach we discussed in Chapter 3. When you have a company (your system) comprised of different spheres of activity and responsibility (subsystems), one broad strategy will never be sufficient for your needs. Remember too that each of those subsystems within your company is made up of individual teams of employees. When you have multiple teams focusing on different and often isolated tasks, it would be illogical to even presume that one comprehensive company strategy could guide them all to success.

Worse, if even one of those employees or teams fails to follow through on your company strategy, there is a ripple effect throughout your organization that can cause the entire enterprise to depart from your strategic plan. That can ultimately lead to the abandonment of the strategy altogether, leaving your company in a state where it is adrift and aimless.

Using the system approach, we develop strategies that bore down to the team and employee level, to ensure that we maximize the strategic value of all of the company's resources to ensure that the various systems and subsystems within the organization achieve optimal results. Your broader, comprehensive strategy for the company must therefore be complemented by strategies that provide guidance and planning at every level of the business. You must have a strategic plan that is focused on each employee, team, and department.

At the employee and team levels, these strategies provide guidance and direction that help to ensure that resources are utilized in the most effective manner possible to achieve daily, weekly, monthly, and longer term goals. At the departmental level, these strategies provide critical guidance that helps those employee teams build and maintain the competitive advantages that can enable your company to acquire and retain customers. At the company level, your strategic plan will enable your company to establish its market presence and enjoy planned and sustained growth over time.

At every level, however, you will notice that strategy is about more than just the "now" of the business. It is about more than just the future too. It is about all of those things that you and your teams do now to ensure that you are not only positioned properly for the future, but traveling down the right path to reach that destination. Your multi-level strategy has to be about winning today and tomorrow, at every level of the business, each and every day.

Think Strategically

Think about when you first decided to launch a business. It all began with a vision. From there, you created a defined mission statement designed to guide you in your efforts. You then move on to figure out exactly what you needed to accomplish that mission, and began to establish your goals and objectives. Your strategy is the sum of those methods and tactics you will need to use to attain your goals and accomplish your mission. Again, the strategy is neither your mission statement nor your goals. It is the detailed plan you will follow to fulfill that mission and accomplish those goals.

Because everything is interrelated, however, it is useful to understand that these components do mesh together in many ways. Your strategic thinking process actually begins with the formation of your vision, usually at the time you identify some problem or challenge and decide that you have a marketable solution. At its core then, business strategy encompasses all of the innovative thinking that helps you determine the best way to position your company so that you can exploit new challenges and opportunities in a more effective way than your competitors.

That requires strategic thinking. If you can identify a potentially effective way to achieve those results and provide that solution, then you can engage the market and customers with confidence that you can succeed. At the same time, you have to understand the risk inherent in moving forward with any endeavor if you have not properly developed your strategy - especially if you gamble everything without testing your strategy first.

The magnitude of your success or failure will always be in proportion to the scale and scope of your project. That is why it is important to recognize the need for minimization of risk exposure. When practical, you need to follow the sound business practice of testing your strategic thinking on a small scale pilot project before you adopt that strategy on a larger scale. Once you are confident that your strategy can be executed without complication then you can pursue it on a larger scale. The ability to consistently execute large scale strategic plans flawlessly is the hallmark of a best in class business. Make that a worthy goal of your company.

Obviously, the strategy formulation stage of your business planning can be the single most critical thing you do. Still, doing it badly can result in a nightmarish scenario where you lock in failure for your business. Why? It's simple: because a poorly-designed strategy can never be executed in a way that creates positive results. To avoid the worst-case scenario, you need to ask some fundamental questions:

1. What do you want to accomplish?
2. What are your goals and objectives?
3. What are your core competencies?
4. What resources are available?
5. Who is in charge?
6. What is the Timeline for Execution?

7. How do you compensate for known weaknesses?

8. What makes it a desirable winning strategy?

Only by answering those questions can you begin to lay out the "how to" plan that will design the most strategic way to complete the job before you. With that strategy, you can then begin to execute the plan, realize your goals, and achieve your ultimate mission.   Also, think of it as a game of chess. You want every move to be a winning move, a smarter move than your opponent.

Remember, the primary objective of all businesses is to maximize their long term investment of resources utilized, including the owner's valuable time. With a formal business plan, you can go through the exercise of identifying and examining your strengths, weaknesses, opportunities, and threats (SWOT). That business plan will clearly define the mission, goals, and objectives of your business endeavor. Your strategic plan will be established in support of your tactical plans, and with the right coordination, timing, and execution, will prove to be an invaluable contributing factor in your company's overall ability to achieve success.

Managing Your Strategy

In any process involving the management of a business strategy, there are different stages that should be followed. Experts have a variety of opinions with regard to how these stages are divided and categorized, but most agree on the basics that underlie the process. For our purposes, we will focus on three stages: development, implementation, and evaluation. However, there is some foundational work that must be done before you are ready to even begin the strategic development process.

That foundation includes both vision and analysis. We have already addressed vision at the beginning of the book, but it is worth mentioning again. The vision question - why you're in business in the first place - is central to the formulation of your goals and objectives. You have to identify immediate and long-term goals, and decide on the best process for meeting those objectives. With that determination made, you should then analyze your business needs and the overall market to identify core competencies, strengths, weaknesses, and available resources. This analysis should also provide you with insight into future challenges, threats, and opportunities that your company is likely to encounter in the coming months and years.

With your vision as a guide and your analysis ready, you will have the tools you need to begin the strategy formulation process. That three stage process may take longer to complete than you might prefer, but it is essential if you want to launch your business in an organized way and avoid the mishaps that can occur when disorder is allowed to prevail.

1. Create the Strategy. The creation of your business strategy is the single-most important part of the strategic process, since the lack of a sound strategy will sabotage even the best efforts to implement and evaluate the plan. A properly crafted strategic plan will rely on the information you derive from your analysis, and will be designed to channel your company's available resources in a way that provides your company with the best chance for achieving your business objectives.

The development of such a plan requires that you identify not only which resources are necessary for achieving each objective, but the best way to use them to achieve those goals. To do this effectively, you will also need to identify any external resources you will need to gain access to, and determine exactly how you will secure and use them. Many a business has failed due to improper planning in this one critical area.

You also have to identify all of the issues that your company is likely to face on its journey toward success. You should prioritize them both by their likelihood of manifestation and by the impact they could have on your ability to achieve success. When evaluating these issues, you have to focus on the various challenges that could arise at every level of the organization, and develop a plan to insulate the company against them, or effectively deal with them as they appear.

Finally, your strategy must have a certain level of flexibility built into its design. Economies are fluid and business circumstances can be impacted by a host of internal and external factors. As a result, your strategy will fail if it is designed to be so rigid that it cannot adapt to reality. Be sure that you have alternative options available for every part of your strategy so that you can effectively continue your business growth regardless of anything that might be occurring outside of your organization.

2. Implement Your Strategy. Just as the implementation of your strategy is meaningless if the design is fundamentally flawed, the strategy itself has no value if it is never implemented. Unfortunately, you may as well not even bother going through the motions of developing a strategy if you lack the commitment needed to actually implement it. Your time might just as well be invested in the latest movie at the theaters or sporting event on television.

When it comes to the strategy management process, the implementation stage is where the rubber meets the road. This is where strategies gain their meaning and prove their worth. For no matter how brilliant a strategy might appear to be on paper, it is a waste of ink if it never gets used in the real world. This is where the real action stage of your planning occurs, and is the point at which you must ensure that your company's organizational design is structured in a way that best facilitates effective implementation of your strategy.

Strategies should conform to a cohesive structure. That is an important truth to keep in mind since a failure to recognize this fact can result in chaos within your organization. Too often, entrepreneurs create their strategies and business structures in ways that fail to provide avenues for integration and effective implementation. If your structure cannot properly implement a sound and effective strategy, then it is the structure that must give way.

Strategy should be implemented at every level of the company. Each employee and every team must be made aware of their responsibilities within their business level's plan, while also being cognizant of the broader strategies that guide the organization as a whole. Only then can the implementation begin in earnest.

The process of implementing your strategy is critically important, and will be covered in greater depth in Chapter 6.

3. Evaluate, Modify, and Implement Changes.

Even after developing and implementing a strategy, your efforts could still fail if you don't ever stop to assess the results. The reality is that few strategies can ever achieve perfect results. Prussian Field Marshall Helmuth von Moltke the Elder, one of the leading figures in the German Wars of Unification in the second half of the 19th Century, spoke to this truth when he observed that:

> "Strategy is a system of expedients; it is more than a mere scholarly discipline. It is the translation of knowledge to practical life, the improvement of the original leading thought in accordance with continually changing situations." (Moltke on the Art of War: Selected Writings (1993) by Daniel J. Hughes and Harry Bell, p. 124)

Like Moltke, it falls to each of us to recognize that strategies seldom survive their first contact with conditions on the ground. No matter how clever we think we are, or how carefully we craft our plans, those plans almost always fail to accurately predict the nearly-infinite variety of possibilities we will encounter once we begin to implement our strategies. Surprisingly, however, many entrepreneurs allow themselves to become frozen with inaction when they discover that their strategies are inadequate for the challenges at hand. Still others continue to follow ineffective strategies long after those plans have failed them. If you want to succeed in the long-term, you have to learn to identify failings quickly, and adapt to your current situation.

The question is how you can ensure that any weaknesses in your strategy are identified quickly enough to provide you the time you need to adapt your strategies to meet your business reality. The answer is simple: continual evaluation. You have to conduct regular evaluations of your business to keep your strategy up to date with current needs. That requires things like employee, team, and departmental performance measurements, and a continual review of all of the major and minor issues affecting your company.

To do that, you have to establish performance parameters that are based on the initial goals and objectives you established when you first developed your business vision, values, and mission statement. You simply measure those goal parameters against the actual results you are achieving with your strategy. With the right focus and continual assessment, you will develop the ability to identify which issues are directly related to any deviations from your strategic expectations, and react accordingly.

Now, if you evaluate everything and find that your strategy is working exactly as intended and envisioned, then you can continue along that path without corrective action. On the other hand, when you see deviations in those anticipated results, you need to return to the strategy development stage to modify your plan. You then implement any modifications and continue to assess progress.

Many can develop impressive strategies on paper, but few can execute them flawlessly; even fewer have gained the mastery of dynamic strategic offset with flawless execution. It is an acquired skill that takes commitment and time to develop. Essentially, you have the ability to compensate for any shortfalls promptly without noticeable negative impact on the final outcomes.

Management by Objectives

There are many tools that you can use in your strategic thinking, and some of them have been around for many decades. One of those tools is the approach known as Management by Objectives, or MBO. This approach to strategic planning, execution, and management was first proposed by Peter Drucker back in 1954, and has been a useful management system for many companies. Though the idea has lost some of its luster over the course of the last sixty years, many of its principles remain sound and useful for entrepreneurs today.

MBO is an approach that focuses your company's resources on attainable objectives to enable the organization to maximize its resources and optimize results. An examination of this approach to management reveals it to be remarkably in tune with our system approach to business, since MBO also focuses on getting the most out of every employee, team, and department within the organization.

For our purposes, the main thing to note about this Management by Objectives approach is its emphasis on quantifiable goals and specific deadlines for achieving them. Because of its structure, this approach necessarily entails exactly the type of delegation that you should be focused on as the leader of your company. Every individual within your organization should be provided with well-communicated objectives that directly contribute to the overall objectives of your business enterprise. With your guidance and ultimate approval, those team members then establish their own short-term result goals that will enable them to achieve their broader objectives - as well as the company's overall goals.

As you develop your strategy, this can be a positive addition to the process when you implement it properly. MBO incorporates many of the key ideas we have already examined, including the need for employee empowerment, clearly-defined objectives, results tracking, feedback, and ongoing analysis and modification of your efforts. It also has the benefit of helping to focus your energies on those big picture issues that will ultimately determine the success or failure of your company, while providing enough autonomy for each employee to effectively meet his or her individual goals without the need for micromanagement.

Remember, though, that goal-setting is of the utmost importance with this or any other strategic approach to business. When we talk about setting goals, it is not within the context of some nebulous desire to achieve some objective at some random time in the future. To create, implement, and properly evaluate any goals, you have to ensure that your objectives are all so well-defined that you can recognize when they have not been met, since they are quantifiable with set deadlines.

That requires specificity on a level that most entrepreneurs tend to avoid. There are good reasons for that, not the least of which is the very natural human desire to limit the risk of being considered a failure. After all, if you have a goal of achieving a certain amount of sales revenue, but have no set time in which you expect that to happen, then who could ever suggest that you are failing? The problem, of course, is that this sort of lack of specificity can limit your growth and opportunity for success since it enables everyone within the company - including you - to simply accept mediocrity instead of striving to meet hard deadlines for your goals.

Without those verifiable numbers and hard deadlines, goals are but words. With no set date at which expectations must be met, any results are acceptable. To avoid that, your strategy must include realistically achievable target dates so that you know when you are not meeting your objectives. Only then will you have the feedback you need to determine that your strategy needs modification to keep you progressing toward your broader goals.

High level strategic thinking, when well executed, is invaluable to differentiate and gain instant credibility and awareness:

Dauphin Technology – A Case of a Winning Strategy

Dauphin Technology began operations in 1989 as a small personal computer firm. At the time of the company's founding, the computer industry had already grown to be quite crowded and fragmented, so there was a minimal cost barrier for those who wanted to enter the market. Even those with only a small amount to invest could start their own companies and declare themselves as leading PC manufacturers. They could claim to have the best product quality and the most favorable prices. And many did just that.

In reality, any one of those companies could have been nothing more than a single operator who was simply ordering parts from different manufacturers, assembling the final product, testing it, and then shipping it off to buyers. The marketplace was so chaotic and fragmented that most companies were just trying to compete on price alone, hoping that they could enjoy enough luck to gain market share and rapidly grow - enjoying some measure of profitability due to the economy of scale. Without that luck, most expected to fail and vanish as quickly as they appeared, and many did just that.

Dauphin Technology, however, took a different approach. Rather than take such an unruly and chaotic approach to operation, the company was specifically founded with the vision of being ahead of the technology curve. Its mission was to position itself so that it would be the future leader in mobile computer and wireless communication.

On the surface, it had a number of advantages that many other startups lacked. After all, it was an off-shoot of an already-established industrial alignment computer company - Manufacturing and Maintenance Systems. That gave it the advantage of enjoying a 20,000 square foot work space, support staff, and positive cash flow. Few enterprises of that era or any other enjoy that sort of start. Still, it is important to remember that the company was formed to compete in a marketplace that was already considered to be saturated and highly competitive. Many wondered at the time how any company - even one with those initial advantages - could hope to stand out from the crowd. How could Dauphin possibly establish a name for itself quickly enough to earn recognition in the industry as an emerging leader? And how could it hope to capitalize on growth in the industry so that it could exploit the market's anticipated expansion?

As the company's founder, I concluded that Dauphin needed to focus on developing the type of winning strategies that could give it the jump start it needed to burst onto the computer scene. We decided to seek two of the largest government portable computer contracts of that era. One was a $125 million Departmental Microcomputer Acquisition Contract (DMAC) II that the Department of the Treasury had been working on for three years without a final award - a fact that rendered its specifications obsolete in the fast-moving world of high-tech. The second contract was being offered by the Pentagon, as it was soliciting bids for someone who could supply it with 75,000 laptop computers called the Lapheld II that were valued at a total of $400 million.

Those types of projects would have given many entrepreneurs pause, but I saw them as opportunities and decided to focus on acquiring the contracts, and did so with a laser-like focus that I was determined to maintain until I achieved the necessary breakthrough. I understood Dauphin's strengths and weaknesses, and recognized that the company had the agility and funding ability needed to develop the three laptop computers that would be required to meet 100% of the contracts' specifications. At that time, none of the other bidders could accomplish that goal.

At the same time, I recognized the areas in which Dauphin had weaknesses, and sought out partnerships with Sysorex Information Systems, Inc. of Falls Church, Virginia, for the DMAC II bid and Sears Business Systems of Chicago, Illinois. As a result of aggressive pursuit of those contracts and timely partnerships to round out the company's core competencies, the Dauphin team secured both contracts. That success had the immediate effect of putting the company on the map and gaining respectability as a formidable competitor in the emerging world of mobile computing.

That success eventually led to the development of the Dauphin mini tablet computer that would end up in direct competition with the Apple Newton - which was an early handheld PDA from the company now best known for the iPhone.

Business Strategies to Consider

Obviously, every business is unique in its individual needs, so no single business strategy will work in all instances. As a result, it is important to recognize all of the many strategic options you have available to you when it comes to developing the plan that's right for your needs. While there are many well-established ideas that many companies consider core strategies - ideas that have been in use for many decades, with little change, new technologies and evolving consumer preferences are beginning to impact their effectiveness.

This is, after all, the information age, and the rise of new concepts like big data and blockchain technology is altering the face of the world's marketplace in ways that many businesses are struggling to understand. The new reality is that smart phones and other interactive technologies are enabling more rapid communication with other people and new ideas. At the same time, the sheer volume of accessible content grows by leaps and bounds with each passing year. As you develop your strategic plans, it is critical that you take these new facts into consideration to ensure that your business is operating in a way that conforms to your audience's expectations.

1. Recognize the New Emphasis on Customers. Forget about all that hype companies used to spew about "putting the customer first" and believing that "the customer is always right." While such assertions were popular fare in marketing campaigns, the reality is that few companies ever actually embraced those concepts as actual ideals to be followed. For most companies, such commitments were little more than surface hype. What little actual respect customers received was based solely on their perceived financial value to the companies involved.

Customers might have tolerated that in previous eras where the exchange of money for goods or services was about as deep as most business-consumer relationships actually went. That was then. Today, increased access to real-time information, greater connectivity, and the broader availability of goods and services in both the online and brick and mortar real world have resulted in a consumer population that has a true understanding of its own value. These consumers recognize that it is they who have the real power in most business relationships, since competition has now provided them with enough choices that they need no longer settle for poor customer service or unmet expectations.

Consumers have power, and savvy entrepreneurs recognize that they must adapt their approach if they are to enjoy real success. You can and must recognize this new reality and adapt your thinking to accommodate these customers' new expectations. A failure to do so can result in catastrophic consequences in an age where online reviews or comments on social media can be devastating for your business relationship. Here's the good news, though: that same potential for harming your business can also be levered to take your enterprise to new heights of success once you learn the new rules of engagement.

- Know your customers. It is not enough to know them when they walk in your store or place an order online. Get to know their buying habits, their preferences, and their expectations. That will enable you to adapt your products, services, and messaging to meet them where they live.

- Engage with them in a comprehensive way. Do not wait for them to find you online. Instead, find ways to encourage them to engage more intimately with your company. Develop a rewards or loyalty program that entices them to become connected with your business on all of the many social media platforms you will use for customer engagement. Encourage their comments and feedback, and let that information guide you as you adapt your services to better match their wants and needs.

2. Get Mobile. Studies have revealed that consumers spend about sixty percent of their internet time engaging with content on their smart phones, tablets, and other mobile devices. Most analysts expect that number to increase in the years ahead, as these technologies continue to become even more affordable. To accommodate that trend, you need to ensure that your company website is mobile-ready so that customers can use it effortlessly. This might seem like an obvious thing, but many entrepreneurs are still surprisingly slow to adapt to these changes.

That mobile-friendly approach to your online presence should be maintained any time you add new websites, conduct marketing, or otherwise communicate in the online universe. Mobile users will continue to make up the lion's share of your online visitors and you need to make sure that the website they visit is one that meets their expectations and needs.

Of course, there is more to leveraging mobile technology opportunities than simply having mobile-friendly sites. You may also want to consider mobile apps, QR codes, and other technological features that are being embraced by customers everywhere.

3. Focus on Content. From a strategic standpoint, content will always be king. Communication is important, but nothing beats communication consisting of powerful, professional content. For many entrepreneurs, the development of content sometimes devolves into stereotypical marketing hype that more often than not turns off a large portion of the audience that sees it. Truly professional content can avoid that hazard and communicate your message in a way that is engaging, enticing, and entertaining.

Here's the thing to remember: content is not just about communicating with words. To be effective, it has to communicate information that the customer wants to see, and do so in a way that delivers real value to consumers. Companies that figure out how to do that in a consistent and effective way end up creating more than just words on a screen or billboard. They end up creating a content brand that serves to enhance their company brand in ways that no stereotypical marketing campaign ever could.

When developing your strategy, never forget about your need for content!

4. Educate your team. One of the hottest trends in recent years is a move toward expanding training opportunities at the company level. Companies are beginning to once again realize that the time and money they invest in enhancing their employees' skill sets yield important results for the business enterprise. This training and continuing education has become even more vital as new technologies and systems continue to develop each passing year.

If you remember the changes that occurred when computer technology began to spread throughout the business world, then chances are you also recall the struggles that many people endured as they tried to adapt to what often seemed to be completely alien devices. Many older workers experienced a great deal of frustration, and there were many companies in which management found itself ill-equipped and unprepared to provide the training their workers needed. No one expects you to accurately predict all of the future training needs your company may experience, but you can include within your strategy a plan for providing and pursuing training whenever it becomes necessary for maintaining your team's skills.

These modern strategic options won't by themselves ensure that you develop a strategy that can work for your business, but they can be valuable considerations for your strategic thought process. There is more to strategy than just focusing on differentiation, cost structures, customer focus, and other factors that help you to create the competitive advantage you need. Those formal, well-understood aspects of business strategy are essential, but they often fail to address emerging realities and new technologies. If you remain in touch with marketplace shifts, you can more effectively create the strategy you need to propel your company into the future.

The Big Picture

As you can see, there is more to strategy than just simple planning. Effective strategies do more than just declare the objectives you need to meet to fulfill your mission and realize your vision, since you do that with your company goals. Strategies do not define what you are trying to accomplish or what your company will look and feel like when all that is done; your mission and vision fill those roles. Your strategy defines how you plan to most effectively use the resources and tools at your disposal to fulfill your vision and mission by meeting those company goals and objectives.

Naturally, all of these elements are essential when you are creating the type of company that will be properly positioned for success. It should also be obvious that it will be next to impossible to create an effective strategy if you have not yet crafted an inspiring vision and a realistic mission with attainable objectives. All of these pieces fit neatly together and help to shape your decision-making process as you craft the type of strategy that you and your team can rely on to guide you to success. Great strategic thinking is an art form that emerges from a deep knowledge of the subject and the opponent. Coupled with boundless practices and self-discipline, the development of winning strategies can become instinctive.

Chapter 6 - Execution

"Without strategy, execution is aimless. Without execution, strategy is useless."

- Morris Chang, CEO of Taiwan Semiconductor Manufacturing Company

****

For many new entrepreneurs, and a sizable number of established businesses as well, strategic development can become such an all-encompassing process that little attention is ever given to execution of those plans. Management in many companies seems to divide its attention between two areas of concern: developing strategies (typically achieved as a result of a seemingly endless series of meetings) and micromanaging employee activities. Any examination of this process in the average business setting reveals that an incredibly large number of well-conceived and detailed strategic plans never receive the type of follow-through they need to achieve the desired results.

Even those businesses that are focused on developing winning strategies spend far too little time emphasizing proper execution and monitoring of those plans. We see it time and time again: meetings are held, ideas are exchanged, and a great deal of priority is given to brainstorming new strategic plans designed to drive growth in the company. Subsequent meetings over time often return to these developed strategies, but these follow-up discussions are often disconnected from any real demonstrable testing of the strategic vision. There is simply more talk, more brainstorming, and perhaps with a few adjustments to the strategy. These decisions are rarely influenced by any measured results, since few companies actually invest time and resources into properly executing their own plans.

Right about now, you may be thinking that this is all hyperbole. After all, there are huge business enterprises out there that seem to be doing virtually everything correct. How then could they be suffering from a deficiency in such a critical area as strategic execution? That is a good question, and there are a number of very good answers that help to explain this phenomenon. Before delving into them, however, it is important to establish the real scope of this problem. According to results from a survey conducted by consulting firm PwC's Strategies & marketplace, executives have some serious concerns about their companies' strategic efforts - in terms of both planning and execution:

- 46% of those surveyed expressed concerns that their business strategies lacked the type of aggressive boldness that is required for their companies to beat their rivals.

- More than a third of respondents - 39% - are worried that their business strategy is so incoherent that it fails to properly leverage critical competencies, resources, and assets.

- 33% recognize that their strategies are so ill-conceived that they don't even address critical concerns like creating value for customers.[1]

As bad as those numbers might seem, the survey results were even worse when company executives were asked about the success of their strategic execution. If you had simply assumed that any concerns over implementation were hyperbolic at best, just consider this:

- 55% of all surveyed executives - a clear majority of respondents - recognize that their companies are not properly focused on executing their strategic plans.

- 42% believe that their strategies are designed in a way that forces employees to actually emphasize competing priorities, or simply address too many concerns at once.

- 42% of respondents believe that their companies have failed to garner the type of buy-in necessary for proper execution. Execution is all but impossible without the entire company being committed to proper implementation.

- 26% cite the company culture as being the primary reason for a failure to execute the strategy.[2] Finally, the overall level of concern is shocking:

---

1   - 1 http://www.strategyand.pwc.com/media/image/img_Executives-see-shortcomings-in-their-companys-strategy1000x700.jpg

2

     [2] http://www.strategyand.pwc.com/media/image/img_Companies-struggle-to-implement-their-strategyy1000x700.jpg

1. 96% of those surveyed are either somewhat or significantly concerned about the existence of at least one barrier to successful strategic development or execution within their companies.

2. Only 4% of respondents believe that their company faces no significant barrier to successful implementation of their strategies.[3]

Those results should dispel any thoughts that this is an overblown concern. The fact is that those survey results just scratch the surface of this problem. If 55% of executives believe that their companies are not properly focused on strategy execution, we need to remember that those are just the ones who recognize that there is a problem. How many of those who believe that no such problem exists are actually correct? There is no way to know for certain, but it is unlikely that even these eye-opening statistics fully describe the true size and scope of this dilemma. These numbers alone reveal that this is one of the biggest issues facing today's businesses.

Why Does Execution Lag Behind Other Priorities?

The obvious question that needs to be answered is why companies spend so much time delving into the process of devising strategies, and so little time actually executing those plans once they are developed. There are many reasons why this happens, but we will just examine some of the most common factors that cause businesses to drop the ball on execution.

• **Strategic Development is Exciting; Execution is Not**

Face it; the real excitement of strategic thinking is found in the creation of a strategic plan. The creative process provides an opportunity for the free-flowing exchange of ideas, and is stimulating for the mind and spirit. Even the seeming monotony of endless meetings seems to fade away when participants are engaged in this type of planning. On the other hand, there is nothing inherently exciting about the hard work required for proper implementation of any strategic plan. Effective execution requires that the various aspects of the strategy be implemented to the letter, so that results can be monitored, measured, and tracked over time. Furthermore, successful execution demands commitment, dedication, and relentless hard work, and that is a lot harder to come by.

3

[3] http://www.strategyand.pwc.com/media/file/Strategyand_Infographic-Strategy-execution-survey.pdf

- **As Excitement Fades, Strategies are Forgotten**

  There is another byproduct of the lack of excitement involved in strategic execution: the tendency to simply forget about the entire strategy once that thrill has passed. There are companies that begin the execution process with somewhat of an air of urgency, but as managers and employees become more engrossed in the day to day tasks associated with just operating the business, that urgency fades. Without that initial sense of excitement and urgency, the entire plan fades into the background and is all but forgotten.

- **Team Changes Can Cause Loss of Focus**

  Even in cases where a sincere effort is made to execute the strategy, the entire plan can collapse due to changes in personnel or management. Often times, strategic thinking is not properly ingrained into the company culture, and that can cause newer members of the team to lack the focus on execution that is needed to succeed with the plan's implementation. Without a competent plan for maintaining team momentum, the impetus for continued execution eventually subsides.

- **Communication is Lacking**

  As important as strategic plans are for the successful achievement of company goals, you would think that management and leadership would give priority to communication with the entire team. Sadly, most businesses that fail to properly execute their plans fail in this one area. Successful execution requires that every member of the team fully understand each aspect of the company's strategy and the tactics that will be used during execution. It is thus vital that these strategic goals and implementation plans be communicated to team members throughout the organization.

- **Strategies Conflict with Employee Interests**

  Many companies devise strategies that run contrary to the systems established for employee performance and incentives. If your employees are being assessed using criteria that are in conflict with those performance yardsticks that need to be done during successful execution of your broader strategy, then those employees are going to ignore the strategy and focus on their own wellbeing instead. Remember, self-interest is the single greatest motivating factor in the world. The key to successful strategic execution is to find the best way to align your strategy with your employees' self-interests. Consequently, the much disliked traditional employee performance review and other incentive programs may be a hindrance rather than of help. Carefully consider if a different approach, such mutual goals review mentioned in chapter 10 of this book, is more effective in aligning employees' interest with company's interests, missions, goals, and objectives in the pursuit of the company vision.

- **Failure to Monitor Results**

  According to some estimates, 85% of business enterprises fail to properly monitor the results of their strategic execution process, and compare them to their original goals. That leaves them generally clueless with respect to whether or not any real progress is being achieved, and unable to effectively modify their strategies even when it becomes clear that nothing is working according to plan. As former British Prime Minister Winston Churchill once noted, "However beautiful the strategy, you should occasionally look at the results."

- **Lack of Knowledge About Strategic Execution**

  There are also many business leaders who simply confuse the development of a strategy with its execution. Much of the business education process is focused on teaching businesspeople how to think strategically. That focus is so pervasive that it is easy for many of these thought leaders to become so enamored of the strategy-creation process that they never come to terms with the fact that execution does not just happen of its own accord. If anyone had ever told you that a well-conceived strategy will basically execute itself, they were probably trying to sell you something.

- **Lack of Conviction**

  Because businesses today exist within an environment that is constantly changing, many entrepreneurs mistakenly assume that they must work to constantly adapt to every little change in the marketplace. While flexibility and nimbleness are important traits for any business, there is also such a thing as being too adaptable - especially when it comes to your company's strategic plan. If you are constantly shifting your strategy in an attempt to chase each day's perceived market trends, then you are denying yourself one of the best tools for strategic success: the ability to track any plan's results over time and assess the viability of your overall strategy. In this instance, patience is not only a virtue but a necessity.

- **Lack of Accountability**

  Many businesses never effectively assign execution accountability to departments, teams, or individual team members. They merely establish their strategic plan, outline the tactics and methods they will use to achieve it, and then trust everyone in the company to make it happen. That lack of direct accountability creates the type of organizational drift that prevents goals from being reached.

  Now, this is not to suggest that you create your strategy and then put team members on notice that a failure to achieve the smaller goals for which they are responsible will result in harsh consequences. That sort of rule by fear is seldom inspiring. At the same time, however, there has to be some accountability, maintained over time, if anything is ever to be achieved.

- **Failure to Keep Score**

  By and large, people are competitive. We continually compare business to sporting activities for one compelling reason: they both involve the type of competitive nature that fosters true emotional engagement. Many companies that fail to track results and develop accountability are missing out on this key to emotional engagement in the workplace: keeping score.

  If you can get your team members, teams, and departments to actually track their own performance during strategy execution, you will have them keeping score of the action. They may be comparing their results to each other, to other teams, or to other departments, but the important thing is that they will be emotionally engaged in the process. Their natural competitive drive will motivate them to execute the plan.

Defining Execution

As I mentioned, one of the reasons why so many business leaders fail to achieve successful execution of their strategies is that they fail to understand the real nature of the concept. Execution is not just a natural byproduct of strategic planning, nor is it something that magically happens when your strategy is sound. Neither is it the concluding stage of the strategic planning effort. Instead, it is a process worthy of its own attention, and one that requires an even greater investment of time, energy, and resources.

Every important strategic plan must be complemented by an execution plan. Without such a carefully-crafted plan of action, your strategy will not be fully implemented and far less likely to succeed. A viable execution plan is needed to guide your team as it implements strategy, and that plan must include the following key elements:

- The execution plan should detail all of the actions necessary for implementing the strategy. That includes key decisions, processes that need to be put into place, and other factors that will impact the ability of the company to achieve its strategic goals.

- To avoid confusion, your execution plan should include an analysis of how various factors will interact, and describe interdependencies within the execution process.

- The plan should assign responsibilities for needed actions and decision-making, as well as any areas where cooperative efforts are needed to move the execution forward. This is the point at which accountability should be assigned as well.

- It is also advisable to include standards for measurement, as well as a tracking and results analysis plan within your execution plan to ensure that progress monitoring is not forgotten along the way.

Your execution plan should provide the guidance every member of your organization needs to translate your brilliant strategy into the best possible performance. All of those tactics and resource allocation plans that form the foundation of your strategy are of little use without a solid plan and system for execution throughout every level of your organization. And while strategy planning tends to involve only a small subset of individuals within any organization, execution must involve each and every person on your team. A well coordinated plan execution is an integral part of a winning strategy. Remember, everything is interrelated. Like a well oiled machine, when all the subsystems are working perfectly; it delivers the maximum performance.

It is also worth noting that time is a critical factor in both strategy and execution. Strategic planning is something that typically requires only days or weeks. In some cases, a sound strategy can be developed in just a few meetings, encompassing several hours total. While strategic thinking can encompass future-centric plans that look out years in advance of today, the creation of such plans requires only a small fraction of that time.

Execution is something that requires that you think both in terms of short and long-term needs. It encompasses not only the need for implementing your strategy over the course of years, but the specific things your company needs to do today, tomorrow, and next week as well. It is a plan that directs individual team members, coordinates their efforts into team results, and channels each team's achievements into departmental and organizational accomplishments that align with your strategic plan and move the company forward toward its goals. It often involves multi stages of strategic positioning as a vital part of the execution.

The Cost of Execution Failure

According to estimates, 60% of all strategies are never successfully executed. If that statistic existed within a vacuum, it might be of little concern. The sad fact, however, is that this failure to properly execute has real and serious consequences for the businesses involved. Poor execution, an incomplete execution process, poorly timed execution efforts, and outright abandonment of execution plans routinely result in a lack of company success, as well as business failure.

Consider the example of a typical concert. No concert director worth his salt would ever contemplate allowing a production to proceed without first ensuring that there is a well-conceived plan in place. That plan would provide details about every task and responsibility, and each would be defined with a great degree of specificity to enable the entire concert team to execute the production within the goal parameters, on time, and in sequence. Each and every act would be carefully chosen, rehearsed, refined, and perfected before the first show would be launched. Why? It's simple: without a precise plan of action, the entire production could easily devolve into a state of utter chaos.

In business, you face the same challenge. All of your great ideas are worth very little if you have no concrete plan for executing your strategies. You can develop the best game plan in the world, but it will avail you nothing if you never figure out how to successfully execute that plan and somehow exploit the opportunities before you. Simply put, you cannot be the best in class if you fail to learn how to execute strategy.

To understand how an inability to execute your strategy can damage your business, it is helpful to consider how that failure can impact every area of your company, as well as customers and others with whom you do business:

- **If execution fails, leadership fails**

  Make no mistake; contrary to what some executives might believe, their job does not end with the development of the company's strategic plan. Far too many leaders assume that there is a clear division of labor at work when it comes to strategy and execution, and that management is responsible for executing the strategies that leadership develops. That is simply not the case. The reality is that proper execution cannot happen without leadership's direct and continual involvement in the process.

  It is leadership's job to work with management to ensure that execution occurs. That is true for one simple reason: execution is not a short-term process; it is an ongoing effort that requires leadership's involvement to ensure that the company's culture continues to support full implementation of its strategy. Most managers find it difficult to maintain focus on any plan for execution, since their attention tends to be pulled in a thousand different directions each day. Without support from leadership, management will simply give up, or will suffer from divided attention that causes the execution effort to lose momentum over time.

Because leadership is so critical to successful execution, when strategies fail to be properly implemented the team's confidence in its leaders can suffer. That loss of confidence can have a cascading effect in every area of the business, and hinder productivity, reduce commitment to the company's mission and vision, and even cause deterioration in employee morale and customer service.

- **Poor execution can cause a loss of focus**

One of the most troubling effects of a failure to properly execute the company strategy is the resulting loss of focus that often follows. The fact is that an organized and concerted effort is always needed if any execution plan is to be successful. When a plan does not get executed properly, it is typically due to a lack of organization, follow-through, and commitment. If you review my earlier list of reasons why execution tends to receive such little attention in most companies, you will see that there is one common theme running through each cited example: a lack of focus.

Now, the reason this lack of focus can have long-lasting effects is simple: if the organization cannot maintain its united focus on the execution of a well-conceived and carefully-detailed strategic plan, how can it be expected to maintain focus on the more chaotic and less-structured details and tasks that fill most work days? It cannot. And when such a broad-based failure occurs at the company level, that failure tends to take root in the company culture and permeate other areas of operational concern. Many businesses that fail to execute their strategies do not suddenly go bankrupt; instead, they lose focus more and more each day and tend to drift along aimlessly for a time. The failure to execute is, in those cases, a mortal wound - but one that causes the company to bleed out slowly over time rather than drop dead in an instant.

- **Team cohesion can be shattered**

When execution fails, teamwork is often one of the first casualties, leading to blame games and politics. Again, this all comes back to the team's united ability to focus on execution. The team that demonstrates that it cannot maintain cohesion during implementation of a strategic plan will find that it cannot maintain cohesion in any area of operations for very long. This is why most failing businesses have decaying company cultures that fail to motivate and guide employees in their daily actions.

- **Customers can sense drift too**

A failure to execute your plan impacts customers too. The average consumer recognizes a lack of focus and can discern when companies are committed, organized, and moving forward in a coherent manner. When strategies are ignored or improperly executed, that has an impact on how consumers perceive your business. They take note of how your team members conduct themselves, and are aware of any lack of consistency in your approach to your market.

- **You'll never be the best in class**

This is the most critical one. As I've mentioned earlier, you cannot become the best in class by accident. Life just doesn't work that way. To succeed in being the best in class, you need a plan. But your plan will not help you achieve your goal if it goes unrealized. You need an effective strategy to score those consistently high category results, and an execution plan to ensure that your strategy is fully and properly implemented. Without the latter, your business will never be more than mediocre.

Developing a Superior Execution Plan: The Keys to Success

Now that we have established the importance of having a plan for executing your strategy, the next and most logical question is how that plan should be developed. There are some clear steps that must be taken during the execution planning stage to ensure that you have put into place all of the elements necessary for successful implementation. Key decisions will have to be laid out in great detail, and a well-crafted action plan will need to be communicated. Your plan will also have to be able to accommodate change, lest the need for adaptation undermines your team's focus and disrupts the implementation process.

Key One: Understanding the Strategy

Before you can design an effective execution plan, you have to make sure that everyone involved in that planning fully understands the strategy. That means not just understanding it from the perspective of process, but understanding as well how it comports with the company's culture, values, and ultimate goals. Recognize that the execution of your strategy will be far more difficult than its creation, and will have a far greater impact on your eventual success.

Because of this fact, it is important to ensure that your strategy is sound before you develop your execution plan. Are the resources, systems, processes, and tools you have at your disposal sufficient to accomplish your strategic goals? Is your culture sufficiently amenable to executing the strategy with a minimum of disruption? What internal and external obstacles need to be overcome for successful execution of your plan? These and similar questions need to be asked at the earliest stage of the process, to ensure that you are not developing an execution plan that is doomed to failure.

Remember also that the execution planning stage may reveal weaknesses in your strategic thinking that will need to be remedied before you can proceed. You may discover that your current culture is not amenable to proper execution of the existing strategy, in which case you either have to modify the strategy or work to change the culture. You might learn that there's a gap in your strategic thinking that seems to have no easy solution. Be resourceful and test it out in a small scale. At times, you may have to reposition the company or even develop a new partnership to fill the gap or compensate for any weaknesses.

As you examine your strategy, it is important to identify any deficiencies and remedy them before you proceed any further. While you cannot implement a sound strategy without a sound execution plan, it is also true that no plan of execution can succeed in achieving your goals if the strategy you are implementing is fundamentally unsound. Once you are confident that the strategy can achieve your goals, you can move on to developing your execution plan.

Key Two: Translate Strategy to Action

With your strategy in hand, the next step in the development of your execution plan involves translating your goals into concrete initiatives that will enable you to make progress toward those objectives. In most instances, your strategy will cover multiple years, and include specific objectives that you expect to achieve within certain time frames. To translate all of those objectives into real-world action, you need to break down larger goals into smaller ones, to provide a more detailed roadmap that clearly outlines the specific path your company will travel.

The reason for this breakdown is simple: without it, you will have difficulty organizing your company's daily activities in a way that makes steady progress toward your strategic goals. Once broken down and aligned with specific initiatives, however, the work that your team does on a daily basis will be in alignment with your strategic roadmap and goals.

Each initiative is simply a concerted effort to foster progress toward your objectives. Initiatives should contain a number of elements that help to define them for every member of your team:

- Defined Actions. You must define the specific activities involved in the initiative, and how those activities are expected to foster progress toward the company's strategic goals. You also need to define expectations in quantifiable terms, so that your results can be measured in terms of anticipated goals.

- Defined Responsibilities. This is important, since accountability at every level of your organization is necessary for success. Identify all of the resources - money, employees, material, and time - needed for implementation of the initiative.

- Defined Timelines. Initiatives need to be time-sensitive. To properly measure progress, define every initiative's beginning and end point.

- Defined Results Analysis. It is vital to track results. Also determine the metrics used to judge performance, and the time periods at which you will closely analyze those results.

- A Defined Modification Process. It is helpful to know in advance how you will handle any needed adjustments.

It is critical to understand that leadership must avoid becoming detached from the execution process. Because leaders view execution as a managerial responsibility, this is usually the point at which many executive decision-makers think they can simply hand off the baton to their managers. To avoid that mistake, remain involved throughout every step of the process. While there is a natural branching out of responsibility from leadership to management and then on to each team member, there must also be a leadership-focused approach to the process. Leadership must insert itself into the tracking, reporting, and analysis part of the execution plan, and maintain regular contact with management to ensure that execution goes forward as planned. Many strategy executions failed due to the lack of top management participation and support. Avoid the costly pitfalls, especially if those strategies that must be executed flawlessly are critical to the success of the company.

Key Three: Implement Your Initiatives

Since your business is a complete system with many subsystems working together to achieve the company goals, it is almost inevitable that you will have multiple initiatives underway as you execute your strategy. Different departments and teams may be responsible for different types of initiatives, and that can sometimes be difficult to properly coordinate without prior planning. To ensure that your initiatives all contribute to the progress you are seeking, you need to work to fully integrate them at the team level, while clearly communicating any overlap among different teams or departments.

To do this properly, it is necessary to analyze how different initiatives will impact one another. From our study of the system approach, we learned that every system impacts other areas of your company. You must remember that lesson while you are considering the interplay between the different initiatives you put into action. Every time you launch a new initiative, you have to do so with the expectation that its execution will place new demands on different aspects of your organization. One initiative might place a new demand on human resources, while another might increase technological stress.

Ideally, the interplay between these initiatives will have been studied and worked out during the planning process. However, it is sometimes difficult to determine exactly how project implementation will affect operations, so it is important to be flexible, nimble, and ready to make modifications to ensure that the plan goes forward.

To prepare for that possibility, it is important to get everyone in management on board early. That includes not only departmental heads, but team leaders as well. Everyone who has a role in leadership at any level must be involved from the initial stages of strategic implementation, and remain focused for the long haul. During the early phase of the execution process, you will want to work on communicating the plan to those team leaders and managers. They should then provide you with details about available resources, with an eye toward ensuring that each member of your team has access to the human capital, resources, and technology necessary to successfully implement the assigned initiative.

Key Four: Communicate

No matter how spellbinding your execution plan might seem to you and others on the leadership team, it will ultimately amount to nothing if it is not properly communicated to everyone in your organization. By this time, your team should have some idea about the overall strategy - the best planners communicate these things in smaller pieces during the planning stage - and find themselves adequately prepared for the more detailed execution plan. The idea behind this level of communication is to seek active engagement from everyone in your company.

To achieve the right level of engagement, you should not only provide the information that each team member needs, but encourage feedback. Sometimes, a line employee may have a better handle on resource needs than management. If you put into place a system that facilitates two-way dialogue during execution, then you will have access to more timely information. It is also helpful to develop a framework for team meetings for updates on execution progress, as well as personal meetings between employees and management to emphasize task management.

Above all else, however, communication must be sustained over time. It is not enough for you to communicate big ideas and plans on day one of the execution process, if you never follow up with regular updates and meetings to measure progress and sustain momentum. If you fail to return to the topic on a regular basis, your team members will lose focus and the execution effort will stall.

This communication effort is designed to mobilize your team, marshal resources, and channel your organization's combined energies into one sustained push to achieve the aims of each initiative that makes up the whole of your execution plan. This mobilization requires buy-in at every level of the company since execution often entails members of your team doing things in new ways. That is another reason why leadership is so critical during the execution process: managers often fail to make the case for this kind of change. As you communicate your execution plan, focus on these critical areas:

1Communicate not only the "what" of the plan, but the "why" as well. If you only tell team members what you expect of them, they may do it but they will never sustain the effort when your attention is elsewhere. If you effectively communicate why you are focusing on these changes that added level of understanding can provide the incentive the team needs to ensure that you get the follow-through you need.

2Make sure that your employees understand how their performance targets are aligned with the company's strategic goals. If there is any competition between employee self-interest and company objectives, you can rest assured that the employee will always choose his own interests over yours every time. Then again, if you were in his shoes, you would do the same. To avoid that choice, align team self-interest with your company's strategic objectives.

3Make sure that everyone has all the information needed to effectively carry out their responsibilities. Since most initiatives of consequence will involve input from multiple team members, be sure to eliminate the potential for weak links in your chain of communication.

4Assign responsibilities and accountability. Create competition where possible, to ensure that everyone on the team is keeping score and motivated to win.

5Establish a process for ongoing communication and updates. That could entail something as simple as a daily email, or more complex processes like newsletters, a departmental website, or regular meetings and workshops.

6Work to ensure that execution of the company strategy becomes a part of the company's culture. That cultural shift should begin during the strategy formation process, as leadership updates the team on any new changes in the strategic plan. From that point onward, the culture's vision, mission, and values should become closely associated with your strategy and execution plans.

Key Five: Track Results

Execution requires constant monitoring, analysis, and adjustments if it is to be successful. If you examine any group of companies, you will find that the ones that are best at implementing their plans are also among the best at tracking their progress and results. They have effective processes for tracking a wide range of metrics, and systems that enable them to accurately assess their results. Their evaluations are periodic, ongoing, and designed with the goal of providing the type of critical information that decision-makers need to properly adjust to the reality on the ground.

To track results accurately, you need to have a culture that encourages everyone on your team to consistently record progress toward initiative goals. As a leader, you should work with team members and management to ensure that the tracking process is not so arduous and time-consuming that it inhibits the real work that contributes to the realization of goals. Instead, progress reports should require no more than a few moments on a daily or weekly basis.

Those tracked results can then be used for the even more critical strategy reports that you should generate on a regular basis. The team member progress tracking provides the information you need to monitor and report on your overall progress toward achieving your strategic goals. They provide clues about where your company stands with respect to its execution timeline, while identifying any challenges that may be slowing progress or otherwise affecting priorities.

That information can often reveal weaknesses that need to be addressed. Unrealistic timeline goals, an unforeseen shortage of manpower or material resources, or just improperly tasked staff members can all create roadblocks that inhibit progress.

Key Six: Review, Adjust, and Repeat

With your results analysis in hand, you can review the progress that you have made and reassess your overall strategy and execution plans with an eye toward identifying areas in need of improvement. As important as it is to follow through on your execution plans once they are implemented, it is equally important to recognize when changes are needed. In a perfect world, every sound strategy and implementation plan would simply be put into place and run on its own from that point forward. This is not, however, a perfect world.

The reality is that your plan - no matter how carefully-crafted will almost certainly fail to accommodate every eventuality that will arise. Even the best estimates about employee allocation, resource availability, and other critical factors will often prove to be less than accurate when all is said and done. Your progress in achieving your initial goals will be excellent in some areas, mediocre in others, and perhaps even downright dreadful on occasion. The one thing that can help you to continue to move forward is your ability to make adjustments even as you are executing your plan. The ability to recognize problems early and promptly make adjustment is a valuable skill set in great execution. Being proactive and resourceful to counter balance or compensate for anticipated shortfalls is a secret to flawless execution.

The key thing to do at this stage is to regularly assess your results and return to the strategy analysis and planning stage of your process. When goals are not met, work to identify the cause of the failure. Was the strategy too ambitious, or was it simply a deficiency in the plan for execution? Go through all of the obvious potential reasons for failure until you identify the weakness in your strategic or implementation plan, and then make the changes you need to overcome those challenges.

Important Execution Factors You Should Consider

Those six keys can help you to get started with your strategy execution plan, but they are by no means the final word on the subject. The fact is that execution techniques are not static, and new tactics, technologies, and theories are being introduced on a regular basis. More importantly, the rise of information technology and instantaneous communication has helped to introduce a variety of future-focused execution ideas. Many of these approaches are designed to accommodate the need for real-time adjustments to deficiencies and quick responses to immediate challenges. The world often seems to be accelerating at an ever-greater technological pace, and businesses need to be able to adapt, respond, and engage more rapidly than ever before.

Think Real-Time

We previously discussed the need to design your plan with built-in flexibility to enable you to adapt quickly. This is especially important when your execution plan involves tech-reliant initiatives, since technological innovation is occurring at such a high rate of speed that today's cutting edge technology will likely be considered obsolete six months or a year from now. Your plan should contain enough flexibility to provide you with options for adapting to new innovation or better systems when they emerge. The world is moving beyond historical indicators and embracing forward-thinking leading indicators to provide the timely strategic execution flexibility today's companies need.

However, especially in large scale revolutionary technologies like digital currency and blockchain at the formative stages, participating at the right time is critical. New technologies always evolve and get better over a period of time. Going all in too early, when many technical issues are unresolved can be risky and expensive incurring a heavy pioneer burden. Consider participating in a smaller scale at the onset but be positioned to scale quickly at the most opportune time. Learn all you can and be a thought leader capable of making the right calls in real time.

Link Delegation to Authority

Focus on empowering employees at every level. Accountability is important, but so too is authority. For your team members, there are only a few things more frustrating than having responsibility delegated to them and discovering that they have no authority to do what is necessary to meet those obligations. Always remember that higher levels of responsibility and accountability should be linked to increased levels of authority to ensure that the job can get done.

Don't Misjudge Managers

As a leader, you may be thinking that execution will never be a problem because that is why you employ managers. Think Again! The problem with that line of thinking is that managers are generally unqualified to execute plans on their own. If you doubt that, just consider the type of courses studied in most MBA programs. There is a strong emphasis on various types of strategic thinking, focused on marketing, finances, and competitive needs. Where execution is mentioned, it is as an afterthought. Everything is planning. And while there are signs that some business schools may be altering that approach to focus more on implementation, that only helps the next generation of business leaders.

We have to deal with the reality of the here and now, and that reality is simple: managers are planners. They are not trained to execute. That can be a problem in companies where managers have had little experience in the execution of plans, since execution is generally something that is learned through actual action rather than in classes focused on theory. The leaders who develop strategies must work alongside their management staff during the execution phase, and cannot simply assume that managers can implement ideas on their own.

View Execution as a Way of Life

When it comes to being the best in class, it is important to recognize that execution of your strategy is more than just a series of actions or even a process. It should become the sum total of every action and process your company engages in as it pursues implementation of its strategies. There are no tricks that can help you navigate some magical shortcut from strategy planning to goal realization. Execution is, at its best, the aggregate result of all of the decisions and actions that you take to fully implement your company initiatives over time. When done properly, execution creates the type of competitive advantage that will make you the best of class in every area of comparison.

Above all, great execution creates the type of competitive advantage that is all but impossible for your rivals to imitate. Product gimmicks, catchy services, and clever marketing can all be copied or imitated by jealous competitors. When you are the best in class as the result of consistently effective implementation of your strategic plan, however, that is something that even the best imitators will struggle to match.

The Big Picture

Of course, there is more to successful execution than just getting that latest product or project launched. At the end of the day, even the most effective execution plans cannot be said to be truly successful unless they manage to produce real and tangible benefits for the company. In many instances, the successful launch of a new service or product is just the beginning of the process with no guarantee of success down the road. It is every bit as important to focus on project management that emphasizes long-term consistency of returns. Additionally, it is also prudent to start out with small pilot projects that are designed to be highly scalable. The ability to execute and launch projects flawlessly is invaluable.

This is why we make plans even for execution, when practical, especially when important and complex strategies are involved. Without a plan, we would fall into the trap that devours so many other entrepreneurs as they are lured by the siren call of new opportunities and never manage to stick to any one strategic plan long enough to allow it to work. Without a plan, every new technology or business model we see would have the potential for leading us astray as we chase one golden dream after another, never fully exploiting any one business opportunity long enough to recover our initial investment or earn a profit.

Being the best in class requires sound strategic planning and consistently great execution. With those two things, and a commitment to harnessing your team's energies and competencies, your strategic vision can be implemented in a way that maximizes your company's opportunity for success.

Chapter 7 - Organizational Structure and Process

"The team architecture means setting up an organization that helps people produce that great work in teams." Jay Chiat

Organizational structure and process are two of the most often overlooked elements of business success. For a whole range of reasons that we'll explore in greater detail throughout this chapter, a lack of sound organization structure can wreak havoc on your company and undercut your efforts to succeed in virtually every area of business activity. And without a well-aligned, flexible structure, and well-defined processes in place, you will find that your company fails to even meet that most basic criterion for being considered an effective business enterprise: the capacity to deliver consistent results for customers day after day, month after month, and year after year.

Still, many entrepreneurs continue to underestimate the importance of structure, or have little familiarity with what it actually entails. Too many business owners simply create their strategies and execution plans and then operate under the false assumption that their company's organization structure and processes will automatically conform to align with their plans. If life worked like that, almost every business would succeed with little effort. The fact that most do not succeed should demonstrate to any doubters just how important properly organized structure is when it comes to successfully creating and implementing any solid strategy.

In this chapter, we will delve into the nuts and bolts of organizational structure and process to gain better insight into why it's so critical for every other aspect of your enterprise, examine its relevance in relation to the development and execution of your strategy, and consider some of the existing organizational structure models in use today. By the time you have worked your way through this critical section of the book, it is my hope that you will have a fundamentally different perspective on the way in which your chosen structural design either enhances or inhibits your company's progress.

What is Organizational Structure?

When most people think of structure in a business, they tend to focus just on the hierarchy of relationships within the organization. They look at how every member of the team relates to every other member, from top to bottom and side to side. While that is certainly one aspect of any formal organizational structure, it is by no means the be-all and end-all of this important concept.

To best exploit our open system approach, I would like you consider that the preferred organizational structure encompasses much more than just an organizational flow chart that diagrams everyone's responsibilities, powers, and areas of accountability. We need to look at structure and process as an integrated package to include all of the people in the organization and their respective positions, the processes, and culture that facilitate and guide those team members' actions, as well as other resources that support all of the company's activities.

While organization chart represents a formal hierarchy of chain of command, in reality, the structure is both formal and informal. Depending on the corporate culture and process, as the different units interact with one another, the structure can also be flexible or rigid. However, in order to gain the best competitive edge, formal organizational structure must not be rigidly enforced as it will stifle the formation of informal structures, which may include spontaneous groups, organized communities, forums, and other social media engagements. In an environment that promotes team and mutual cooperation such activities are very beneficial communication channels for information sharing and the creation of new ideas. They can be an invaluable extension of the formal structure.

Furthermore, to be truly successful in business, it is crucial to recognize that strategic planning and execution must rely heavily on appropriate organizational structure, coupled with well defined and efficient processes that enable it to function like a well-oiled machine. To avoid redundancy and for better clarity, the word "structure" used in this chapter is inclusive of processes, policies, communication, and procedures covering both formal, and to a limited extent, informal groups.

At times, you design project specific structure, define the process, and provide the necessary support and resources involving multiple teams and departments. Dynamic and fast growth companies constantly create new structure and process, involving multiple departments, as they embark new projects. Beyond just the hierarchy organization chart, think of structure and process as part of a master logistic plan, involving command and control of communication as well as the allocation and deployment of resources. Structure and process can be created or modified as deemed necessary to best accomplish the mission involved.

To truly appreciate the vital importance of structure and process, and how they impact your company's ability to achieve its goals, try to imagine that your business is a football team (or any other similarly organized enterprise with a common objective). When you think of the average football team, chances are that you see the coaching and teamwork.

You almost certainly see the great players, dynamic play-calling and unexpected big plays that can swing any game's momentum in the blink of an eye. What you may not have noticed or considered is the degree to which the structure of any given team organization directly impacts everything that it does on the field during game day - or how established processes help to prepare it for success.

On the surface, the elements of structure are visible to anyone who takes the time to look for them. Every good team has a clear chain of command that starts with the head of the organization. Whether that is the team owner at the professional level, or an athletic director of a college, their role is the same: they select the coaches that are responsible for the day-to-day management of the team. Those coaches, in turn, hire assistant coaches, trainers, equipment managers, and others who help them develop the type of structure needed for success. Those coaches and staff members then assemble a team of players, each of whom has his own unique set of skills.

You probably recognize those surface elements of organization within the context of a football team. Of course, there is much more to creating a successful team than just gathering those personnel elements. Like an onion, every football team has an overall structure that consists of many different layers of sub-structure, process, culture, and strategy. If gathering the best coaches and players together into one team was all that was required for victory and success, then the New York Yankees would have won even more World Series titles than the impressive collection they currently possess.

When a football team experiences success on the field, spectators see great players, effective communication, solid coaching decisions, and critical plays made at just the right moments in the game. They see the play-calling both from the sidelines and the huddle. They bear witness to the various players working in concert to execute the team's game plan. They watch as the mission, goals, and objectives are achieved through a concerted and consistent application of leadership on the field, strategic adjustments during the game, and solid game execution from every position.

Those spectators do not see the many elements of structure and process that empower that success. Few pay much attention to the well-developed sub-systems put into place throughout the organization to provide nutritional guidance, strength training, and ongoing medical care for the players. Likewise, many fans are only minimally aware of the attention paid to scouting, game film, and highly-organized practice regimens designed to ensure that every player, formation, and play can be executed with the right level of precision and consistency the team needs if it is to enjoy success against its rivals.

From team owner on down, the hierarchy of any football team is just the outer layer of visible team structure. The organizational structure must be designed to ensure that every member of the team and coaching staff, every piece of equipment, and every element involved in preparing for good game play achieves the level of synergy needed to create a winning product each and every time the team takes the field.

Your business is no different. Your leaders, managers, and other team members are just the outer shell of your organization structure. Beneath whatever hierarchy you have established, there needs to be a solid structure of processes, technological tools, and overall company culture to support what your team does on the business field each and every moment of every business day.

The Importance of Structure in Organization and Process

Organization and process is vital in any system approach to business. Once we accept the premise that your company is a system made up of many separate yet interdependent sub-systems and components then we also need to accept that those elements' ability to directly and indirectly impact other areas of the business is reason enough to work for consistent excellence throughout the entire organization. After all, weakness in one area weakens the whole entity. A well-designed organizational structure can help to prevent that from happening.

If you find yourself designing your company structure with an organizational chart as your guide, chances are that you are focusing on titles, and things like who reports to who rather than important issues like which functions need to be performed to achieve the company goals. It means that you are designing your organization to satisfy individual team member egos rather than designing a concrete structure that can get things done. An organizational structure can help to avoid those deficiencies by outlining the functions, as well as where authority rests within the organization. An organizational chart can still be helpful, if it is designed to show the formal structure and chain of command rather than an over emphasis of the hierarchy, status, titles, and formal reporting requirements.

All of this is critical for your business planning efforts, since the way that you structure your company will ultimately determine how you perform in a variety of different areas of concern:

- A structural diagram can help to ensure that everyone in the organization understands the company's priorities in terms of functions that need to be performed, how different processes relate to one another, and where accountability rests within the business environment.

- A solid structure can better facilitate the pursuit and realization of specific business goals by helping to coordinate and channel the company's efforts and energies.

- Structure provides safeguards and checks throughout each stage of every process to ensure that progress is consistent with expectations.

- Organizational structure eliminates most instances of duplicated efforts. There should be minimal overlap where responsibilities are concerned, in order to affect optimal productivity and efficiency. Without structure, work distribution can be confused or even wasteful. A good example of this is seen in the organization of many governments, where multiple departments and agencies have overlapping jurisdiction and responsibility over various concerns leading to duplicated efforts, bureaucratic waste, and ineffective processes.

- Individual "turf" conflicts can be minimized. Organizational charts that lack structure based on function often end up leading to battles over who has authority over any given area of the enterprise. Rather than promoting teamwork, the strict organizational chart model can create division and conflict where there should be unity and teamwork. The right structure can ensure that the entire team focuses its attention on achieving objectives that satisfy functional requirements rather than worrying about which team leader or manager has authority over minor decisions.

- A sound organizational structure facilitates sensible planning. Because well-structured systems more effectively outline the relationships between human capital, resources, and important business functions, leaders can more effectively plan for the future. More importantly, the business will be better positioned to ensure that those plans are able to be implemented and target results achieved.

- An effective structure can encourage teamwork, while helping to promote employee self-actualization within the organizational framework. Whereas an organizational chart can tend to limit employee freedom, the right kind of structure can organize the business in a way that maximizes every team member's autonomy, providing to each employee his or her own area of responsibility and authority. Done properly, this can help to create a strong network of interconnected team members, elevate morale, and improve the overall effectiveness of the team effort.

- Communication can be enhanced. Proper organizational structure has a positive impact on effective communication in ways that typical organizational charts often fail to accomplish. Instead of being limited by a chart's strict chain of command, something that often leaves employees afraid to communicate ideas or problems to anyone other than their designated superior, team members have the benefit of clear communication lines that negate concerns about turf battles or wounded egos.

- Employees are encouraged to innovate. The higher levels of morale and self-autonomy engendered by a successfully designed organizational structure can provide employees with the encouragement they need to express their creativity and contribute positive ideas that can help the company be more innovative. These types of structure can leave team members feeling more empowered and appreciated and that can have lasting impact on the quality of their work.

- Structure makes it easier for leadership to balance priorities. While everything matters within your business system, some things will be more relevant at certain moments in time. Moreover, some functions are so critical that they must always receive a higher level of priority than less critical functions. How you structure your company can help to determine how such differences in priority are addressed.

- Sound organizational structure simplifies the process of adapting to new technological innovations. In organizations where the emphasis is on people rather than function, adaptation to new technology can often be a painful and time-consuming process. Where structure focuses on function, however, the application of new technologies tends to be a simpler process since everyone is already focused on how the company's available tools and resources come together to achieve its objectives.

Put simply, organizational structure and the processes it helps to define are indispensable elements of any successful business. You can try to run your business without a clearly defined structure (I say "try" because structure will settle in, whether you design it or not), but in the end you will only be handicapping your ability to become the best in class.

The Connection between Strategy and Structure

"Unless structure follows strategy, inefficiency results." - Alfred D. Chandler

"Structure follows strategy … as the left foot follows the right." - Henry Mintzberg

There's a reason this chapter follows closely on the heels of our examination of strategy and execution in chapters five and six. Many business owners start their companies with the belief that structure and strategy are somehow separate and distinct from one another. To make matters worse, there are company leaders who devise strategies that are totally misaligned to their existing organizational structure and processes and simply assume that the latter two elements will be forced to align with strategic plans during execution. That false assumption is actually one of the biggest reasons strategies fail.

Without the right structure and process in place, you will find it all but impossible to properly execute your strategy!

So, what do entrepreneurs typically think of when it comes to organizational structure? What positive impacts do they view it as having on their business success? A large number of new business professionals simply see structure as an avenue to creating the culture, teamwork, efficiencies, and cost management that they need. Those with a little more experience often recognize structure and process as a way to increase the overall level of synergy within the organization. None of them are wrong, by the way. Organization structure and process can be vital to achieving those goals. The problem is that anyone who sees structure as having no value beyond those areas is missing out on one of the most important truths in the business world today:

Strategic planning and execution must rely on appropriate organizational structure and process if they are to succeed.

As we discussed in chapter six, there are many reasons why strategies fail during the execution stage of the process. Many of those reasons stem from a lack of appropriate organizational structure and an improperly designed process. In many instances, companies completely alter their strategic plans and then fail to address the structural changes necessary to enable those plans to be carried out in any effective way. There are some simple truths governing the relationship between strategy and structure that reveal why this is a mistake.

The most fundamental reason is the most important, however. Structures have a sort of gravity that can defy strategic planning when the two are not properly aligned from the outset. When you design a strategy without considering how it will fit within your existing structure, or simply fail to revise your structure to make it more conducive to your strategic needs, then you will quickly discover that those efforts were wasted. Structural gravity will take hold and subvert your strategy to fit the existing environment.

The reason for this is simply: strategy tends to conform to structure. No matter how brilliantly you design your strategy, and no matter how flawless you think your execution plan seems to be, the reality is that your organizational structure will invariably determine the success or failure of the endeavor. Remember always that structure ultimately supports strategy. It precedes it, facilitates it, and empowers everyone within the organization to meet your objectives. In any situation where there is a misalignment of strategy and structure, the latter's natural gravitational pull will serve as a drag on the former, preventing forward process.

Worse, you will ultimately discover that your strategy will have been altered - sometimes to the point where it is all but unrecognizable. When this happens, leadership often blames some element of the original strategic plan: management's presumed inability to execute the strategy, or even employee resistance to the plan. What has actually transpired in most cases like this is that the strategy itself has shifted organically, as it conforms to the existing organizational structure.

That's how much impact your organizational structure has within your company. Structure is powerful enough to overcome even the best laid plans when the two are not properly in sync with one another. Because of that simple truth, it is essential that your structure be considered in depth prior to any attempt to execute a strategic plan. Remember what we learned from our exploration of the systems approach: everything is connected and interdependent. Everything is impacted when you make changes to any single area. Where strategy and structure are concerned, the important thing to understand is that structure will always win out in the end.

So, once you recognize that fact, the obvious question is this: how do you leverage that relationship between structure and strategy to benefit your company? Start by coming to terms with the need to balance strategy and structure. Your strategy encompasses everything that your company does to achieve any goal or objective. Your structure encompasses all of the personnel, resources, and processes you've put in place to enable you to execute your strategy. Once you understand how those two things are connected to one another, everything else will begin to fall into place.

To better understand why this matters, imagine that you have an organizational structure with a defined relationship system between employees and processes. If you develop a business strategy and execution plan that fails to take that structure into account, what do you think will happen? Will your company managers and employees adjust their roles to accommodate the new strategy? If those team members' career paths are tied to the effectiveness of functions and processes at odds with your new strategy, which is likely to receive greater emphasis, their own perceived self-interest or the plan you are attempting to put into motion?

The answer is not surprising. Structure is critical precisely due to the need to ensure that each component and system within your organization is focused like a laser on providing support for your company vision and mission. That culture that you work so diligently to create becomes a tangible force within your company - a force with such gravity that it can take even your best-laid plans and remake them in its image.

We see this in business all the time: companies that attempt to impose strategies on structures that are not designed to support them inevitably find that the strategy changes to conform to the existing organizational structure. Managers tend to focus on results, so it should come as no surprise that they attempt to execute the plans they are given - without considering whether or not the existing structure is designed to facilitate those plans. Leaders often hand down plans without considering that managers are ill-equipped to revise structure on their own. And employees tend to remain aligned with whatever status quo satisfies their career self-interests.

Now, none of this is to suggest that your attempt to force a strategy onto an incompatible organizational structure will fail right away. It probably won't. But the reality is that it would almost be preferable if failure did occur immediately, since at least then you could avoid weeks or months of wasted effort and stalled progress, and simply move to change the strategy or the structure so that they are in better alignment with one another. That seldom happens, however. The more commonly seen pattern is that employees attempt to perform the tasks given to them, managers attempt to force the strategy to conform to the structure, and the strategy itself ends up being something radically different than what you actually wanted.

There seems to be a golden rule at work here: if you attempt to forcibly impose a strategy on an organizational structure designed with other strategies in mind, and fail to modify that strategy first, the existing structure remains faithful to the original plan and co-opts the new. That leads to a host of undesirable consequences, of course. To avoid those, you need to have a plan of action that addresses the deeper structural changes necessary for successful implementation of any strategy. That requires a concise and detail-oriented approach to creating change:

- Don't think that a directive from leadership will be enough to implement strategy if the structure cannot support the plan. No matter how well you define your objectives, overall vision, and direction, your action plan can only work when your company's daily operational systems are built to support your strategic efforts. Your leadership is critical in this area, but only when applied in the proper way.

- Recognize that change in strategy almost always requires change in structure. The only exception to this is when your new strategy has already been designed to be in alignment with your existing organizational structure. Any time you are modifying strategy or creating new strategy from the start, you need to carefully assess how it will be impacted by your company's current way of doing things, and adjust either the structure or the strategy to accommodate any identified areas of conflict.

- Remember that structure is a form of strategy. As Chandler noted, structure follows strategy. When it does not do so - when the structure is designed in a way that facilitates systems that cannot effectively drive strategic execution - then you have inefficiencies, or worse. At the same time, strategy can follow structure as well. This occurs in cases where conflicts between strategy and structure are organically resolved in favor of the latter due to structural and cultural gravity.

- As a leader, your strategic thinking must emphasize not only your short and long-term objectives, but the type of organizational structure that will be needed to reach those goals. You need to align the functions within your company in a way that supports your strategic goals and execution needs.

- Once you identify your goals and the strategy you need to execute to achieve those objectives, your very next step must involve a comprehensive evaluation of your existing structure. You must determine all of the ways in which your team members, management personnel, functional divisions, and processes will either contribute to or detract from your ability to execute that plan.

- Try to think in terms of cause and effect during this evaluation process. How will your employee's current self-interests impact their willingness and ability to execute your strategy as currently envisioned? Which functions currently receive the highest level of focus from management, and what effects will that emphasis have on execution? Are your existing company functions structured in a way that supports or inhibits strategic success? Do you have your processes designed in a way that can ensure efficient and sustainable execution?

- Once you identify deficiencies in your structure, analyze them carefully to determine if and how those areas of your organization can be altered to better facilitate strategic execution. If you find problems that you cannot resolve with structural changes, then it may be necessary to revisit your strategy and make modifications to the plan.

- Implement changes where needed, and then re-evaluate the modified structure to ensure that it is both viable for the company and supportive of your strategic goals.

Clearly, strategy and structure have a relationship with one another that is far more intimate than most entrepreneurs first realize. For that reason, it is always important that changes in your structure be considered in a measured way, with an emphasis on creating that perfect alignment of form, function, and plan. While you never want to change structure just for the sake of change, you always need to ensure that structure can support whatever strategy you are pursuing at any given time.

A Note on Cooperation...

It is also important to remember that not all attempts at cooperative efforts achieve the desired results. Within the structural context, this can often be explained by the inability to achieve true cooperation rather than collaboration or coordination among team members. To maximize the group dynamic, it is important to recognize the difference between these three group dynamics so that you can properly implement them within your organizational structure:

> **Coordination:** At its core, coordination is about arranging groups of people to ensure that they are able to work together in an orderly manner. This ordered approach to organization can help an enterprise guarantee that team members and departments are all moving forward in concert with one another, in pursuit of a common goal. Coordination tends to be focused on process, measured goals, and incentives for individuals.

Collaboration: The idea behind collaboration is simple: it defines how individuals and groups work in parallel relationship with one another. It is directly tied to the work being done, and the way in which employees relate to one another as functions are performed. There is little or no emphasis on the outcome of those efforts. Collaboration is a form of teamwork that often relies on interpersonal feelings and relationships and tends to be more informal in nature.

Cooperation: This is the most intimate level of the team dynamic, where the individual needs of team members are taken into account by aligning structure, employee goals, and strategy to ensure that each person's talents are directed toward the achieving of the group's intended output. With the cooperative approach, teams focus their joint energy on achieving something greater than themselves, with the expectation that the entire team shares in the resulting glory of accomplishment.

All three dynamics have their place within any organization. The key is to recognize when to use each. Obviously, cooperation is the most productive of the three and thus remains the preferred target dynamic for companies that want to maximize their results. Still, there will be times when cooperative groups within your organizational structure will need to engage in coordinated or collaborative efforts with other teams and departments. This should all be defined by your chosen strategy and the structure you put into place to facilitate the execution of those plans.

Define Your Structure or Let It Define You

Earlier, I used the word "try" when I referred to the decision to operate without a clearly defined structure. I also noted that structure will eventually take root, regardless of whether you choose to design it or simply let it happen organically. My reason for making both of those points has to do with a concept we examined when we considered your company culture. We discussed how your personal vision, mindset, and beliefs can help to create your business culture, even when you are not aware that it is occurring. Well, structure is similar to culture in that regard.

The fact is that human beings are, by their very nature, creatures that tend to flock to structure. Much has been written about how humanity has spent most of its existence under the thrall of various strongmen and despots. America's Founding Fathers spoke and wrote about this history of subjugation and how individual liberty had always been the exception in mankind's historical experience. The American Revolution and the subsequent enshrinement of protected personal liberties within a well-structured governing system of checks and balances was the direct result of those wise men's recognition of the inherent weakness of the human condition.

The fact is that history clearly demonstrates at both the societal and corporate level that human beings who are left to their own devices almost inevitably gravitate to some perceived center of influence, power, and authority. At the broader societal level, a lack of organizing principles and structure results in a state of chaos that almost always ends with some strong authority figure seizing power over the masses. Even in societies that have flirted with things like democracy, a failure to adhere to structure and legal principles has often led to the collapse of governments, chaos, and eventual authoritarianism.

This does not occur because democracies are an inherently unstable system of government. Nor does it happen because chaos or tyranny is preferable to liberty. Instead, it happens due to simple human nature. When weak governing systems are in place, or when there is a culture that lacks respect for whatever structure is seen as maintaining order, chaos inevitably results. And chaos always leads to the formation of some type of organized structure. Unfortunately, it is a rare thing indeed to see a positive structure emerge from the confusing ruins of chaos.

The problem is, as I noted, human nature. In a perfect world, every person could be a self-governing, autonomous, sovereign in his or her own right. There would be no need for firm organizations to maintain order and secure sound societal processes. Obviously, this is not a perfect world. The world in which we live is one in which human beings need guiding structure to rein in baser impulses and self-interest so that greater societal goals can be realized. And the choice between guiding structures has always been essentially a binary one: a system where that structure is obtained through the consent of the governed and protected with strong checks, balances, and concrete limitations on power - or a structure imposed by an authoritarian who emerges from the chaos of de facto anarchy, seizing power by flattery, force, or the clever garnering of influence over time.

Now, what does that have to do with your business, you ask? Good question! The reason this is important is that human nature is human nature whether those human beings are operating within a larger societal venue or in the more isolated environment of a company. And since human nature is what it has always been, we can draw certain conclusions about what happens within business organizations that fail to create their own well-defined structures.

1. Human nature historically reveals that people do not long exist in a state without some type of organization directing their activities. Self-autonomy without guiding principles and directives has never been a recurring theme in the history of planet Earth.

2. There are almost always those who are willing to step into any perceived vacuum and impose their own structure on those around them.

Sometimes it is one person assuming the role of structural enforcer; other times it is a small group. In some of the worst examples, there are multiple factions that emerge to create a patchwork structure of inconsistencies and confusing processes.

3. As destructive as those tendencies can be in society at large, they are absolutely fatal for any business environment. No business can prosper in an environment in which the structure of the company developed organically from within due to a failure by leadership to develop the right organizational framework. Power will be mismanaged, accountability will be difficult to manage, and processes will lack the integration and interdependence needed to create efficiency, productivity, and profitability.

As Harold S. Geneen observed, "Every company has two organizational structures: The formal one is written on the charts; the other is the everyday relationship of the men and women in the organization." Your concern as a business owner has to focus on designing the type of formal structure that can help to achieve your goals, while also providing the type of environment within your company that encourages an informal employee relationship structure that is in alignment with your formal organizational structure. That is the only way to guarantee that the organic structure that will inevitably develop does not come into conflict with your established structural design.

The fact is that there is always organizational structure in any company. It can be intentionally designed and put into place in a formal way, or come about in an informal, organic manner. In many instances, both informal and formal structures are in existence simultaneously. That element of human nature that demands some sort of order will give rise to an informal structure whenever an entrepreneur fails to implement his own designed system of organization.

One thing that you cannot change is that employees will form their own groups based on how they interact with one another, their personal preferences, and their interests. Your job is to ensure that you have created a system and culture that can help those employee-created structures to contribute to the success of the company by promoting a positive mindset. If you fail to do that, you will likely end up with an employee-created organizational system that does nothing but promote an atmosphere that negatively impacts every area of your business enterprise.

We often see this phenomenon in companies with loose management systems lacking in any defined organizational structures. Because companies like that lack the basic organizational structure employees need, there is no guiding set of processes and systems in place. By accident or design, the employees in those companies often end up creating an informal culture that ends up focusing on the interests of one or several individuals. This culture often becomes ingrained, and becomes the default organizational structure for the entire enterprise - more often than not, to the detriment of the owner's company.

Other instances where this type of informal structure can come about include business environments in which the various areas of responsibility, authority, and accountability are ill-defined. When authority and responsibility are not properly designated, companies often end up with situations in which areas of authority simply overlap, reducing the ability to refine control by delegating power and accountability. That establishes an environment of inconsistency due to a lack of formal structure, which leads to a greater loss of control that engenders confusion and frustration among team members throughout the company.

That uncertainty and frustration leads to a loss of employee engagement and reduced motivation that lowers morale, decreases productivity, and negatively impacts profitability. If you've ever seen a company where the employees seem to do just enough to get by, then chances are that you have seen exactly this type of environment. Those companies are usually filled with employees who are deprived of leadership, struggling to understand their role within the organization, and unsure about what they are expected to do. This situation is surprisingly common!

At its core, the problem is easy to understand. When employees are not organized as a team and provided with clear structure, process, and easily-quantifiable goals, objectives, and deadlines, they tend to gravitate toward their natural human instincts. Without leadership to inspire them to achieve something larger than themselves, they become fractious, lean toward faction, and gradually succumb to whatever informal organizational structure develops in the absence of formal systems.

Your job is to ensure that you help them to avoid an atmosphere that fails to give them standards to which they can aspire. And you can do that by establishing the clearly-defined organizational structure and processes that they need to properly align their self-interests and motivations to the goals of your business enterprise.

Structure Defined by Need

As we discussed earlier in the chapter, there are many different ways to structure a business. However, truly well-managed companies design their organizational structure with function and the successful completion of projects in mind, rather than people. The reason behind this approach is simple and particularly important to understand if you are a small business owner. Individuals should be hired and trained to fit within positions that are established based on necessary company functions. You cannot simply hire individuals and then change the nature of the position to fit their talents and personalities.

The latter option is one that is commonly seen in many family-owned enterprises. Husbands, wives, children, and other members of the family are brought in - often just to provide them with gainful employment, and there is little attention given to whether or not they can meet the requirements for any function-based position. Since they are often incapable of meeting those skill-based standards, the actual nature of those positions gets adjusted to fit the employee. Naturally, that leads to weaknesses in the system, as other employees end up performing many of tasks and functions originally allocated to those positions. Over time - and often not much time at that - this places so much stress on the small family business that it simply collapses.

Being the best in class requires us to focus on function first, and then hire the best candidates to meet our functional needs. And even after we make those hires, we must focus tirelessly on training with an eye toward continual enhancement of each team member's skill set and productivity. We choose our team based on their skills, ability, knowledge base, and experience, and then train them to not only precisely meet the requirements of their tasked function, but continue to grow and develop in those positions as they provide consistently excellent performance.

The emphasis on function is important because that focus in organizational structure tends to provide optimal flexibility for structural changes to accommodate strategic shifts. And, unlike structures that are designed around titles and personnel, a functional focus helps to ensure that the essential needs of the company are met as it endeavors to meet its strategic goals, service customers, and achieve profitability and growth. It also helps to ensure greater continuity, since turnover issues are not as disruptive as they often are in companies that highlight job titles and hierarchy over meeting functional need.

In this model, your culture is even more important than ever before. While there is a strict chain of responsibility, authority, and accountability in place, it is much less restrictive than many other options. To make it work, you have to cultivate a company culture that emphasizes team spirit within an environment that offers clear-cut chain of command. Tha spirit of team cooperation is essential for ensuring that all employees effectively communicate with one another and coordinate their efforts to deliver maximum results.

At the same time, it is important to ensure that you avoid overlap of responsibilities and authority as you promote that atmosphere of mutual cooperation and shared responsibilities for mission success. Remember always that truly exceptional results are only accomplished when your systems are designed to prevent duplication of effort and miscommunication due to confusion about who is in charge of and accountable for what functions. Properly coordinated team efforts and perfect execution are essential to maintain the type of harmonious environment needed for optimal results.

At each level of your structure, need should drive form. This will still result in the same type of formal organizational structure seen in title-centric organizations, but one that will enjoy all of the benefits we have already examined. Formal structure is critical for its ability to properly define communication flow in a vertical manner both up and down the chain of authority. It facilitates quick and accurate reporting and feedback, which are essential for achieving efficient and productive coordination of all of the many elements within your company.

Authority is essential, and should be well-defined. At every level of leadership, the person with the ultimate authority should be the one to make each final decision. That final call on matters at hand must be honored by members of the team, for better or worse. In many businesses, the opposite holds true. Authority figures at the intermediate level of management are often delegated powers by their boss, only to find that boss continually issuing orders that contravene management's instructions. That lack of coordination between executive leadership and management at any level can create a culture of confusion, uncertainty, and fear. Team members learn to distrust management's decisions, which can create even more chaos throughout the company. This is another form of duplicated effort - in this case, duplicated delegation of authority and responsibility. In spite of its destructive potential, this is a problem that seems to occur with disturbing regularity.

Where need is concerned, the need for recognizable and easily-understood authority structure is critical. Individuals who are entrusted with the authority to make important decisions for the company must be allowed to exercise that authority without constant counter orders stymieing their efforts. Those decision-makers are responsible for making decisions that work toward ensuring that the total efforts of the team are channeled in an efficient and effective manner that promotes the best interests of the company. And while those decision-makers may or may not be given the authority to delegate some of their authority to others for efficiency's sake, it is they who are ultimately accountable for all of the results produced by their decisions.

Types of Organizational Structure

While it is important to gain greater insight into the various elements of structure and process, the rubber really hits the road at that point where you have to decide upon the type of organizational structure that will work best for your business. Sure, it is great to understand what organizational structure is and why it is important to your company's success.

It is helpful to grasp the relationship between strategy and structure and recognize how the disparate elements within any company come together to form a larger entity that is greater than its component parts. Those things are all valuable for you to know. Ultimately, however, the philosophy and theory must give way to the hard reality of the doing of a thing. And before you can begin to establish the type of structure that can best facilitate your strategy, you need to have some understanding of the types of structures that are possible.

In almost every business setting, there is at least some rudimentary formal structure in place. Some companies have well-established organizational charts with boxes and directional lines representing functions, managerial positions, and employees tasked with certain jobs. Vertical lines are used to connect these boxes in a way that clearly delineates how authority flows both downward and upward within the entirety of the organization. Within this chart, we see command authority, directives, and other orders flowing down to lower levels, while feedback, reports, and queries of all kinds get channeled up the chain of command to those highest levels of authority.

Some of the largest companies utilize organizational structures that are highly complex, rigidly enforced, and focused like a laser on achieving company goals. Sometimes these structures become so rigid and complex that communication and cooperation are stifled, leading to a failure to share knowledge and experiences. Cultural affections can break down, leading to deterioration in the level of empathy employees feel for one another and reducing the incentive others feel to contribute.

Many smaller companies take the opposite approach, with loosely organized structures that often leave everyone in the business reporting only to the company owner. These structures too can become unwieldy, particularly when the leader of the company is unskilled in critical areas needed for the proper management of the business. In such environments, employees can suffer from a lack of confidence in leadership's abilities, feel abandoned, or simply lose interest in the group dynamic.

Fortunately, there are a wide variety of different structural options between those two extremes. We will briefly examine four of the most common organizational models here so that you can get a better idea of how structure can be aligned with strategy. There are other structures as well, and I would encourage you to research them in greater detail to learn more about your options.

Before we begin, let's be clear about one thing: there are virtually no limits on the options available to you when it comes to how you arrange the functions, personnel, resources, and processes in your company. You can choose to have accountants stuff envelopes on the loading dock if that's what makes you happy (though you probably didn't need this book to recognize what a poor use of personnel and resources that would be). However, there are some tried and true structural archetypes that you might want to consider before you make your decision.

Let us begin...

The Functional Organizational Structure

If you are familiar with just one or two structural archetypes, this is almost certainly one of them. It is the most common way to organize your business, and does so by grouping individual team members together in accordance with the functions that they are hired to perform. This is the type of structure that typically divides different functions into separate departments, with management of each being distinct and apart from other areas of the enterprise. For example, companies that divide their employees into groups like sales and marketing, accounting, human resources, etc., are utilizing the functional structure.

There are advantages to this structural device, obviously. If there weren't, it might not be so popular. The biggest advantage is that it meets the need to ensure that functional requirements are met within every area of the business. Each function within the company is separated in accordance with the expertise needed to meet its challenges.

Each department handling these distinct functions is set up to be managed independently of other departments, with all of the different department heads answering only to the central manager above them in the hierarchy of authority - whether that is another layer of management or the company executive. The compartmentalization inherent in this structural design is a clear benefit, as is its easily understood organizational chart. Everyone within the company can not only identify his or her place within the company, but the clear chain of command, responsibility, and accountability as well.

There are two clear disadvantages as well. The first is that the entire system can become dysfunctional if there are weaknesses at the top of the executive chain. Bad decision-making, weak organizational skill, and other failings can result in breakdowns in interdepartmental communications, which in turn leads to gross inefficiencies and cultural rot throughout the company. The second disadvantage is that this division of function into departments can reduce their ability and willingness to collaborate and cooperate with one another.

The Customer Organizational Structure

This type of organizational structure tends to be used by companies targeting specific industries. For example, healthcare companies are often well-suited for this type of structure. Other service-oriented businesses often find certain aspects of the structural model useful for their needs as well. The whole goal of this structure is to ensure that each customer's individual and unique needs are met with a flexible approach to customer service.

The structure's usefulness for healthcare is obvious. Patients seldom require the exact same treatment regimen. Outpatient needs are very different from inpatient needs; so different areas of the company are segmented to ensure that specific groups of customers receive the service they need. Each of those areas has its own command structure, with managerial staff who report to others above them in the hierarchy. Redundant service, overlap, and confusion can all be reduced using this type of structure.

The Product Organizational Structure

With this structure, many larger companies can better manage a wide variety of product types and service offerings. Functions are directly related to individual product lines, and those products are segmented - often into separate subsidiary entities that focus only on their specific offerings. The chain of command has executives at the uppermost part of the hierarchy, with product managers reporting directly to those executives.

There are a couple of clear benefits offered by this structure - both of which can be essential for the efficient operation of large enterprises. Since products are segmented from one another, it is often easier to implement vastly different processes within each segment. That can be essential when your offerings range from canned food to toiletries. An equally important benefit is that communication between different product line segments is, for all practical purposes, unnecessary. That enables upper management to exercise more targeted control over each individual area of the company, which can help maintain tighter focus on company goals while avoiding the chaos that often occurs in large enterprises that lack tight formal controls.

The Matrix Organizational Structure

As the name might suggest, this is a structure that is more popular with media companies than most other types of business. It is characterized by a combination of horizontal and vertical reporting, with employees who often serve on functional groups while also contributing their efforts to other groups at the same time. Members from different functional groups routinely combine their efforts to create and produce new products. Examples of this type of structure can be seen in many music companies, video game firms, and movie enterprises. Team leaders are charged with directing squads of individuals who all have different areas of expertise, combining their efforts to produce things like albums, video games, and movies.

This approach has obvious benefits for the businesses that adopt it. It is more open and conducive to creativity than most other structural models, allowing employee talents to be used on a variety of projects, and in different ways. That makes employees responsible for their own departments as well as projects that encompass functional aspects from every part of the organization.

The challenge with this structure is related directly to its looser style of organization. Because there is a somewhat less strict hierarchy involved in the matrix structure, it is common to see competing directions coming from different areas of the management team. Employees can also experience difficulty when it comes to prioritizing their various project responsibilities.

The Big Picture

In any business, organizational structure and process plays a critical role in your ability to succeed. To obtain the optimal results, you need to achieve efficiency in your efforts to generate maximum yield. In almost every instance, you have to accomplish that feat with a finite quantity of resources. Everyone within your organization needs to be provided with the infrastructure and resources needed to ensure that exceptional performance can be delivered on a consistent basis. That is all part of the winning formula for success.

Your business philosophy and management style will naturally play a large role in determining the best way to organize your structure, allocate human capital, and manage your resources at every level. As you come to understand the different types of organizational structures available to you, that process becomes clearer. In the end, the decisions you make in the area of organizational structure will go a long way toward determining just how successful your business ultimately becomes.

Chapter 8 - Delegation

"No man will make a great leader who wants to do it all himself or get all the credit for doing it." - Andrew Carnegie

Among all the tools available to you as an entrepreneur, there are few more powerful than the ability to delegate. In fact, delegation is considered by most experts to be one of the most effective ways to maximize productivity and optimize return on your limited human resources. It can also be the best vehicle through which you can train your employees for future leadership positions within your firm. When exercised properly, delegation can enable you and your managers to accomplish more with the same amount of available human resources. Moreover, by assigning others to do various parts of your job, you can free yourself up to focus on more important tasks, duties, and responsibilities.

As vitally important as the art of effective delegation can be to the success of any business enterprise, few companies give it the level of priority and commitment that it truly deserves. Take payroll and related employee expenses, for example. These often make up 30% or more of any company's operating costs. And yet most companies have the same reaction whenever any sort of bottleneck occurs and there is a struggle to deliver results: they hire an additional employee to help boost productivity. That is, if they can afford to do so. That reaction, though, raises an obvious question: why don't more companies rely on delegation to better manage those human resources and avoid those types of bottlenecks in the first place?

Part of the problem is that delegation is misunderstood by most managers. On the surface, it sounds so elementary that it seems almost deceptively simple. For many managers, the very notion of delegation evokes thoughts of simply assigning tasks to subordinates to ensure that they remain busy and gainfully employed. Often times, these tasks are assigned with the unrealistic expectation that the results will be identical to those that the manager would realize were he to simply do the work himself. Other times, there are few expectations other than expecting that the work will get done. For untrained managers with little experience in delegation, this can present a dangerous trap. All too often, these managers end up just doling out work in an attempt to keep their employees busy.

Things are not often much better at the higher level of delegation. Here too management delegates by assigning tasks to subordinates in an attempt to maximize their own ability to get things done. These managers delegate due to constraints on their own time and an inability to get everything done without help, or simply because there are tasks they prefer to leave to underlings. Again, though, the problem ends up being a simple one: delegation based on the hope that everything will work out fine and the job will be done properly often ends in disappointment.

Delegated tasks that result in poor execution and weaker-than-expected results remain one of the biggest challenges confronting managers, management consultants, senior executives and business owners alike. There is an old axiom that this situation brings to mind, and it is one that often times proves tempting for leaders and managers who experience delegation problems:

"If you want the job done right, do it yourself."

For reasons that should be all too obvious, that old saying is one that smart business owners and managers would do well to discard from their catch-phrase toolbox. The reality is that most sensible leaders eventually have to come to terms with the fact that they just cannot do everything on their own. Those who think they can will find they are only setting themselves up for one type of fall or another.

And yet this remains a common line of thinking for many small business owners. It is a way of thinking that often leads to burn-out, exhaustion, and an extremely high level of frustration. Business owners and managers who try to do everything on their own quickly become overwhelmed, lose sight of their priorities, and end up reacting to demands as they manifest instead of proactively exploiting opportunities and resolving problems.

The Failure to Delegate

Any good leader or manager has to understand that his or her primary responsibility when it comes to employees is to ensure that others are doing everything that they need to do to ensure that the organization's mission and goals can be achieved. When managers fail to delegate, they limit not only their own ability to meet their responsibilities but they also limit their employees' ability to properly advance the company's interests.

The question becomes then, why would any manager refuse to delegate? As it turns out, there are many reasons:

1. As mentioned before, there is a common belief among many in management that their subordinates simply are not up to the task. This line of thinking involves an assumption that employees are unable to effectively do the job as well as their leaders and managers.

2. Managers sometimes distrust employee commitment to a give task. They sometimes believe that their subordinates lack the motivation and drive necessary to accomplish certain tasks, and will thus be less focused on doing a quality job.

3. Some managers simply feel that delegation will somehow make them less indispensable. This attitude can create a whole host of problems, as management effectively hoards responsibility and accountability for fear that their jobs will be less secure if their superiors discover that others are capable of doing what they do.

4. More conscientious managers may be hesitant to assign more work to their employees, particularly if they believe that those workers are already overburdened.

5. Managers may mistakenly believe that delegation and oversight will prove more time-intensive than simply doing the job themselves.

Sadly, however, managers who fail to properly delegate can upset the entire structure of any company's operations. After all, the very reason for having a manager is to ensure that other employees are better organized in a way that ensures smooth operational efficiency and maximum productivity. When managers attempt to inhibit delegation of tasks and responsibility, they short-circuit that structure and the processes that make it work. Instead of cooperating with others in management to develop plans for improvement, creating new strategies, or developing their own skill sets with new technologies and innovations, these managers end up wasting their time doing work that they should be leaving to others.

Finally, there is a direct negative impact on employee development when delegation is ignored. One of the most important benefits that delegation can provide to any business is in the area of employee leadership development. Delegation provides an invaluable opportunity for management to identify employees with leadership qualities, and provide the training those subordinates need to increase their value within the company. At the same time, the very act of delegating responsibility and accountability to an employee can be one of the best ways to establish a deeper sense of mutual commitment and loyalty between managers and their teams.

To understand just how important delegation really is, try to think of your employees as members of a sports team who are sitting on the bench during the middle of the game. At some point during the competition, your strategic thinking will require that some player hears his number called. That player will be assigned with the task of going into the game and given the responsibility of taking the place of another team member for a time. Now imagine how poorly they will perform if he is sent in with no instructions about what he should do, and no information about what is expected of them.

Effective delegation has to begin at ground zero. It is most successful and invaluable when the processes used to implement delegation strategies start at the top to ensure that every act of delegation is properly aligned with the company leadership's vision and mission.

The fact is that there is a radically different management philosophy at work when companies focus on hiring and training employees with delegation in mind. Those companies are laying the groundwork for ensuring that every team member is properly prepared to accept any delegated responsibility and execute tasks in the manner that meets company expectations. Like the members of a team that has been properly trained and coached, each employee has been prepared to assume multiple roles when necessary and are always ready when called upon to give their best efforts on behalf of the company.

Alan Yong

This is the art of delegation at its finest and can give your company the head start it needs to ensure that it is the best in class. It is precisely the type of investment that every company needs to make in its systems and people. When you can make effective delegation training and leadership development an ongoing endeavor within your enterprise, you can better achieve the exceptional performance and high employee morale you need for long-term sustained success. And when you begin that process by hiring the best A+ employees who align with your business culture, your odds of becoming best in class are dramatically improved.

The Challenges of Effective Delegation

Most of us are so accustomed to assigning work to subordinates that it is only natural that we assume that everyone knows how to delegate effectively. The reality, however, is that this is simply not the case. All too often, tasks and duties are assigned by managers and end up not being completed in accordance with expectations. In other cases, the work is simply ignored and never gets done at all. Sometimes that failure to complete delegated tasks goes unnoticed until the work is already overdue or other negative consequences have manifested. There are so many common problems that can arise due to ineffective use of delegation that it can be difficult to narrow them down to a manageable list.

Here are some of the better known difficulties that can result from a weak or otherwise ineffective delegation process:

7Employees can be confused about the chain of command when delegated tasks are involved. Often times, they are not sure who they are supposed to report to, or who is actually tasked with the responsibility for directing their actions.

8Incoherent information flow can also be a problem. Whenever you fail to establish clear lines of communication, you can end up with a chaotic situation where multiple people are issuing directives to the same people - and this can be particularly troublesome when those orders are in conflict with one another. Productivity is directly impacted, goals are impeded, and frustration can quickly set in.

9Changes are not properly communicated. This is one big area of delegation that often gets neglected. When assignments are modified, the person who is ultimately responsible for the task often fails to convey the changes in a timely manner. This too can lead to frustration as work is done improperly or ends up being completed later than expected due to last-minute alterations.

10Subordinates are also sometimes called away by other managers or leaders without anyone bothering to notify the manager responsible for any delegated tasks.

11Managers are often given delegated responsibility without the requisite authority needed to ensure that the tasks for which they are responsible can effectively be completed.

One of the worst effects of poor delegation is its impact on employees. In far too many instances, a failure to develop good inter-company delegation skills can result in the company cultivating so-called "bad" employees who are often seen as incompetent or incapable of being trained. In many cases, the problem is that these employees become so frustrated by the chaotic delegation processes in play around them that they simply lose motivation. In other instances, they are simply pulled in too many competing directions, distressed by an incongruity between delegation, responsibility, and authority needs, or suffer from a sense that they are not being properly managed.

As a manager and leader there is something that should always be remembered: if you earnestly believe that everyone around you is stupid, then you are setting yourself up to be surrounded by idiots. Does that mean that the employees you are managing are actually incompetent? Perish the thought! What it actually means is that if you believe that your subordinates are only capable of handling the simplest tasks, then that is all that they will ever be able to manage. Recognize though that if you choose to be one of those managers who get into the habit of only assigning the most undesirable tasks to your team members, then you should expect that they will lose motivation, commitment, and interest in their jobs.

Begin at the Top

The most effective way to master the delegation mindset within any company culture is to have it be supported and promoted from the uppermost echelons of management. The development of great delegation skills that permeate throughout the enterprise from top to bottom is one of the smartest human resources investments any company can make. As a result, mastering the art of delegation must be part of the corporate mission of preparedness and leadership development, rather than an afterthought that exists only in response to immediate needs. Once mastered, the delegation skill set is one that equips managers and employees to achieve optimal results for themselves, other members of their team, and the broader company.

Delegation remains one of the most effective management skills, and is an important part of being able to get things done through subordinates. That skill can provide managers with an expanded opportunity to achieve more from the team without overextending his physical and mental capacity. And, of course, the proper use of delegation remains one of the chief tools management can use to identify, develop, and test future leaders and successors.

As the leader, mastering the art of delegation is something that must start with you. Now I understand that this is one of the most difficult things any business leader can ever attempt to do, since most of us have a natural human tendency to consider ourselves indispensable - especially within our own businesses. The thing is, though, that you must cultivate a mindset that envisions you as being dispensable. Your goal must be to become the best coach you can so that you are striving to help others be even better at your job than you are, so that they could take over for you at a moment's notice.

Communicate that message to them using clear and concise language that details your strategy for implementing effective delegation. Say things like, "I want you to learn to do my job better than I can, and I will teach you all that I know. That way, if management needs me to start another project you won't miss a beat. In turn, I want you to have the same attitude towards your subordinates. Coach and inspire them all everyday and acknowledge their contributions with sincere appreciation every time. That is the best advice and encouragement I can offer you for your career advancement in our company. We are all a team; the A Team."

There are three key elements of delegation:

Responsibility: When tasks are done, they need to be done under the supervision of whoever is assigned the job. When you delegate a task to the best person available to you - whether from your team or another team, that person (or team leader if the delegation involves a group effort) is also given the responsibility for completing the assigned task. Now, if you have taken the time to properly train your team members, they will know exactly what you expect from them as they begin. They will understand instinctively what their role in the process is, and how to utilize teamwork, timing, and execution to complete the task successfully.

Authority: Whenever you are delegating any responsibility, you are entrusting your subordinate with the necessary power and authority to do what you are requiring. One of the biggest mistakes you can make is to assign responsibility without authority, since that almost always leads to failure, frustration, and fear of future assignments. Consider your delegate as an extension of yourself and grant to them the same type of authority and resources you would wield were you doing the job yourself. Of course, you want to ensure that the person chosen shares your high standards, style, and management philosophy, and that they will work closely with you to ensure that the outcome is as successful as if you did it yourself. Central to this effort is your commitment to remaining interested and informed about the project, and your ongoing efforts to serve as a coach and inspiring presence. Your involvement will be necessary to ensure that the highest level of performance is achieved and delivered.

Accountability: Accountability is one of the trickiest things to manage in any company, and especially where delegation is concerned. When something goes wrong, whose fault is it? Who ultimately should be held accountable for mistakes and failures? You? Your managers? Their delegates? The entire team? Accountability is not something that can be delegated. Ultimately, it is always the people at the uppermost levels of leadership and management who are accountable in the strictest sense of the word. At the same time, though, there are lower levels of accountability that should be maintained and communicated to team members. If you assign responsibility and authority to a subordinate, then that employee should understand that there is a certain level of accountability that goes with that power. As long as they do everything as they should, then they will meet their accountability threshold.

The important thing is to avoid situations where delegates are assigned task, given power, and then held accountable for every little thing that goes wrong. Mistakes - whether operational or strategic - should be speedily identified and remedied, but accountability issues should always be managed in the most positive and constructive manner possible.

Important Factors for Effective Delegation

- *Be Clear About the Importance of the Assignment When You Delegate it*

Regardless of whether you are assigning a small task or a major project, you should always take the opportunity to clearly define why successful completion is important. Tie in company goals, the mission, current objectives, and even vision and philosophy when appropriate. Reinforce the importance of teamwork, customer satisfaction, and high standards. Never forget that our goal here is to construct a mindset that will enable you to be the best in class. Proper communication is an essential part of ensuring that delegation accomplishes an array of important goals.

- *Delegate More than Just Undesirable Tasks*

You should avoid the habit of just dumping your least enjoyable tasks on subordinates. Mix in other tasks and functions that are interesting, educational, challenging, and rewarding. Sure, there will be plenty of more mundane functions that need to be handed out, but you can maintain your delegate's interest by tasking them with those more desirable jobs too.

- *Delegate Gradually*

It is important to work into the delegation process, so that you train your subordinate properly. Avoid just dumping a series of assignments on them as that will just set them up for failure. You have to be genuinely dedicated to their success, and that requires a more gradual introduction to new assignments. Commit to coaching, inspiring, and empowering them so that they are motivated to go beyond expectations. Acknowledge the importance of their contributions and be appreciative at each step of the process. Gradually increase the workload over time, perfecting your delegation model first and then replicating it.

- *Delegate in a Timely Manner*

Try to avoid waiting until the last minute to delegate some task that you know needs to be done. The surest way to achieve delegation failure is to wait until work has reached a crisis moment. Managers who do that generally need some help getting more comfortable with the delegation process.

- *Maintain Proper Communication*

That means informing all departments, teams, and personnel who need to be aware of specific assignment delegations. That can help to ensure that teamwork is more cohesive, eliminate confusion, and smooth out the inevitable conflicts that arise when no one knows why things are happening the way they are. Be sure to alert all relevant personnel to the fact that your delegate has the requisite authority and responsibility to complete your assigned job.

- *Delegate and Then Back Off*

Once you've assigned tasks and empowered a subordinate to finish the job, step back and let them manage it. You have given them the parameters of the job, the power to carry it out, and the expectations that must be met. If you continually step in and interfere, you will only frustrate everyone on the team and reduce the chances that the task will be successfully executed. Let them decide how to accomplish the task using the resources you have provided, stepping in only when absolutely necessary. And even then, it is wise to consult with your subordinate in private, to ensure that you do not disrupt the authority you have delegated.

When you do intercede, do so in a constructive way, offering advice about your positive experiences using certain techniques or strategies. Be subtle, let them know what has worked in the past and serve as coach and inspiration rather than intrusive boss. Above all else, be sure to acknowledge their good work, be appreciative, and encourage them in their efforts.

- *Be Consistent*

Do not change expectations after the project is underway unless absolutely necessary. And if changes are needed, be sure to thoroughly discuss them with the subordinate to ensure that you are both on the same page going forward.

- *Praise in Public, Critique in Private*

This is an important rule of management that is applicable in every area of your business. Good leaders understand the importance of publicly praising their team members. That builds enthusiasm, engenders good will, and keeps everyone happy and motivated. At the same time, it is equally important that individual critiques be conducted in private. If there is a problem such as poor results, review the issues in a private setting with the subordinate.

- When you do so, be sure to allow them time to give you their assessment of the project and their efforts before you critique them. Then shape your criticism to focus on how things could have been done differently to achieve a more favorable outcome. Remember, leadership entails showing, not telling. If you still believe that the employees have the potential to fit within your delegation plan, then work more closely with them on the next assigned task to help them master the process. Different employees develop different skills at their own pace, so be prepared to be flexible.

Of course, there will be times when your subordinate seems completely unable to adapt to the delegation process. At that point, you will need to assess their skill set and value to the company, with an eye toward determining whether you simply need to leave them with their typical daily duties, or replace them altogether. As harsh as that sounds, there are times when employees simply do not fit within a company's structure. If your "B" employees show no sign that they can be transformed into "A" superstars, then you need to think about replacing them to ensure that your company remains on track to being the best in class.

Chapter 9 - Employees – A Pillar of Business Success

"Everyone talks about building a relationship with your customer. I think you build one with your employees first." Angela Ahrendts

Have you ever heard some business guru declare that employees are your most valuable asset? If you listen to business leaders and industry experts on a regular basis, you might be forgiven if you assume that this is a universally-accepted belief. Everyone talks about the fundamental importance of finding and retaining quality employees, and about how they are among the most indispensable assets within any sound organization. The question is, however, does anybody actually believe that? Judging from the way in which most companies fail to properly leverage this asset, it is reasonable to conclude that far too few employers truly believe in the value of their workers.

That is, of course, an apparent contradiction that can be difficult for the average person to reconcile in his mind. Given that most people agree that human capital is the most valuable asset any company can possess, how can it be that this belief is not reflected in the way firms treat and manage their employees? The answer is clear: today's business owners and managers lack the ability to effectively harness employee talents and capabilities in a way that maximizes their contribution to the attainment of company goals. In short, those valuable resources are significantly under utilized.

It is important to remember that your employees are the most dynamic asset you can possess. They can and should serve as the nucleus of your organization and its culture and play an active role in every area of your business operations. Like other business assets, however, they often lose value over time unless you actively invest in them. Companies used to understand this fact, but much of that understanding has gone by the wayside in recent decades.

The One-Employer Life of the Past

Many young people today would be shocked to learn that just a few short generations ago the average person's career path was vastly different than it is today. Back then, when you went to work for a company, you often did so with the intent of working there until retirement. That was true for a wide variety of career paths - from factory jobs to white collar occupations. Employers hired the best people they could find, with the intent of keeping them on staff for the long haul.

That desire for a long-term relationship between employer and employee necessitated the creation of corporate cultures that emphasized investment in every employee. Since labor was an asset that needed to be sustained over time, employers recognized that they needed to do everything in their power to build loyalty, competence, and the broadest possible range of skills sets. They invested heavily in training and other avenues of employee improvement that were designed to enhance each worker's value to the company. That investment paid off over time as employees became ever more productive and valuable to their firms. Consequently, we benefited from decades of rising wages and benefits that went hand-in-hand with sustained corporate profitability.

That era marked the largest expansion of middle class America that the nation had ever witnessed, as millions fulfilled their dreams for themselves and their families. Employees were treated like members of the company family and in turn they gave their talents and loyalty to their employers. Today, we look back on those times with an air of nostalgia, mindful of how much things have changed in just a few decades. Few, however, lament the passing of that status quo. For most people, there is just acceptance of the fact that today's marketplace makes that sort of symbiotic relationship obsolete.

But does it really? Is there some unalterable law of business in effect today that demands that employees be viewed as entirely disposable objects that can be replaced without any serious negative consequences? Many businessmen today worry that any serious investment in their employees is a waste of finite resources, since most employees migrate to other companies before that investment sees any serious return. It is true to say that turnover is high, the bonds of loyalty are all but gone, and long-term decision-making is becoming a lost art. But does that mean that there is no way around the current status quo?

I would argue that there is still much value to be realized from the attempt to develop employee skills and loyalty. With the right kind of leadership, a commitment to recognizing employees as valuable assets worthy of investment, and a strategy for embracing personal and professional growth at every level of your organization, you can capitalize on what the lessons learned by business owners long ago. Companies that treasure their employees will find that those employees become their greatest treasure.

The Perceived Problem with Employees

It may sound somewhat naive to believe that employees can once again be viewed as the vital resource that they truly are, but commons sense and historical experience demonstrate that this is an attainable goal. Yes, globalism and its increased international competition have caused companies to alter their internal paradigms in ways that give less thrift to the value of employees. However, there is no immutable law that says that this must be the case. Nor would I argue if this is healthy for this trend to continue. In the end, it all boils down to the type of culture you strive to create and what you are willing to do to achieve your ends.

As we've learned throughout the preceding chapters of this book, your company culture will come into existence even if you take no steps to create it. If you actively plan its development, you can largely shape what it eventually becomes. If you fail to take an active role in creating a culture, one will take root on its own - and it will, as often as not, end up being a culture that does little or nothing to further your company goals. It is for that reason that I consistently urge entrepreneurs and managers to diligently work to create precisely the type of company culture that will best facilitate the attainment of the firm's goals. There is no substitute for this.

What we often see, however, is a complete lack of planning when it comes to building this cultural foundation - though that failure seldom receives attention when companies fall short of their goals. More often than not, business failures are attributed to bad management or an abundance of bad employees. Those two problems are so interrelated that one is seldom seen without the other. Both are also contagious in any business, which means that once bad managerial habits and bad employees begin to take root, their example can spread like a virus contaminating every aspect of the enterprise. They can affect morale, product quality, customer service, productivity and profitability, and so much more.

Worse, the negative impact on your operations can be so severe that even top-notch products are often insufficient to see you through to success. If your business struggles and your first instinct tells you that your employees are failing you in a major way, you wouldn't be the first entrepreneur to have that thought. The fact is that far too many business owners find themselves doubting the value of their employees at one point or another.

In my experience as a management consultant for more than a decade the most common reasons many small business owners cited for their lack of success consisted of three main complaints: 1) It's just too hard to find good employees these days; 2) We were handicapped by a large number of employees who were only here to collect a paycheck; and 3) Most of our employees lack ambition, refuse to take responsibility, and have no desire to excel at their jobs.

These common perceptions are shared by a large contingent of frustrated business owners who feel that employee-related issues are at the heart of many of their most pressing operational problems. For many of these entrepreneurs, those perceptions become their reality and end up being something that they are forced to continually struggle against.

I am often reminded of Douglas McGregor's "Theory X" which he outlined in his 1960 book, *"The Human Side of Enterprise"*. McGregor focused attention on the traditional view of management (he called it "Theory X") that had held sway for many years. That widespread viewpoint held that the average person - and by extension, the average employee - shared a number of basic characteristics:

- They tended to lack personal and professional ambition

- They generally worked as little as possible, doing only what was necessary to earn their pay

- They typically focused on their own self-interests

- They were fairly gullible

- They usually disdained responsibility

- Most preferred to be led

As a result, McGregor observed that the only way to get the best out of them was to ensure that they were tightly managed and controlled at all times. They needed to be persuaded using a system of punishments and rewards - in much the same way that many adults deal with their children... or pets. What is striking today is the fact that this more than fifty-year-old mindset remains quite common, even today. In fact, I have often encountered it among small business owners I have met over the years.

After years of hearing entrepreneurs describe their employees in this way, I felt compelled to challenge what was apparently a firmly-held view among many business leaders. One day I decided to gain greater insight from one business owner about this odd viewpoint and asked, "Tell me, when you advertised to fill job openings, did you say, "bad employees wanted" - or did you hire the best employees and then turned them into bad employees over time?"

As you might imagine, I never did get an answer to that simple question; I only received a puzzled look by way of response.

Over my many years of consulting I have noted a number of disturbing things when it comes to employment issues. Take family members, for instance. Quite often, when a business owner has a family member in need of a job, he or she will provide that relative with employment. Now, don't misunderstand me, there are many examples where family members can turn out to be among your most loyal and productive employees. However, it is often the case that these relatives get hired just to ensure that they have paychecks and then end up being improperly managed. That can create serious employee problems with ripple effect throughout your organization.

Here's the thing, many struggling small business owners believe that their businesses would be seeing tremendous successes if they could just somehow find and keep great employees. Now there is much truth in that sentiment. Your employees are the engine that drives your business forward, and are a vital component and integral part of your execution strategy. They are, of necessity, involved with and central to everything that the company does. They are an extension of you and allow you to multiply your own talents and efforts in ways that you could never do working alone.

At the same time, even one or two employees can drag your company down if they are behaving in ways that run counter to your company's goals. And when you have a large number of employees dragging down productivity, disrupting your business processes, and otherwise impeding progress, that dynamic can literally run your company right out of business.

Employees can be your Biggest Dysfunctional Component

Employees can indeed prevent your business from achieving the success you seek. Of course, every situation is unique in its own way, and there is no single solution. However, it is also true that you cannot actually resolve a problem until you recognize that it exists, honestly want to solve it, and actively seek out solutions. And when it comes to employees, you can expect that at some point or another in the course of your business life, this will be a problem.

No matter what you do and how hard you try to avoid it, the fact is that you will eventually experience a situation where employees are not meeting your expectations. When those instances occur, you need prompt attention to the problem if you are to have any chance of correcting it before serious damage occurs. The decision to act quickly must become the rule rather than the exception, given the important role employees ultimately play in your business success. They are the most critical components in your organization and any poor performance - even on the part of just a few team members - will inevitably degrade the final score of the whole and prevent you from being the best in class.

It is vital to understand the types of systemic problems that tend to lead to the creation of most of these unproductive and disruptive employees. These problems include things like:

- Poor recruiting

- Hiring friends and family as a favor rather than as a sound business decision

- Undefined rules and expectations

- Lack of mutual respect

- Failure to show appreciation and recognition

- Management that permits an unproductive and confrontational environment

If you can make improvements in these areas, you will see a noticeable improvement in the type of management practices that work to create and cultivate happy and productive employees.

Poor Recruiting

Poor recruiting processes are among the most common of these problems and are especially prevalent in struggling small businesses that have ongoing difficulties attracting quality workers. This often occurs with companies that find themselves short-handed and in need of bodies. Often times, these companies fall into the trap of being forced to compromise standards just to get enough people hired to maintain some semblance of productivity. While this is understandable to some degree, it is also something that can cost you the success you seek.

If you are continually frustrated by an inability to get your employees to accomplish what you need to see accomplished, or if their performance is continually below the expectations that you have set, there is a very good chance that you have employee recruitment issues that need to be resolved. If your employees are repeatedly failing to show up on time, engage in gossip or discuss personal problems on a regular basis, or otherwise act in an unprofessional and unproductive manner, then you almost certainly have employee issues that are eventually going to lead your business to disaster.

It is important to identify the source of the problem and narrow down the exact flaw in your recruitment process. It could be that you simply have a case where your poor recruiting process is the result of being in a position where you have to hire people quickly. Or it could be that you are hiring unqualified people from within your circle of friends and family. In either of these instances, the important thing to do is to begin with a concrete set of standards from which you will not deviate. It is not enough that someone is willing to work for you; they must also be a person who adds something to your organization.

Identify the personality traits that you want to see in your business and recruit only those candidates who meet your criteria. Start with your best current employees. Review their personalities and other qualities and use that as your measuring yard stick. These are the types of employees who can help you to build a foundation for lasting success and every effort should be made to find as many of them as you can Let them serve as your core group. Then, when you are assessing new candidates, let each one know your exact expectations. Stress the importance of critical factors like teamwork, as well as the environment and company culture that your enterprise promotes. Carefully interview and assess to determine whether the job is a good fit for both parties.

When your hiring process is operating at peak efficiency, every new employee should be showing up for work with an air of excitement and a willingness to learn and adapt to the new work environment. It means that you have to be showing a strong interest and commitment to helping those new hires get acclimated to your business culture. You also have to inspire others on your team to do the same. When you do that, any hires that are not a good fit will be shown to be out of place in rapid order, and when that happens it is your job to ensure that the situation does not fester overly long. Take immediate action to determine whether the problem can be corrected with training or whether more drastic measures are needed.

For my part, I generally meet with the employee's direct supervisor first, and then hold a follow-up meeting with both the manager and the employee. At that meeting we discuss the problem and try to determine whether a resolution is possible. Then, if things still cannot be worked out, we simply come to a mutual agreement that recognizes that the business relationship is no longer in either party's best interest.

I have personally terminated the employment of people at all levels, and this is how I typically address the event:

"We always have very high hopes for all our new employees and invest heavily in training them so that they can thrive in our culture and work environment because we sincerely believe that a successful career path is important to everyone. Unfortunately, not everyone is a good fit for reasons we already covered in our previous meetings. For those reasons we have decided that this is not the place for you to continue to have a successful career. Here is your last pay check, paying you in full up to today. We have included two weeks' severance pay as well. John will be here shortly to help you move."

After delivering that termination notice, I shake hands and depart. There is no further discussion or negotiation allowed, since by the time we reach that point in the process everything that might change the situation has already been tried. I should also note that I have a strict policy of never rehiring anyone who I have previously fired.

Hiring Family and Friends as a Favor

Almost all larger companies have some sort of written policy that prevents hiring within the same departments. Thanks to such policies, there is often little danger that supervisors will hire unqualified family members or others with whom they share a close personal relationship. Sadly, that is rarely the case where smaller enterprises are concerned. Those types of hiring policies are a great way to avoid even the appearance of a conflict of interest, and thus enable larger companies to escape the damaging consequences such conflicts can cause. There is no denying that it is virtually impossible to manage in an objective and effective way when personal relationships are involved. All too often, that leads to the type of compromise that can cause you to set aside established rules, procedures, and even traditions. To not have such rules in place in a large enterprise is tantamount to management malpractice!

Where smaller businesses are concerned, however, the implementation of that type of concrete policy could be devastating. After all, many small business enterprises are dependent at one time or another on friends and family members' participation. Many of these relatives and friends are hired as a favor, but just as many are hired because the owner needs inexpensive labor, people that he can depend upon, or even their unique talents and abilities. In many instances, these people start out as temporary workers and end up making full-time careers out of the job.

In many instances, however, these employees turn out to be problematic at best. Sometimes it is because they never go through an official hiring process. Other times it is because their status as sons, daughters, or friends of the owner causes them to assume that they are somehow above the rules and entitled to special status and treatment. Whatever the reason, the problems can become very severe very quickly.

When Mommy and Daddy's favorites are made a part of the team, existing family rivalries and longstanding negative feelings can boil over in the workplace and taint everything. There are few unrulier examples of unproductive workplaces than those in which there is serious family-employee infighting. There is constant gossip, backstabbing, and other chaotic behavior that can lead to a toxic work environment that destabilizes every aspect of the enterprise.

Even little things like allowing family members to show up whenever they desire can lead to the downfall of the company. It makes the workforce inherently unreliable and unpredictable and fosters resentment among the larger body of employees in the firm. In the end, it won't even matter that the vast majority of your employees are loyal, productive team members; they can do everything they can to keep the company alive and it likely won't matter at the end of the day. When you have that sort of structural problem it degrades every other component in your system. Without correction at a foundational level you will end up with a systemic failure that will prevent you from being the best in class.

Still, a policy that would prohibit you from hiring family members to work for your small family-owned business would simply be impractical. The fact is that family members and friends are often invaluable for that type of business endeavor, but you have to consciously work to make that scenario possible. That requires an open discussion about well-established rules, guidelines, procedures, expectations, and the ways in which those requirements will be enforced. The problem with most familial work relationships is that there are often role conflicts associated with family members working in close proximity to one another. Those conflicting roles lead to confusion about expectations and even abuse of the family relationship. The best way to minimize the chance that such conflict will occur is to act preemptively to avoid any illusion about such dual roles.

It needs to be perfectly and clearly understood by everyone in the organization that anyone who works there are employees, and they are all subject to the same rules and expectations. It matters not whether those employees are spouses, sons, daughters, other relatives, or childhood friends. Each has to know that when he or she shows up for work they are all employees until the work day ends. They will all follow the same set of rules. If any of them cannot handle that status, then it would be best that employment be found elsewhere. Your primary and most important job as a business leader with family or friends working for you is to enforce this policy diligently to prevent any potential for role conflict.

Undefined Rules and Expectations:

Undefined rules and poorly communicated expectations often lead to great frustration and misunderstanding. When there is no clear message about what is expected from employees on a daily basis, management and employees alike are placed in an awkward and untenable position. To counter that potential hazard, it is important that everyone in the organization be made aware of specific rules and guidelines.

Ideally, every company should have an employee handbook. If you haven't gotten around to creating a handbook, at least design a single page list of all of the most important rules and expectations so that your employees can see them in writing. It is generally wise to present every employee with a copy of whatever rule sheet or book you create and have them sign something that acknowledges that you've provided them with these rules and explained them where necessary. If that is not possible right away, then post a copy on the notice board where everyone can read it.

Lack of Mutual Respect

In business as in life, both positive and negative attitudes can be contagious. When mutual respect is lacking in any area of life, it can result in the type of bad attitudes that can lead to a host of other destructive types of conduct. Persistent bad attitude is typically a sign of poor management. That is, as you might expect, something that is inherently bad for your business. It can lead to escalating employee conflicts, poor team work, and unproductive work environment, and deficient customer service. It is your job to inspire your team members to come to work with a positive attitude and an eagerness to treat everyone with respect. Be on the alert at all times for any sign of a negative attitude and move promptly to correct it when it rears its ugly head.

As the leader it is incumbent upon you to consistently promote mutual respect for the mutual benefit of everyone in your organization. Positive attitudes combined with mutual respect to cultivate the type of healthy and happy work environment can make every work day a rewarding experience. In this type of environment, employees are far more likely to leave work at work, use their time off to rest and relax, and then be excited about coming back to work the next day. You will find that your employees are more caring, creative, and collaborative, with a stronger commitment to achieving organizational goals and objectives. Equally important is the fact that this positive attitude will be reflected in their interactions with customers and others in the outside world.

Lack of Appreciation and Recognition

Truly great leaders do not attempt to claim credit for the success of their organizations. Instead, they are humble and actively seek to either share credit with others or allow their team to take credit for any successes. It is common for business leaders these days to miss that simple fact and many fail to appreciate and provide recognition for all that their employees contribute to the company. That can be a costly mistake. As soon as employees begin to sense that they are overlooked and unappreciated, the entire organizational culture is at risk.

The reason this is important is that cultural changes of this type can degrade employee morale and the motivation to contribute anything more than the bare minimum necessary for maintaining employment. All of that can lead to a feeling of indifference toward the company and its goals. Once that atmosphere begins to take root, many managers respond by becoming even more demanding. They grow frustrated and determined to exercise tight control. Naturally, that leads to even more alienation in the workforce, makes even more employees unhappy, and creates a vicious cycle that can drag your company down before you even realize anything is amiss.

If you've done your job well at the hiring stage, then even your worst employee is surely doing something right. If there are problems, it is important to politely point out areas where improvement can be made - but do so even as you maintain focus on praising him for all those things he is doing well. Let the employee know why his quality work is important to you and always be sure to add some words of recognition and appreciation. "Great job for that, I really appreciate it."

With leadership, the best examples are those that communicate by showing rather than telling. As a leader you need to consistently express recognition and appreciation for good work, no matter how small the contribution might be. Your employees will pick up on that example and adopt it in their own dealings with other members of the team. Over a period of time that style of interaction will become a part of your company culture. That, in turn, will inspire everyone to try harder since they will know that their contributions are both noticed and appreciated.

Permitting a Confrontational and Unproductive Environment

Workplace drama is a very common thing, but nowhere is it more common than among small family-owned businesses. In the end it really doesn't matter what conditions give rise to such disharmony; it always leads to a confrontational and unproductive work environment. If management and leadership permit such conditions to continue, morale and company efficiency inevitably suffers. A permissive confrontational work environment is inherently bad for business and must never be allowed to continue.

It also doesn't matter who is right and who is wrong. All conflicts within the workplace need to be resolved in private settings lest they spread and infect the broader culture. The solution to these situations is almost always the same: you need to cultivate an inspiring and positive environment to elicit the positive organizational and behavioral changes you want. And to do that you have to ensure that employees are happy and confident in their ability to contribute to the company's success while advancing their own careers.

Employees are Your Best Non-Binding Partners

As global competition and mounting regulatory burdens continue to drive up the cost of doing business there is a renewed and urgent need to re-examine the traditional relationship between employer and employee. That old custodial concept that saw employers create pension plans to ensure that their employees' financial needs were taken care of upon retirement has been deteriorating for decades and is now on the verge of going extinct.

The fact is that the vast majority of today's employees are struggling to secure their own financial futures. Naturally, that creates the type of uncertainty that leads to high stress, low productivity, diminished loyalty, and a high rate of employee turnover. In most cases employees simply wish that they could find an employer who would offer them the opportunity to prove themselves and build a career in the way employees of previous generations often did. Those employees of old were effectively non-binding partners in the business relationship. They often owned not even a single share of the companies at which they worked and yet they were so in tune with those organizations that their loyalty was complete. It would be a rewarding and refreshing state of affairs if today's employees could be inspired to feel as if they too share ownership in your company.

Sadly, many small business owners are not doing any better themselves. Underfunded retirement plans and a constant struggle to meet payrolls and keep pace with withholding taxes is something that is becoming the rule rather than the exception. Many small business owners have to resort to high interest credit cards just to supplement their cash flow. Even things like high transaction costs, charge reversals, and credit card fraud are putting a damper on the average employer's ability to support pay raises or better facilitate job growth and expansion.

The vast majority of small business owners and wage earners both struggle with a declining level of income and a related loss of purchasing power. Both share in the most negative effects of a rapidly changing global economy. With that said, there has never been a more urgent time for employees and employers to come together and create a new mindset of partnership to confront these new realities and secure their common interests.

Recruit the Best Fitting Employees

Employees are by far your most vital business components. You are the driver of your business vehicle, but it is they who serve as the integral parts that keep that vehicle in operation. They all serve different functions, and you select them based on their individual strengths. You look for those that best fit your business needs and select them based on the roles and functions they are able to perform.

Think of your recruiting process the same way you would approach capital investment. You hire employees based on a long-term outlook because you believe in them. When you hire them it is with the intent to keep them in your company forever. You want to empower them so that they can be as successful as possible in their careers, and in turn help to make your company more successful as well.

Encourage Employees to Find Their Best Fit

Your employees will always be at their best when you have them doing those things that are best aligned with their own unique natural strengths. To get the most out of them and have them become your best marketing tools and evangelists, you need to find those things they love to do, and then join them with projects that they can be passionate about on a long-term basis. When you can do that you will find that they come to work with a positive attitude and will be upbeat and tireless - relentlessly pushing themselves to deliver the best results they can while taking their own productivity to its highest level regardless of their current compensation.

Often times, when you talk to people who feel that they are well-placed in their companies and doing things that they care deeply about, you hear things like "I am willing to do it not just for the money, but because I love it." When that ideal is reinforced by a meaningful career path that captures their imagination, that type of empowerment can be a powerful motivator. With the right type of inspirational and caring leadership team, you can develop many exceptional employees in that type of environment.

As a general rule, however, these are not the type of employees McGregor characterized as the "Theory X" group. McGregor also observed that there was another group of employees that he referred to as "Theory Y" workers. These people treat work as just another daily routine like play or rest. These workers can be motivated and inspired to exercise maximum self-control and self-direction and channeled into contributing to the accomplishment of organizational goals.

Just as there are differences in talents and skill sets, there are clearly different levels of employees - ranging from poor to exceptional. Few of those who are exceptional actually started out at that high level of attitude and performance. Instead, they were developed to that point through exceptional coaching, training, and inspired leadership - along with their own hard work - over a period of time. On the other end of the scale you have those who continue to be below average in the workplace no matter how hard they work or how much you coach and train them.

To give your company the best chance of success you have to hire employees the same way you would recruit for a championship team in sports. You have to recognize that great intentions are not enough. The fact is that not every candidate will be able to do the best job for you regardless of how much time and effort you put into making them suitable. You have to pick the best of the best from your "A" team and understand that even some of those will be cut. For that reason, you must be prepared to make necessary adjustments when you must. No matter how great you are at hiring quality employees, you will make bad choices from time to time. Just remember that you are unlikely to form an "A" team when you mistakenly hire anyone possessing the characteristics described by McGregor as "Theory X." Always adjust as needed.

The thing is that you know you want to be equal to or better than your competition. You want to build an exceptional company. You can either dream about it or position your company right out off the gate to make it happen. You start by hiring the best employees who you believe can effectively work for your company and then you weed out your mistakes. You have to begin by treating every new employee as if he or she is exceptional. You inspire them to be exceptional and coach them as best you can. You are working to form your first exceptional core team. Those team members will share your vision, believe in it wholeheartedly, understand your values, share your culture, and will be fully committed to helping the team accomplish your goals and objectives. This will be the elite team that serves as that first and primary extension of you.

You have to inspire them and coach them by showing rather than telling them what it takes to build the type of exceptional company you are trying to create. These team members will be your evangelists and will have a new and powerful personal mission that drives them to inspire and coach those who end up reporting to them. They will be driven to ensure that new converts continue that mission all the way down to the bottom of your organizational ladder and horizontally throughout every department. Potentially, they are your championship team and are either actively playing or waiting on the bench to enter the game and give you their best performance night-in and night-out. With little or no further instructions given they will know their roles and execute them flawlessly. The point is, however, that they just don't reach that level of quality unless you have coached them well and they have worked hard to develop their performance level.

While workshops and group training are valuable and essential tools, the best way to ensure that your workforce is as well-trained as possible is one-on-one training from inspiring coaches - preferably an immediate supervisor. Most of us have the potential to be coaches and inspire our employees, but it often does not happen as naturally as we would prefer. We may even feel out of place. You have to make it your mission to create a culture of teaching and assisting others to become as exceptional as you are. Your management and leadership team has to send a strong message that declares that the ideal goal is to make you dispensable. That means that you have to become great at training your subordinates so well that they could take your job if you needed them to do so.

You have to demand the same of your employees. Each must be willing and excited to train his subordinates to the point where either of them could move to the next higher job level. That helps to create an environment in which everyone sees before them a plausible path to a more successful career. That environment is one of the best employee retention plans out there, and the best way to inspire employees to achieve the highest level of self-actualization within their career paths.

It is up to you to provide your employees with opportunities to thrive within your firm. Thriving employees are happy employees who come to work excited every day. Thriving employees are energized, engaging, and have a great positive attitude and drive to promote mutual success for everyone and the company. Your employees are your most valuable assets. They are your partners. You have to empower them in a way that makes them feel like they are owners and partners of the company.

You have to create the most productive conditions for employees if you want them to be inspired to do their best for the team and the company. They have to know that their extra effort is being appreciated and that their company has their best interests in mind. That entails creating a new culture, in much the same way that you would create an ideology or a religion. It has to be engineered in a way that allows it to replicate itself. You just have to learn how to do it right so that you can create the most favorable environment for it to grow and spread.

Character Traits of Exceptional Employees

Remember, your exceptional employees will form that critical foundation on which your company's ultimate success or failure rests. The more of them you have the more your company will have the type of solid foundation you need. If the rest of your employees end up being good or great employees rather than exceptional, you will still come out ahead because you will have built the foundation you need to work toward being the best in class. Your company will already be well-positioned to exceed expectations relative to your competition. You will just need to continue to inspire them and promote peer coaching and mentoring at every level of the enterprise while continuing to stress how important it is that every employee strive to achieve those traits that characterize your most exceptional employees.

Those traits will include a great understanding of the company's mission, goals, and objectives and the ability to effectively contribute to and influence strategic decisions and their execution. Those traits include the type of proactive self-motivation that enables employees to make a positive difference for the customers, their colleagues, the company, and anyone they interact with on behalf of the company.

Employees with those traits will have excellent people skills and a great ability to build exceptional teamwork based on mutual respect and consent. They will consistently perform beyond what is expected of them. They are the type of employees who constantly propose new projects and opportunities for the company and are always prepared to head up new projects with little concern about additional compensation. They earn the admiration of other employees and are always a joy to work with. They are not only valuable resources they are also your most valuable role models.

Growing the Value of Your Most Valuable Asset – Employees

Success in business does not happen by accident. Instead, you need to start out with a great product, a service that is in high demand, or an amazing technology that easily captures the imagination of people who hear about it. Ultimately, your company's success is highly dependent on the strategic vision of the top leadership and the execution of your strategic plans.

A successful and flawless execution demands exceptional teamwork and coordination of your most highly skilled and motivated team members. Each team member has to be prepared to contribute and perform their roles like a bench player at a championship ball game.

If you can rise to the challenge of becoming that coach of a championship team - inspiring, coaching, training, and preparing each and every one of your players to jump in at a simple hand signal knowing exactly what to do – you will have learned the mastery of unlocking your company's most valuable asset: your employees. You will have gained the huge competitive edge you need to truly be the best in class.

Chapter 10 - Beyond Employee Performance Appraisal – Mutual Goals Review

Employees are your most valuable assets, which is why they are one of the four pillars of business success. Human beings have a unique place among the living creatures of this world and are gifted with extraordinary talents, capabilities, and a propensity for combining their efforts and strengths in organized groups. When they act in concert with one another, they develop ingenious processes and tools that enable them to take the resources they find in their natural environment and harness them to accomplish both individual and collective goals. That type of organized effort has, over the course of many centuries, helped mankind to achieve the level of civilization that we now think of as "the modern world."

As a species, we have made inexorable progress in many areas of material living with technologies that continually improve, companies that grow and innovate, and societies that generally see each new generation enjoy a better standard of living than its predecessor. It is important that we note, however, that at the individual, group, and company level, some have done significantly better than others.

That fact points to one sobering conclusion that many in the business world often fail to realize: there is no exact science when it comes to success. No management experts can conclusively cite any single factor or accumulation of factors that can be said to be solely responsible for determining any given person or company's success or failure. We do, however, have no shortage of theories on the matter.

From a theoretical standpoint, management theorists are convinced that certain management philosophies are more effective than others when it comes to harnessing human talents, resources, and processes in a sustained effort to achieve company goals. The real point of disagreement focuses on which of the many philosophies out there in the marketplace today are actually the most effective for accomplishing that objective.

The fact is that we have made remarkable advances in many areas. As a civilization, we have seemingly mastered the art of managing extremely complex projects, and the logistics required for the flawless coordination of multiple teams working in concert with one another. Despite those impressive achievements in management capability, we still seem to lag in one critical area of importance. At almost every level of business, we struggle to effectively and accurately evaluate the performance of our employees. That failure has wide-ranging ramifications for all businesses, and is a weakness that desperately needs to be addressed.

In this chapter, we will examine the many employee performance review challenges that still need to be resolved, and propose an alternative way to appraise employees and their contributions towards the success of the company and their career development. This review method can be significantly more collaborative and rewarding, and can better assist you in your efforts to promote your employees' career advancement by focusing on a unified purpose-driven approach that ensures that employee development is perfectly aligned to the fulfillment of your company's goals, mission, and ultimate vision.

The Employee Performance Review

Management experts have long recognized the importance of the employee performance review and have been laboring in vain to perfect its process for decades. While nobody expects you to succeed in making that process perfect, you must recognize its importance and endeavor to make such reviews as efficient and useful as possible if you want to become and remain the best in class. Performance reviews deserve your utmost attention since such evaluations are filled with many pitfalls. In fact, they can be so challenging that many small businesses have simply abandoned them altogether.

A performance appraisal consists of a formal annual review of each employee's performance, conducted by the manager. As you might imagine, this is traditionally an anxious time for employees as they are about to discover just how the management team has rated their work performance over the course of the last year, and whether leadership feels that pay raises or other rewards are in order.

As an example of how such an appraisal is conducted, consider an employee who is being rated in twenty categories of performance, using a rating scale of 1 to 5, with total maximum possible score of 100. Using this scale, the rating numbers could be defined as follows: 1=poor performance; 2=fair; 3= average; 4-good (or above-average); and 5= excellent, or some other complementary description. The employee is scored in each category, provided with the overall assessment, and informed of any shortcomings where improvement might be needed.

This evaluation assessment is typically provided in written form using a standardized form or report. The appraisal is completed, reviewed with the employee, signed by everyone involved, and filed away in the employee's permanent records. Because everything is so formalized and focused on identifying weaknesses, there is a strong tendency to emphasize shortcomings. Employees are thus informed of problem areas and expected to correct those areas of weakness on their own.

While that process might seem useful for at least identifying employee weaknesses, it does little to help them meet expectations. For small businesses, however, it rarely even accomplishes that goal. Why, you might ask? Well, the fact is that the practice of conducting regular and scheduled annual employee performance appraisals is by no means universal throughout the marketplace and many small businesses avoid these reviews altogether. Some may have tried to conduct appraisals early in their business operations, but failed to see any benefits and simply abandoned the concept. The truly sad thing is that companies that fail to conduct these reviews properly are probably better off avoiding them - especially considering just how few managers are actually capable of doing them properly.

The fact is that, regardless of whether these are scheduled events, part of company policy, or simply done as requested by consultants or the company's leadership team, most managers who are tasked with these reviews lack the training necessary to perform them properly. A performance appraisal is among the most sensitive encounters management can ever have with any employee, and can result in the unleashing of a wide range of emotions. That, of course, can make the process an uncomfortable one for managers unaccustomed to dealing with such sensitive matters, leaving them eager to just get the process done as quickly and painlessly as possible.

Of course, one can hardly fault these managers, since it's not like they are the exception to some imagined standard of excellence in employee appraisal. On the whole, employee performance evaluation has been a serious industry concern for a very long time. Many attempts have been made to create and gain acceptance for a proven system, but most of those efforts probably did more harm than good. After all, without clearly defined quantifiable objectives that are well articulated and fully supported by top management, there are too many common pitfalls that will almost invariably lead to unintended consequences.

Used to Criticize and Record Employee's Poor Performance

In the more authoritarian-based leadership work environments, it is still common practice for many business owners and managers to use performance evaluations as an opportunity to criticize and make record of an employee's poor performance. While that might seem like an eminently reasonable approach, it is instead a very poor use of this important management tool. Management should never be in a position where annual reviews are seen as the ideal setting for such criticisms.

Here's the problem in a nutshell: if your employee's performance is below your expectations, chances are that your management team is aware of that fact long before appraisal time. The question then becomes: why exactly would you wait for that review process to address inferior performance?

In any instance where management feels that an employee's performance is unacceptable, action should be taken immediately to address the concerns. It is important to promptly meet with the failing worker to determine the exact nature of the problems and devise a plan to correct any deficiencies. It is very poor management to wait for several months - or worse, an entire year - before taking corrective action.

Granted, this most often occurs in settings where the owner or various supervisors hate to "play God" or fire their subordinates. Many times, these managers simply wait until they are forced to act. That's irresponsible and unfair to both the company and the employees.

There's another issue to worry about here as well. This type of disdain for normal processes can lead to a higher potential for abuse of power against certain employees based on personal judgment, revenge, discriminatory opinions, or other prejudices. This is the type of abuse that can place the company in a precarious legal position, leaving it open to potential lawsuit.

In most cases, such an approach creates the type of demoralizing work environment that can have even your best employees feeling uncertain about their futures. When they find themselves the target of such practices, they can quickly lose interest in cooperating, become less productive, and begin to harbor feelings of resentment as they realize just how unappreciated they really are. The truly dismaying reality is that this type of approach to managing employee appraisals is more common than you might assume, and often leads to the loss of good employees and a rise in employment discrimination suits.

False Negative and False Positive Render Appraisal Useless

Imagine if you will, what would happen if medical lab tests were handled by untrained technicians who were asked to perform their jobs without the right test equipment or procedures. Naturally, the results would be wildly inconsistent with an almost absurd range of variations. Those results would be judged to be useless by every medical doctor who ordered them. To a large extent, this accurately describes the vast majority of performance appraisals. Their results are consistently inconsistent with wide ranging variations.

Those who are given the power to play "judge and jury" with these evaluations are rarely provided with the training they need to render such judgments. Most of the forms that are used for these assessments are so rigidly designed to serve as "one-size-fits-all" management tools that they lack the flexibility and nuance needed to accommodate the wide-range of more individual issues any evaluator is likely to encounter.

For example, an appraisal form used to assess a salesperson whose primary responsibility involves meeting specific sales revenue targets is unlikely to be sufficient for assessing senior executives whose responsibilities extend to issues like recruitment, planning, organizing, coaching, and inspiring others. If the employees' jobs and roles are different, it is folly to think a single review form can meet your needs.

Add to that the fact that there are no real standards in place for most appraisal programs and you have a recipe for disaster. There is almost always far too much room for subjective personal judgment, and many managers resort to the use of vague terms and expressions that provide little opportunity for employees to determine where their perceived weaknesses lie. Managers often criticize by saying things like "your work has been sloppy lately" and "I have not been exactly happy with your performance for some time." Ask yourself what, if anything, an employee is supposed to make of that sort of appraisal.

On the other hand, even seemingly positive remarks are not always useful. Feedback like "I am generally happy with your performance and I am going to give you high marks across the board" could just be a false positive, since so many supervisors have a desire to keep everyone as happy as possible. The problem, of course, is that when you start to worry about disappointing employees in the review process, then you end up with the type of inaccurate feedback that inhibits positive change. That's never a good thing.

When employee performance standards are not easily discerned, your workers will often be confused about which personal traits and contributions are valued most by your company. When those expectations are left to the good graces and judgment of the evaluating manager, you are left with an ineffective and delusional review system that can only leave chaos and damage in its wake. The fact is that you have to be honest with employees. They want to know how they are doing so that they can determine what kind of future they have with your firm.

Let the Employee Do the Rating

Standardization is critically important when you are developing an evaluation process. It is impossible for appraisal managers to be totally objective and fair when everything is not properly recorded, quantifiable with a dateline, and verifiable in every respect. Everyone arrives at these sorts of processes with different value judgments, and it is too easy for them to be influenced by internal and external factors when there are no safeguards are in place.

For example, managers are human just like the rest of us. They have good days and bad days, and they - like us - confront the challenge of viewing any given day through the prism of their own current emotional and mental state. That can result in extreme rating variations from day to day. Since these types of reviews are so difficult to standardize for many companies, the results cannot always be trusted.

And then you have the managers who simply don't like to judge such things as performance. For them, it is a little like playing God, and they worry about hurt feelings or damaged careers - even to the point where things get overlooked and the company ultimately suffers. This style is equally as damaging to the employees and the firm.

One option in this instance is to establish a system wherein the employee rates himself with the manager then adding comments once the completed form is turned in. Self-rating works well in many settings, including ones in which great teamwork, similar mindsets, and a culture of strong mutual respect are encouraged. This culture motivates team members to accept that they all will benefit when the group's mutual goals are met.

It is extremely common in those environments for employees to adopt a more selfless approach where they think of the team first rather than focusing on their own needs or taking advantage of teammates. Many managers like to employ self-rating in this setting, since they know that most people are their own worst critics. Still, there are some who will instinctively overrate their own performance. Some do so because they honestly believe themselves to be more effective than they actually are, while others do it because they seek raises or other personal benefits.

Regardless of the reason why it occurs, the fact that such erroneous self-ratings do happen must give management pause. Managers who use this approach quickly discover that it is unacceptable - especially when the score is used to help determine merit-based pay raises.

It is easy to see why employee performance appraisal has always been one of management's toughest challenges. To be frank, management often lacks the skills to effectively and accurately evaluate whether other managers are adequate in their job performance. Given that fact, it should come as no surprise that managers often fail to properly evaluate the employees in their charge. Appraisals of both management and employees must then be considered a top priority for any business owner who is serious about being the best in class.

Management is an ongoing process that works to execute the business plan by harnessing the talents and abilities of a team of employees all united in their effort to accomplish common goals. To accomplish that feat, appraisals have to be properly focused on helping the company to develop employees, build cohesive and effective teams, and advance core objectives. While there is a natural tendency to associate performance reviews with annual pay raise decisions for certain job categories and titles, the focus of any appraisal should always be firmly on the person and not the job position he or she occupies.

In a small business setting, resources are often limited. That means that great teamwork often consists of workers covering for one another, especially when tough deadlines need to be met. Team players often need to represent the firm's internal and external interests in ways that can be difficult to assess. It is not uncommon for an employee's greatest contribution in any given year to have taken place outside of the bounds of his normal position-based duties. The problem is that, unless the evaluator is a direct supervisor, he or she may not be aware of that extra effort and accomplishment.

Sadly, there has been an ongoing controversy for many decades over the best way to manage performance appraisals, and that lack of consensus is still a widespread fact of business life. Much of the dispute centers on how things should be measured; which tools, forms, training, and standards should be developed and implemented; and precisely how management should be trained and prepared to conduct these reviews. To date, many companies have simply lacked the top management support and total buy-in from lower-level managers that is required for proper implementation of a truly effective system. As a result, the full usefulness and potential benefits that performance reviews could provide have simply never been realized.

For a time, it had appeared as though that might change. The 1960s were the start of what should have been a promising period, coming as they did on the heels of Peter Drucker's `1954 publication of "The Practice of Management" - a book that first outlined the concept of Management by Objectives (MBO). That book led to three decades of tremendous excitement over the fact that there was finally a management tool that could help managers to effectively and objectively evaluate employee performance.

Management by Objectives

Management by Objectives is essentially a participative or team management approach geared toward the ultimate achievement of a common overall corporate goal, through the integrated efforts of all the subunits and individuals that make up the company. The MBO concept, therefore cannot be fully practiced to give the company maximum benefits under authoritarian leadership, since that leadership model relies upon an opposing philosophy for utilizing human resources. As a matter of additional perspective, it is also important to understand that there have been two highly notable philosophies or styles on management, which still holds sway today: reactive and pro-active management.

Reactive management style - also known as management by reaction - hardly plans any activities with predetermined objectives or alternative courses of actions designed to manage certain actives. The manager just reacts to whatever develops. Even in those instances where there is a plan, frequent changes are made either because there is no time to consider alternatives or as a result of the lack of predetermined objectives.

This leads to managers who use their own "hunches" to resolve problems as they appear. Instead of managing the problems, they are often managed by the problems and they tend to make their decision impulsively, especially if they are under pressure to handle more than one problem at a time. This leads to a chaotic work environment where constant compromises are made in response to unexpected problems that are beyond management's immediate ability to resolve.

To be fair, these managers may indeed work extremely hard under this system, vainly doing their best to resolve unexpected issues as they arise. While they may not be capable of dealing with these problems, they do at least struggle to meet the challenge and want to do the best they can. They may even be convinced that they have done an excellent job for the company. Unfortunately, they rarely understand how to prioritize what is important, and thus fail to realize that their efforts would have been better spent focusing on more important operation concerns rather than reacting to situational issues.

The lack of concrete strategies, predetermined objectives, and ordered priorities makes it difficult to determine how well the manager has been doing at any given point in time when it comes to his efforts to facilitate the over-all goals of the company. That assessment is particularly difficult when it comes time for his performance to be evaluated by his superior. Ideally, his superior should be most concerned about how effective that manager has been in working toward the ultimate attainment of the company's goal of maximizing its long-term return on the resources it employs. This is, however, seldom the case.

It is common for companies to fail to provide concrete expectations to let the manager know what he is supposed to be achieving and that can result in the appraising superior being more likely to simply judge that manager by his personality traits than by his hard work and actual achievements. The problem is that hard working employees who find themselves hampered by reactive philosophies of management are more likely to score poorly in their annual review and feel frustrated, underappreciated, and even unfairly treated.

Pro-active Management Philosophy, which became the foundation of Management by Objectives, (MBO), advocates for planning out everything that can be planned well in advance of need. The manager is provided with his priorities and the objectives that form his overall mission. Often times, he even has a contingency plan that provides for alternative courses of actions just in case his original plan does not work out. Wherever possible, goals are established in quantifiable terms that include a timeline for completion so that results can be easily compared against the targeted achievement. Most importantly, his mission objectives are designed to be fully integrated into the overall goals of the company.

This arrangement makes it possible for the superior to determine how well the manager is doing, both in meeting the objectives of his particular mission and the central goals of the organization, at any point in time. Any significant deviation will be noticeable and corrective action can be taken immediately when necessary. Most important is that the superior have a set of figures at hand so that he can objectively measure how well the employee has performed in the mission to which he was assigned. When definite objectives and priorities are well stated in writing, every manager's efforts are more likely to be focused on important matters as opposed to just reacting to events as they occur. That will result in fewer wasted efforts and a better-coordinated plan to meet the overall organizational goals.

Every company wants to maximize its long-term return on its resources and that includes the human capital that it employs. To be most effective in achieving this goal of maximization, a company must have a well-coordinated plan designed to achieve a set of objectives. In more complex organizations and larger project settings, this often involves multiple teams or departments. Flawless execution is dependent upon highly-skilled coordination that is designed to ensure an orderly arrangement of the overall group effort to achieve the common goal. Company goals are always achieved through the combined efforts of groups of unique individuals, but optimal results can never be realized without real unity of purpose and action. To accomplish that unity of action, the team members need to share more than just a common goal. They need a complete understanding of their determined roles, and how their efforts can be best combined and coordinated to meet their objective in the most effective and efficient manner possible.

In his book, "Management – Tasks: Responsibilities: Practices", published in 1974, Peter Drucker stressed the importance of coordinated efforts and predetermined objectives and pointed out that:

"Each member of the enterprise contributes something different, but all must contribute towards a common goal. Their efforts must all pull in the same direction, and their contributions must fit together to produce a whole – without gaps, without friction, without unnecessary duplication of effort. Performance requires that each job be directed toward the objective of the whole organization. In particular, each manager's job must be focused on the success of the whole. The performance that is expected of the manager must be directed toward the performance goals of the business. His results are measured by the contribution they made to the success of the enterprise. The manager must know and understand what the business goals demand of him in terms of performance and his superior must know what contribution to demand and expect. If these requirements are not met, managers are misdirected and their efforts are wasted."

Going back to the two theoretical extremes between Management by Reaction and Management by Objectives, it is important to realize that neither one is likely to exist in its purest sense. No manager can possibly plan every event before it happens to ensure that he never has to manage by natural reaction. Nor do we find too many managers who work without any sort of plan and deal with everything by reaction.

One thing is for certain, however: management efforts are always more productive and effectively utilized when the manager understands and knows his role. He has to know what he is expected to do, in quantifiable terms, so that he can work toward meeting the overall goals of the organization. When he is given predetermined objectives to meet, the manager will better understand his priorities - and that is particularly useful when he is under time constraints. When priorities are well-ordered, he can focus on doing what must be done right now rather than focusing on what he thinks would be nice to be done.

This management philosophy yields better results in terms of proper utilization of each manager's time, results in fewer wasted efforts, and enables him to focus on matters of the highest priority. MBO advocates also claimed that another end result of the management by objectives system is that it provides a valuable basis for a more objective performance appraisal. That in turn serves as a very useful tool for preparing managers for higher level positions.

In the decades that have passed since the 1960s, these arguments have led many management theorists to believe that management by objectives tends to have many advantages over the conventional approach of activities-oriented management when it comes to managing human resources. Many companies, including Exxon, General Electric, Hewlett Packard, and the Washington Post, had implemented MBO as a manpower planning requirement, compensation benchmark and over-all performance assessment for a period of time but appear to have migrated to a modified version of it today.

The management by objectives concept sounded so deceptively simple that it might have actually misled and disappointed many managers who were looking for fast and easy payoffs. The fundamental principles of setting meaningful, quantifiable, and measurable goals are well practiced in modern management today, but pure management by objective as a program has, unfortunately, been fading away.

The problem seems to have been that, in the absence of relentless support from top management, these types of formal programs became difficult to administer in the face of changing priorities. Even though many believed that it was highly useful as a planning tool, it was very difficult to maintain and sustain the amount of continual updating that was necessary to make it work. As happens with so many management concepts, difficulties with implementation and general neglect caused its popularity to decline in recent years.

Though they continue to be problematic, traditional employee performance appraisals are still commonly used among smaller to mid-sized companies, while others have moved on to adopt new techniques. Many larger US companies have adopted the Kaplan and Norton's "balanced scorecard" approach for good reasons.

The balanced scorecard, created by Dr. Robert Kaplan (Harvard Business School and Dr. David Norton) in the early 1990s, is a strategic planning and management system. It evolved from the original concept that we know as the performance measurement framework. As a whole, it is not a measurement system but a strategic management tool that uses expanded metrics to track four key areas considered critical in the execution of strategies used to accomplish the company's vision.

These days, thanks to increased popularity and demand, software is being developed to make implementation of balanced scorecard easier. This software allows you to select criteria in each of four key categories of perspective: financial, customer, internal process, and learning and growth. You can be sure that this new management tool will continue to evolve and could have expanded features in the future to help it become a complete and functional software tool for evaluating multiple layers of performance. With increasing computing power, advances in artificial intelligence, and the great strides being made in programming skills, this new tool holds the type of promise that makes it a project worth watching in the months and years to come.

Beyond Employee Performance Appraisal - Evaluating and Nurturing Your Most Valuable Assets

As discussed throughout this chapter, no matter what system was being used as a tool to appraise employee performance annually; whether to measure accountability, disciplinary enforcement, manpower enrichment, or the reward of employees through pay raises, there were always pitfalls and obstacles. It is troubling to observe that despite those shortfalls, employees continue to be evaluated in a way that suggests that the process is little more than an annual ritual deemed too sacred to abandon; often with results that are damaging to both the employees, as well as the company. Perhaps that is one reason why so many small business owners have yet to even think about implementing an appraisal program.

The thing is that most management tools sound deceptively simple when they are first presented. That is certainly true in the case of management by objectives and employee performance appraisal. The balanced scorecard is no exception. The fact is that any of them can be successfully implemented if the company is blessed with the dedication and commitment of top management personnel who are willing to invest resources with a long term view. The plan has to be well-designed to ensure that it meets the intended goals and objectives. More than that, though, it must be well-executed and then maintained over time with continual training if it is to be sustained on a long-term basis. When this is done correctly, the initial launch can be quite exciting and the results can be spectacular. If it is neglected, however, or not well maintained by knowledgeable personnel, that excitement will diminish over time - especially for an annual event like the employee evaluation.

The one thing that will make the biggest difference is the mindset of the top leadership with regards to their employees. To be the best in class, the prevailing culture has to be aligned in a way that enables you to nurture and treat your employees as your most valuable assets. Remember, they are one of your pillars of business success. The extra commitment and investment in time and resources is essential and justifiable to help develop the largest number of exceptional employees relative to your industry peers and to make your company better than the competition.

Employees are at their best when they are treated like long term partners with mutual interest and benefits. That motivates them to strive for optimal career development, while being inspired to go the extra mile in their contribution to the team's common goals - the success of the company and the success of their own careers.

The thing is that you don't want to settle for mediocre. You want to build a best in class business and you have hired and retained employees who share your vision. They are now a part of your "A" team – the championship team. Where others are failing you have excelled, with a success-oriented philosophy centered on a willingness to see things differently and do things differently. The employee performance appraisal process - something that has always been a problem for others - is an opportunity for your company to differentiate. Until you can do it objectively and productively, you need to stop rating your employees by their weaknesses. You either let them go or focus on their strengths in an attempt to ultimately diminish those existing weaknesses.

The fact is that you want to have the best employees. It is important then to realize that your employees are most happy, proud, motivated, and dedicated when they believe that they have found an employer who is committed to providing them with a successful career path. Unlike most traditional employee performance evaluations where the primary intent is to point out employees' shortcomings - with the goal of using the power of the office to induce change - your new approach should be one that focuses on mentoring to promote career development and team building. It should also be an approach that seeks to direct employees toward contributions that provide maximum mutual benefits that are aligned with the company's mission goals, objectives, and strategic vision.

Wherever and whenever practical, all employees should be given an opportunity to advance their careers. Instead of one annual review, this program can be designed to include multiple employee conferences throughout the year. The conference can be a meeting between the manager and his subordinate individually or with all of his subordinates as a group. This is a management tool designed to help all the employees in a leadership position better prepare their team members for career advancement through coaching and self-improvement, while working and coordinating as a team to accomplish the company's missions.

Mutual Goals Review

The Mutual Goals Review is a strategic management tool based on the systems concept that everything matters because everything is interrelated. It is an ideology focused on a commitment to a shared vision of being the best in class in everything. It is a mindset of being equal to and better than the competition in every aspect, predicated on the recognition that the only way to be the consistent winner is for the company to be committed to outperforming its competitors in every category. It is a believe system that, when both the company and its employees share a common goal of mutual success, all parties will continuously strive for the best outcome in whatever they do. It is a self-motivating driver that thrives on collaborations for mutual recognition and mutual benefits. At its best, mutual interest trumps self interest, resulting in great teamwork and collaboration. It changes the mental prospective from self to group; from I and mine to we and ours.

Mutual Goals Review is a scheduled conference to encourage, train, and assist employees so that they can get on track with their career advancement. It is also an opportunity to ensure that each individual's goals and efforts are aligned with the company's goals, missions, and vision, with feedback from management.

Mutual Goals Review acknowledges that there are four key pillars or components vital to the success of the company:

- The Founder/CEO

- The Employees

- The Products/Services

- The Customers

These are the key foundation blocks on which everything else is built, including all of the financial and non-financial aspects of your business enterprise. Employees are the most valuable assets but are commonly underutilized for a wide variety of reasons including the lack of an inspiring work environment that promotes career advancement. This program, when implemented properly throughout the organization with sustained support and participation by top management, will greatly enhance the efforts of every employee and unite them so that they are working together towards the achievement of common goals in the fulfillment of a shared vision.

Mutual Goals Review is the byproduct of a leadership culture based on a philosophy that believes that everyone, given the opportunity, inspiration, mentoring, and training, can become a better manager, a better leader, and be more prepared to advance their career path. It is a philosophy and a conviction of top management that a common mindset of shared vision, missions, goals, and objectives across the entire organization, is the most effective and enduring approach to excellent performances with sustained consistency.

Unlike the traditional employee performance review, the Mutual Goals Review process focuses on employees' strengths and contributions with great appreciation from management. Together, the manager and employee review, renew, and revitalize their commitment to current and future projects with the mindset of remaining the best in class while focusing on how they can do things even better for the mutual benefits of the employer and the employees. It is an approach that seeks synergy between a company's goals and an employee's career advancement needs, aligning them and treating them as mutual goals that will benefit the best interests of all parties involved.

Mutual Goals Review takes place at a scheduled conference, conducted at least four times a year or as often as management deems necessary. It can be conducted in a group setting or between a manager and his subordinate; either formally or informally. The meeting agenda may include discussions about general management philosophies and practices as they relate to the employee. It may also include a general discussion on one or more chapters of the book, "The Four Pillars of Business Success". The intent is to ensure that all parties share the same mindset regarding the importance of working together towards the attainment of common goals. The next step is to move to the review of newly completed projects, ongoing projects, or potential projects. Mutual Goals Review can be incorporated with other management tools and survey results, such as the standard customer satisfaction survey.

Every company and every situation is different. As a result, it is most effective for senior management and key managers to come up with an agenda for each conference, covering recently completed, current, and future projects. Make it inspirational, productive, and relevant to the parties involved. It should be about the members of the team working together for the mutual benefits of everyone and the success of the company. At the launch of the program, it is helpful go over some basic management principles as they relate to planning, goal setting, project management, strategy development, execution, and others. It is a good thing to always treat learning and training as part of work.

Company Objectives:

- To provide the most productive and educational environment where employees are inspired and mentored to excel so that they advance from good employees to become great employees, with a primary focus on mentoring to promote career development, better leadership, and team building.

- To inspire employees to be intimately in tune with the company vision and missions while being empowered to help develop strategic plans that are well executed to accomplish those missions, goals, and objectives. Those goals include both financial and non-financial concerns.

- To familiarize employees with the company's culture and mindset - with an emphasis on being the best in class, as well as being equal to and better than the competition.

- To continually recognize that everything is interrelated. While everything matters, the four key pillars are the most important of all. To that end, emphasize the company's commitment to great customer satisfaction and employee career advancement.

- To determine whether employees need help and discover what other resources they need to overcome obstacles. Be a great listener, genuinely caring and helpful.

Chart the employee's career path. Is the employee on track going forward?

Employee Objectives:

- To promptly acquire the best knowledge of the industry, familiarize yourself with the company vision and mission, culture, philosophies, and your job functions. A mastery of the book "The Four Pillars of Business Success" is highly recommended.

- To promptly develop strategies that will help you become a great employee by setting meaningful and measurable goals and objectives that are well aligned with the company's goals, objectives, missions, and vision. You should strive to be the best team player and be a shining example to others.

- To be passionately committed to help generate and identify opportunities or projects that could contribute to the success of the company and your career. Think how else you can contribute to the company's success.

- To position yourself so that you become dispensable, and acquire and develop the skills and knowledge that can aid you in your efforts to coach, train, direct, and manage all subordinates reporting to you with a goal that after a period of time one or more of them can take over your job with short notice.

- To, as soon as possible, position yourself to move up in the company. Go the extra mile and be the best among your team. Indeed, you should always be positioning yourself for the top job. Master the skills of your manager and be ready to take over his job if needed. Don't forget Henry Ford's saying, *"Whether you think you can or you think you can't. You're right"*

Chart your career path. Are you on track going forward?

Inspiring, coaching, training, and managing employees are all core responsibilities that should be the foundation of your management philosophy. You are the leader and the coach, and as such must be constantly helping your team to always be at their best and ready to take on the next challenge. They can achieve this by being dynamic and always striving to be better than they are today.

As part of the training and employee empowerment, is it recommended that the supervising manager and subordinate take a rotating leadership in conducting each of the conferences. Every situation or conference is different and unique. It is dynamic and dependent on the goals, objectives, and outcome of actives or projects since the last conference. To this extent, each conference is custom-tailored accordingly. Go over key projects or activities in terms of meeting quantifiable goal achievement. Evaluate strategies and execution. Acknowledge any positive accomplishment with appreciation for the best efforts. Mutually explore any room for improvement, and if deemed necessary, make adjustment for future projects. The fact is, "where you are right now is of less consequence than where you are going from here." Use this opportunity to review and refine projects goals and objectives of on going projects based on the mindset of always wanting to be the best in class.

Like everything else, if Mutual Goals Review is to remain successful it must be promoted and maintained with the full and sustained support of top management. Additionally, a mastery of this book "The Four Pillars of Business Success" with continuing education is a prerequisite to the best benefit of both parties – the company and the employee. There must be a deep knowledge and understanding of the business philosophies, tools, best business practices, leadership culture, mindset, and other crucial concepts discussed throughout the book.

Chapter 11 - Products - A Pillar of Business Success

Regardless of whether your great idea involves a product, a service, or both, your starting point must always be focused on your commitment and passion to be the best in class. You must have the goal of becoming equal to or better than your competition at the earliest opportunity. It means that you have to develop ongoing strategies to ensure that you are better than your rivals in every respect, especially as you continually strive to build the most successful product line possible.

Irrespective of the product you are offering to customers, your ultimate goal should be to consistently deliver that "wow" factor that enables you to surpass their expectations. To do that, you must instill within each member of your organization the same mindset that drives you to seek that level of success. Their mission must be to deliver the absolute best product possible, and back those products up with a relentless commitment to great customer service and consumer satisfaction at every level of engagement. This is one of the key pillars of success that will help to determine just how effective you can be in realizing your business goals.

Focus on your brand, commit to making it synonymous with excellence, and promote it with pride. Remember a successful product line forms the solid foundation your business needs for real growth and sustained profitability. With consistency and enough time, that foundation will offer you the support you need to enjoy your best chances of market dominance.

The things that you produce and sell represent the true lifeblood of your business and are in effect the reason why your company exists. At the same time, however, you must be in business to actually make money. Your ability to realize a profit must always be the primary benchmark you rely upon whenever you make decisions of any kind - including hard decisions involving product launches or product discontinuations. You must maintain sensible business objectivity about it all so that your wisdom is not blinded by product or service sentimentality.

Many small business owners went into business with the unspoken notion that what they are doing amounts to little more than a hobby. Others are bored and see the challenge as just one more thing to do to pass the time. Unfortunately, starting out with the wrong mindsets are recipes for failures. As much as it may sound harsh, I have reminded entrepreneurs that it is of vital importance not to mix up business with charities or hobbies. You are in business to make a profit. Accordingly, always keep that in mind with your product or service offerings, including product discontinuation. If you have no chance of making a profit, let it go no matter how much you love to keep the product or service.

Always be prepared for the fierceness of competition with a relentless commitment to manage the best business in all of your decisions. When appropriate, take advantage of opportunities as they emerge. With focus and a drive, you will gain the highest probability of advancing your company towards those upper echelons of market success.

It is important to be selective, strategic, and focused like a laser on your goals. You must understand that success will not be determined by the sheer number of different products you offer, but by the sales revenue and profit that each individual item is able to deliver. One of the mistakes I commonly see involves new entrepreneurs - flush with excitement and filled with a seemingly endless supply of bright ideas- who spent all their time developing new products, even at the expense of cannibalizing their old offerings. They are engaged in what I like to refer to as a "build and destroy" strategy. That path leads to nowhere fast. And you can go bankrupt doing it.

Do not build and destroy. Whenever you create a new product, focus your energies on exploiting it to its fullest so that you can maximize its potential and achieve an optimal return on your investment with the best possible sales revenue and profitability. Any time you abandon efforts to increase your ROI from a product, you must be sure that it has reached its maximum potential already. If it has not, then you are failing to fully take advantage of your prior efforts, and essentially denying yourself revenue just for the sake of trying something new.

Now, that does not mean that you should be complacent. When it is time to introduce new products or move on from older offerings, then do so and do so without regrets. You must always be striving to provide better value for your customers and that often entails the introduction of new products and services or the improvement of existing product lines. So, even as you work to maximize each existing offering's profitability, you should be cognizant of potential improvements that can be made while also focusing on the development of new products that you can release to the public at the appropriate and most opportune time.

Knowledge is Real Power

With very few exceptions, business continues to be about competing for the largest share of a given market and delivering the highest amount of value with the maximum profit margin possible. Knowledge will be your most powerful weapon as you set out to accomplish those objectives. If you have not done so already you must strive to learn everything you can about your competitors and the industry. When you have commanding knowledge of your industry and your competition you have the type of advantage that can be easily translated into a true competitive edge.

To achieve that edge, you need to study your leading competitors and learn everything you can about their products and services. You must have an inquisitive mind that seeks to unearth as many details as possible about how and why your competitors do the things that they do. You then need to determine how you can do what they do, but do it in a way that increases value to the customer while lowering costs. In the earliest stages of your enterprise, that often means striving to do more for less, just to gain a competitive edge in price and provide you the momentum needed to achieve an economy of scale your competitors cannot match.

Of course, your knowledge must extend beyond understanding your competition. You must also have knowledge that enables you to develop a deep and full understanding of your customers and potential customers. Often times, customers are not really effective in letting businesses know what they really need. They lack the ability or determination to effectively articulate their individual preferences and requirements. Furthermore, it is important for you to realize that while the customers may always be right, in a certain sense that does not mean that they always know what they want.

As the expert in your field you need to accept that your customers are not always aware of what is possible or even practical. In many instances, customers do not spend much time thinking about such things anyway. Granted, each situation is different and attitudes can vary from industry to industry. Still, there are three basic types of needs: the needs that everyone is cognizant of on a daily basis, the specific personal needs of which only the customer is aware, and the unique features that only you know how to add or otherwise provide. To achieve a synergy between these needs, it is wise to develop forums or other avenues for communication that allow you to directly engage your customers and learn more about their wishes and desires.

In short, leave no stone unturned in your quest to achieve a fuller and more dynamic body of knowledge about your industry, your rivals, and your customer base. This information is critical fodder for strategic planning, execution, and results assessment throughout your company's life. As Sir Francis Bacon once noted, "Knowledge is power."

Determine Your USP

Products are important, but they can accomplish little if they are never purchased. Your fundamental challenge as a business owner will be to convince consumers to purchase products from you rather than from your competitors. To convince them you need a unique selling proposition (USP) - something that demonstrates the superiority of your offering by clearly communicating its "wow" factor. The proper development and communication of that USP is essential to long-term success.

Here's the thing to remember: if you cannot explain why a customer should purchase your product rather than another brand that he has been relying on for years, then how can you ever break through the marketplace noise and establish your company as a real player in your industry? If you want to achieve business revenue and growth, you have no choice other than to figure out that unique selling proposition that will attract customers to your products.

Naturally, when you have products or services that are somehow different than everything offered by your competitors, then you have something that customers can only get from you. Of course, that does not mean that you strive to be different just for the sake of being unique. What it does mean, however, is that when your company can truly say that its idea is different in a way that makes customers' lives better, then you know that you have the idea you need to fuel your success.

All of this means that you must emphasize new and improved ideas at every level of your enterprise. Additionally, you will have to learn what customers want, develop an understanding of how those needs are currently being served or under-served, as the case may be, and then develop the messaging that can convey why your product can better fulfill those wants and needs better.

Selecting Growth Markets

To be successful your idea must also be directed toward a market that offers the potential for revenue growth. The economy is like a living organism and like most living things it often experiences injuries and illness in different areas of its "body." If your idea targets a market that is currently in a state of downturn, then it can be difficult to leverage the odds of success in your favor. To avoid that pitfall, it is important to do one of two things: either target a growing market, or focus on a market niche that has not yet been either fully realized or exploited. When growth potential is certain, your ability to deliver improved product or service features and better selling value propositions will often be sufficient to gain enough competitive advantages to secure success.

Successful entrepreneurs often see business opportunities differently. They react to identified challenges and problems that have previously lacked a solution. Where the business environment is fragmented, there are many opportunities that can provide high profit margins as well as significant and often sustainable growth potential. This is especially true when product innovation is not the main factor in your product differentiation.

At the same time, efficiency and economy of scale are the most common weaknesses in any fragmented industry. As a result, any entrepreneur who can develop and execute the right strategies to gain greater efficiencies and economies of scale, while delivering products with a compelling value proposition, can enjoy the type of business success that provides steady growth potential for many years - with limited competition in that niche market.

Finding the Right Market Position

As a good example, Smokeys Daylily Gardens of Coldwater, Michigan, USA, became a success story by exploiting a void in the highly fragmented daylily business that was dominated by hundreds of backyard gardeners selling daylily plants online as a hobby. With an initial investment of $500 in 2007 it has grown to be one of the largest daylily growers in the world today. With almost 80,000 registered cultivars, the daylily is one of the top perennial plants yet to be discovered by most gardeners. Its stunning beauty has attracted a large number of breeders or hybridizers with a passion to create their own cultivars and sell a single newly registered plant for as much a $100.

Smokeys Gardens seized the opportunity to take a popular hobby and manage it as a business with a commitment to be the best in class. By reinvesting its earnings in acquisitions, equipment, and well refined processes, Smokeys has reached a scale of planting, harvesting and shipping more plants efficiently in a week than most of the competitors manage in an entire season. The company is positioned for high growth for many years to come. Once established, the plants multiple quickly with nearly zero cost of goods sold. With more than 3,000 cultivars and over two million plants in a single 38-acre farm, Smokeys Gardens is now the lowest-cost producer with the largest selection of popular and premium daylilies.

The fact is that great ideas can encompass everything from basic product concepts to truly disruptive technologies. They also involve new business systems and services that offer customers an opportunity to eliminate middle men. Even products that offer only slight benefit improvements can provide an outlet for success, just as long as they improve customers' lives. That's important to remember, given that truly groundbreaking innovation is such a rare thing in history.

For example, almost everyone now understands that the Internet has been one of the greatest technology revolutions in human history, and is now used and enjoyed by more than 3 billion people worldwide. It has been massively disruptive to traditional financial services, news publishing, bill payment services, and many other industries. Led by companies like Amazon and EBay, E-commerce has created a gigantic new industry causing great disruption and retrenchment to brick and mortar stores. Email has forever changed the delivery of written mail communications, causing great hardship to postal services. The social media platform Facebook has attracted 1.4 billion users. While being disruptive and damaging to some, the Internet has also provided countless others with massive new business opportunities. Great wealth has been created with millions of new jobs spread across the globe, propelled by great visionaries and innovators.

Many people are dismissive of new and disruptive technologies in their early stages of development. While every human being possesses imagination at a personal level, humanity as a whole often clings stubbornly to what it already knows. The process of large changes in the history of mankind have always been more complex and taken a lot longer than early pioneers wanted.

The vast majority of people simply cannot see the full potential of any new technology until it is already proven. Additionally, large scale changes and mass adoption takes years, decades, or many generations to take root in any given society. The first Industrial Revolution took place during the 18th and 19th centuries. Recorded history witnessed the transition from predominantly agrarian rural societies to an industrial Europe and North America with urban societies over a time span of multiple generations. During that time, many individuals and families met with financial loss due an inability to adapt to the changes that were occurring around them.

Simultaneously, others achieved great wealth by being imaginative to recognize emerging trends and nimble enough to take advantage of opportunities. Many early adapters made their fortune with the convenience of money as a medium of exchange, a store of value and a unit of account, while creating a massive number of new jobs in different industries, including banking and financial services. The utilization of steam engines and other machineries brought about immense productivity gain. Yet even that success often came only as the result of a great struggle that saw full productivity improvement being achieved only after a new generation of managers replaced the older generation. Large scale changes are never quick or easy.

The second Industrial Revolution took place from 1850 to 1914 when automation and mass production kicked into high gear. Electricity and fossil fuels quickly became the catalyst for the newly invented combustion engine. Again it took decades for many new inventions to evolve and gain mass acceptance. New fortunes were made and millions more jobs were created. Productivity continued to improve.

Since the end of World War One we have been in the Third Industrial revolution. Within this period of time we have been witnessing many technology revolutions, causing impressive productivity gain as the result of great improvements in efficiency. Hundreds of millions of new jobs have been created and the standard of living dramatically improved around the world with enormous fortunes accumulated by a relatively small percentage of the population.

One of the most significant changes was the transition from analog to digital technology that intensified in the 1980s, at the emergence of personal computers and cellular telephones. We are now living in the digital age and almost anything that can be digitized will be digitized, which includes money, in case you were wondering. Companies like PayPal and others have already been paving the way toward making consumers more and more comfortable with the idea that their money exists in a form that they can neither touch nor see.

The best advice for any human being alive today is to get used to the term "digital asset." That term includes every kind of digital currency - the ones you have probably heard about, like Bitcoin, and hundreds of others that may be less familiar to you. Digital assets are something that we all need to learn to embrace and learn about. The alternative is to resist the tide of history and live in fear of the future. As we embrace that future, we will gain an even greater understanding of why digital currency and blockchain technology are poised to bring about the greatest technological revolution since the advent of the Internet Age. And that is a revolution that has the potential to improve the lives of billions of people around the world as the digital currency and blockchain industry launches a massive increase in the number of business and job opportunities enjoyed by the world over the coming decades.

Like the Internet, digital currency and the immensely innovative blockchain technology will impact many billions of people around the world, including the more than 2 billion people who are currently unserved or under-served by the world's existing banking and financial industry. Digital currency can enable anyone with a cell phone or Internet-connected computer to send and receive money and other assets of value between two parties - at virtually no cost, and without the participation of any central authority. Essentially, with a cell phone you have the potential to become your own bank.

Of course, participation in the early stages of a historic technological revolution like Bitcoin, blockchain, digital currencies, and the other financial technologies that comprise FinTech presents many unique challenges and pitfalls. Technologies are never perfect at the early stages of development and always evolve over an extended period of time with the participation of many players and innovators. Furthermore, technologies often get ahead of regulations which can create a high level of risk and anxiety due to the lack of regulatory guidance, and the justifiable fear that central planners may eventually impose burdensome regulatory schemes. What could be a first-mover advantage now may turn out to be a heavy pioneer burden later that could take years to overcome.

That's why many people simply choose to wait for new innovation revolutions to take root before they act. For entrepreneurs, however, such delays often lead to missed opportunities. Although most people may be more comfortable to follow, good timing and carefully crafted strategic positioning can provide you with great opportunities and greatly improve your odds of succeeding. Bitcoin alternative DNotes is an example of how opportunity can be seized in just that way. It started out as a potential opportunity, evolved into a great idea, and launched as uniquely branded product, much like other great products.

After several months of careful and deliberate study of the industry and great attention to product development, DNotes was launched on February 18, 2014 and immediately set out to compete in a crowded field of more than 1,000 cryptocurrencies. Because its founders were determined to ensure that it would be a long-term, purposeful, and viable currency, DNotes was positioned very differently since the day it was launched. It has focused on building a trusted global digital currency that would elicit participation from everyone around the world - with the ultimate goal of meeting the full function of money so that it could become a viable supplement to existing global fiat currencies.

At the time it was launched, DNotes was entering an industry plagued by signs of troubling behavior. It was an industry that had attracted many bad actors whose "get rich quick schemes" were causing high volatility and providing fodder for frequent negative headlines. It was also an industry that was clearly dominated by younger males who were exhibiting aggressive and destructive behavior that was often reflected in the vast majority of community forums. Leadership and industry cooperation had clearly been lacking. The industry was also facing many of the same struggles many nascent innovations experience in that early success attracted copycats seeking a quick buck. That in turn led to a high rate of failure and investment losses. Biased, inaccurate, and misleading reports and news stories soon followed. Finally, early attempts at regulation - such as New York's BitLicense framework - proved to be prohibitively burdensome. Meanwhile, many other jurisdictions lacked any sort of legal guidance whatsoever.

Succeeding in highly innovative technology during its formative stage - a time when conditions are volatile, dynamic, and chaotic - is challenging and risky under the best of circumstances. It is of vital importance that the participating entrepreneur develops a compelling long term vision coupled with well-defined missions, goals, and objectives. When multiple programs are involved, it is most beneficial that they are all strategically linked so that they generate the most powerful synergistic effect. Careful timing and flawless execution are all very important considerations.

DNotes took all of those different factors into consideration and crafted a long term strategic plan that would see the company take a different path than that followed by the rest of the industry. Its founders decided to go beyond the common practice of just launching a digital currency as many others in the industry had done - often with the hope of cashing in once the price increased sufficiently.

Instead, the DNotes team decided to travel the road less traveled. It is pursuing a vision that will ultimately end with an established and trustworthy digital currency that enjoys worldwide participation in an inclusive way that even today's fiat currencies fail to achieve. That is obviously a powerful vision and a massive undertaking. However, this can only be accomplished by systematically creating building blocks that are all strategically linked and perfectly aligned, with everything working toward the common goal of achieving mass acceptance of the currency within the next five to ten years. The ultimate goal is for DNotes to meet the full functions of money as a unit of account, as a medium of exchange, and as a store of value. Only then, can mass acceptance be expected, allowing DNotes to be a supplement to fiat currency in global commerce.

Since the advent of the Industrial Revolution, history has clearly shown that entrepreneurs are never short of ideas for a product or a service. However, a great idea alone is not enough. Unless you have the time and resources to model it, produce a quick prototype, or publish a white paper clearly framing your concept to the extent that it resonates and survives a peer review, it will end up joining the millions of other great ideas that have never been translated into reality or accomplishment. I have often said that, "a great idea is worth the price of a cup of coffee, if you agree to pay for the tips." This is especially true when you are a startup with no track record of previous success. If you are, you have to work to never be offended by resistance to your great idea, no matter how confident you may be in its awesomeness.

Instead, simply do more research, take the idea as far as you can, and continue to refine your pitch. Make your presentation short and compelling, and remember that your success in presentations will directly correlate to your ability to substantiate your case. Listen attentively and always take notes. You'll be surprised by what you can learn that way. Sometimes, your listener's concerns may have absolutely nothing to do with your product or idea.

After selling my restaurant business in 1981, I founded Manufacturing and Maintenance Systems, Inc., an industrial computer company. We developed a propriety industrial computer for the alignment of rotating equipment such as generators, compressors, and pumps. Being a highly specialized niche market, the company was very profitable and enjoyed sales revenue of about $1 million.

Being young and ambitious, I used the cash flow and started a mobile computer company, Dauphin Technology, in 1998 and began to develop a line of laptop computers. As the market became overcrowded, I decided that the company needed a major break in order to differentiate from our competitors. My great idea was to design a line of computers that would meet the exact specifications of known government contracts for portable computers at the request for proposal stages. I was absolutely certain that I had a great idea but no one took me seriously. I was told that we would not even have a one in a million chance of winning any major government contracts without substantial financial resources and a proven track record - both of which we were lacking at that time.

I took the comments seriously and partnered with Sears Federal Systems of Chicago, Illinois. We then submitted a bid for a $400 million contract with the Department of Defense. Additionally, we teamed with Sysorex Information Systems, Inc. of Falls Church, Virginia to bid for a $120 Million contract with the US Department of Treasury. We won both contracts. Great ideas are most valuable when they are executed flawlessly with sound strategies.

Remember, a great idea does not sell itself. If you are certain that you have a great idea, do all you can to showcase what you have. Create a product mockup or produce a prototype for your show-and-tell. Be relentless and listen carefully for concern and recommendations for improvements.

Coming up with ideas is not hard. Most people do it on a regular basis. The hard work comes into play when you are trying to develop a total package that converts the idea into a product or service that can meet the targeted customers' wants with the required level of satisfaction.

It can be a basic product, an innovative concept, a better solution to an existing problem, or a highly innovative and disruptive technology. Each has its own unique challenges. In each case, you are likely to experience more problems than anticipated, be forced to deal with higher costs than you expected, and exhibit patience as the process takes longer than you had imagined. It helps to remain agile for as long as you can. Being agile and nimble will give you the flexibility and the ability to quickly adapt and make changes to control costs and manage risk. In the real world few things work perfectly at the first trial, so flexibility is a trait you need to cultivate.

It is always prudent to test any new concept or product on a small scale before launching into full scale production. Do not get ahead of the game by overestimating demand and investing heavily in production inventory before there is a proven demand and established distribution system. On the other hand, do not ship to any customers if the product fails to meet your quality standards. It is far better to lose the sale, cancel the order, and refund the money. Protect your brand and reputation with a commitment to customer satisfaction as your company brand is crucial to its long-term success.

Great ideas come in many different forms and are never in short supply. Be selective and stay focused on the things you are most passionate about and that complement your strength and the strengths of your organization. With few exceptions, you will be participating in an existing market with known competitors. At a minimum your products or services must be their equal in all respects. Ideally, they are significantly better. Most important of all, you must have better solutions to known problems and a system-wide commitment to delivering great customer satisfaction and value.

You have an ultimate goal to deliver "wow factors" beyond your customers' expectation with a mission to deliver the best value product possible. What you produce and sell is the lifeblood of your business. Your product or service is thus one of the most important links to success. Like a pillar, its strength is a vital contributor to the integrity of what you are building. For better or for worse, its strength or lack of strength affects everything else that you will do.

Chapter 12 - Customers: A Pillar of Business Success

"A business is simply an idea to make other people's lives better." — *Richard Branson, Founder of Virgin*

Customers are the most vital component for any business organization. Indeed, no company can survive without them. For this reason, they are one of the four pillars of business success and the one that is most relevant to why you are in business. Sure, it is a common thing for any aspiring entrepreneur to cite the desire to "be his own boss" when asked why he was motivated to launch his own business. Still, there is truly no such thing as "being your own boss" - not entirely, anyway. The fact is that entrepreneurs have bosses too. If they are at all fortunate, they will have many bosses.

The reality is that every single customer whose purchases provide the revenue your company needs to succeed is, in essence, your boss to some degree. That's because you ultimately answer to their desires and needs and must respond to their changing wants if you want to remain profitable. In the end, it almost won't matter how good your business idea is or how great your employees are in the performance of their jobs. Even if you have done everything you can to properly position yourself to lead your company toward success, that success will never be realized unless and until you find and retain enough customers to provide your company with the revenue it requires for sustained success. Without customers, all of your projected goals and hoped for achievements are nothing but pipe dreams.

You may, in fact, believe that your idea is the best thing since sliced bread. You may even have a clear vision of where you want your company to be five or ten years from today. You can pack your business plan with a series of powerful mission statements and support them with a whole host of impressive goals and objectives. That is not enough, without a viable and sustainable pool of customers to fuel your business.

After all, what is your business anyway? At its most fundamental level your business is the customer. Your company will not be defined by its name, or your own credentials and record of past achievements, or even by the amount of publicity your innovative ideas receive. Ultimately, your company will be defined by how successful it is at satisfying your customers' product and service wants and needs. As a result of this simple and obvious truth, it is clear that the fundamental mission and purpose of every business is to satisfy its customers.

That is the most compelling justification to explain why the customer is one of the four pillars of business success. It can and should be argued that this is also the most important pillar of all. Customer satisfaction is the core component upon which all business success is built. As the founder of your company, your ideas are the ingredients that must be perfected and marketed, but your company can only be successful if a sufficiently large number of customers want and need them.

It is for that reason you hire employees to assist you in making your product or service available. It helps to imagine this as a four-link chain that consists of you, your products, your team, and your customers. That chain, when constructed with care and effectiveness, links to success. If the last link is problematic or weak, then you can expect your company's overall performance to be problematic or weak. And if you allow those conditions to persist your company will maintain nothing more than a precariously weak link to success. Worse, if that weak link eventually breaks altogether you would have no customers and would have no need for either employees or products. Your company would be left only with you and you would be looking for a new job.

To avoid that possibility, you must always remember that properly serving your customers is the primary reason you are in business. From a strategic standpoint, your ability to serve those customers better than your competitors while providing them with a higher level of customer satisfaction will put you on track to be better than your rivals. You must, of course, always remember that this is only one of many categories that will matter in your quest to achieve a high degree of excellence. To be the best in class, your organization must consistently deliver excellent results across the board. This can only be accomplished by working in harmony as a team with everyone fully committed to achieving one common goal: the ultimate level of success for the company.

With that in mind, it is of the utmost importance that customer satisfaction be fully embraced at the highest level of your organization. It must be relentlessly promoted and practiced across every level of the organizational structure. This is the mission of all missions and must be accomplished through full and complete participation on the part of every employee in the company if you are to be better than your competition and remain on the path to being the best in class. Everything is interrelated on a systems level with internal and external systems and subsystems intimately connected. And with the present level of hyper-connectedness by which the modern world is now defined, what your customers say about you matters more than ever before. Good word of mouth remains the best form of positive advertising, but poor word of mouth can quickly spread across social media and severely damage your brand.

When Problems Arise

Obviously, your goal should be to strive for maximum customer satisfaction at all times. As a practical matter, however, it would be unrealistic to assume that every single transaction will always result in a satisfied and happy client. You will have unhappy customers. Some will be unhappy for very legitimate reasons, while others may have reasons that you will never know. The important thing is how you handle unhappy or dissatisfied customers.

When an issue arises, the first thing you must do is learn everything that you can about that customer's history with your company. Then, you respond promptly and as courteously as you can and work to gain an objective understanding about what actually occurred. As a general rule, with very few exceptions, you should always give the customer the benefit of the doubt. Exceptions can include previous abuse of employees by a customer or instances where the customer is a first time buyer dealing with a long-time and trusted employee. Even in those exceptional instances, however, it is vital that you listen attentively, take notes, and do not offer justifications or excuses during the complaint session. This first encounter is critical if you are to obtain that customer's confidence and assure him that you are advocating on his behalf as he attempts to resolve the problem. This is a golden opportunity to develop rapport with that customer.

To be successful with customer complaint resolution, you need to learn to treat that customer as if he or she is the most valuable client you have. Remember, your mission is to resolve the issue and prevent additional damage to the relationship. At the same time, you must recognize this as an opportunity to win that client's heart and mind by providing the best possible customer service experience. Never forget that your ability and willingness to go the extra mile and do things that your rivals will not do can place you in a position where you can one day do things that others cannot hope to match. As you do more for each customer you develop the type of significant competitive edge that will prove invaluable for the company's long-term success.

With sound customer service techniques, you can get a second chance to make a good impression if the issue is addressed properly and the customer doesn't just switch brands after that first bad experience. This is important since new customer acquisition is costly, time-consuming, and far more difficult than a sound strategy focused on customer retention. Just remember that customers are more likely to tell their friends about negative experiences than they are to report on a positive one. Even when you seem to be doing everything right, one negative incident can cost your company customers if it is badly handled or neglected.

Consider this possibility: a long-time customer who has enjoyed many excellent experiences dealing with your company for years could be put off by the bad attitude of a new employee. When that customer has a complaint and finds that his problem is not dealt with in a prompt and appropriate manner, then another such incident may likely result in the loss of a great client.

It does not really matter if you agree that "the customer is always right". Any time there is a customer complaint of any significance or a problem occurs that is not immediately resolved, senior management should be promptly informed. There must be a policy and procedure in place to handle damage control. At a minimum, the management must promptly get involved to correct the problem with the goal of salvaging that customer relationship and turning an unhappy customer back into a satisfied one. Attention to that goal can help to eliminate the potential for negative word of mouth. Every opportunity to interact with the customer is an opportunity to demonstrate that your company is all about serving the customer and that your entire team has a strong commitment to customer satisfaction. Naturally, you won't succeed every time. Still, it is important for your company to have a dedicated and consistent commitment to turning a bad experience into a good customer experience. Again, always do more than your competitor would at every attempt, were he in the same situation.

Prevention is the best form of damage control and a major contributing factor to successful customer satisfaction and retention processes. You will naturally have defined processes and product quality standards. Never skip any of those processes or standards just to cut corners and meet deadlines. Never be so desperate to fill an order or make a sale that you ship before your product is good enough to be worthy of your brand. It is better to call the customer and refund his money rather than deliver something below his expectations. In most cases, you will find that your customers are reasonable and understanding, provided your communication is prompt, respectful, honest, and sincere.

No matter how hard you try, mistakes will be made. If they go on unnoticed or unreported, it can become systemic and result in high customer churn and costly consequences. When there are options and choices for similar products or services, even at a higher price, the majority of any unhappy customers will just switch brand rather than complain and seek resolution.

It is vital for your company to develop and incorporate a tracking system that can measure the level of customer satisfaction. If you can implement it correctly and with the right level of management support, it can be an early indicator of poor quality product, poor quality customer services, and other systemic problems. It can help you to catch problems as early as possible, regardless of who might be at fault. Once identified, you should correct any such problems using your new procedures so that similar mistakes are not repeated in the future.

Customer Satisfaction Surveys

If you do not have a customer satisfaction survey in place, you should make it a high priority to implement one at your earliest opportunity. It is an invaluable way to get objective feedback from the customer and reinforces the company's commitment to great customer satisfaction when it is properly used. The objective is to see how each customer rates his or her experience with your company, product, and customer services, and how likely it is that they will continue to do business with your firm. Highly favorable ratings are good indicators that your team is doing a good job in promoting great customer satisfaction, good customer service support, and great products or services. These surveys are great predictors of customer retention. High customer satisfaction and retention must become the goal of everyone at every level of the organization since the customer's experiences, both good and bad, are generally not limited to a single touch-point but multiple encounters.

Keep the survey short and sweet and try to limit it to no more than ten questions with exceptions for specific cases. You may have your preference on the format and rating scale; examples can include a survey rating that uses a scale of 1 through 10, with 10 being the best. Nonetheless, the most important goal is to get an objective and accurate reading of the customer's experience dealing with your company as it relates to the products or services purchased, customer service support, relative value proposition, and likelihood of repeat business. Define your objectives and avoid asking unnecessary questions that might lead to irreverent answers. Avoid being biased and hypothetical as that can be annoying to some respondents who might end up being turned off and thus not complete the survey.

Direct contact and telephone salespersons are the best ambassadors for the company, and should always promote the company's commitment to providing great customer satisfaction. They all should be inspired and encouraged to promote this philosophy at all times and build a great relationship with the customers at every opportunity. A standard part of their conversation could include comments like "Customer satisfaction is very important to us. If I may ask you a one question; on a scale of 1 through 10, with 10 being the best, how do you rate your experience with our company?" This type of communication can be embedded as part of a friendly conversation and used at the appropriate time to supplement formal surveys. With proper training and reporting, the feedback from informal surveys can be invaluable. Keep to a single key question and take good notes if the customer wants to tell you more.

Customer support requires specific skill sets that may not be possessed by every employee. As the business owner it is important that you have the right team supporting you. Training a team to support this delicate but important function is absolutely vital, even if some of them just serve as part-time or backups. They must become very knowledgeable about the product or service, the competition, and the industry. They must also be able to deliver a prompt, understanding, and respectful response to complaints and requests for support.

Depending on the situation, some customers may already be irate and disappointed by the time they get around to expressing dissatisfaction of a product or service purchased. Patience, understanding, and a polite demeanor are highly essential skill-sets for the customer support team. Listen to the complaint very carefully, politely repeat it, and then ask the customer if your understanding was correct. Once confirmed, communicate to the customer that you now understand the issue and will work as his or her advocate to see that the problem is resolved as soon as possible.

If the problem cannot be corrected promptly, it is important to let the customer know what to expect. Never leave a frustrated customer languishing without answers. Actively communicate with the customer to inform him of any update on his complaint. Be empathetic, courteous, and always helpful and engaging, to the extent that the customer feels like you understand the problem and that you have taken ownership of it. You will have accomplished your mission if the customer is convinced that you are doing more than any of your competitors would, given the same situation. No matter how challenging the customer or the situation might be, if you genuinely came across to the customer as an advocate at the onset and quickly became a friend you will have gained the upper hand. Irrespective of the outcome, you have won the battle. Customers prefer to do business with friends rather than antagonists.

Much has been written about the importance of customer retention and by now most entrepreneurs are well aware of the benefits that they can enjoy by focusing a great deal of effort on retaining the customers they already have. After all, it costs far more to acquire new customers than it does to ensure that your current customer base remains satisfied. Customer acquisition is very costly. Public relation advertising, lead generation for prospects, nurturing those leads, and closing the sales costs a substantial amount of time and money.

Beyond having great customer services and problem resolution, your efforts at customer retention can be expanded to include an incentive program for high value customers. As a sign of appreciation, it may be beneficial to introduce rewards programs for your best customers, or simply focus your efforts on enhancing their customer experience to ensure that they continue to be amazed with your company's results.

We all like to be recognized and appreciated. This leads to some old memories of my first business venture – a Chinese restaurant named May Ling in Glen Ellen, Illinois that I opened after receiving my MBA from Northern Illinois University in 1976. With a little help from our families and friends, along with about $25,000 in savings, my wife and I acquired an existing restaurant property and turned it into a cozy authentic Chinese restaurant. Armed with the new knowledge I had learned from business school, I proudly did several months of research and product tasting to ensure that we differentiated our products from the Americanized Chinese restaurants with which we would be competing.

That focus on an authentic menu did eventually pay off for us, but those first six months were anything but easy. With our limited advertising budget, we were almost entirely dependent on word of mouth, but it took time for word of mouth to reach enough people who could appreciate why we offered an authentic menu at a significantly higher price - in some cases three times the cost of a good Chinese dinner at the time. It took time for people to recognize the value and not just focus on the price. As a result, we practically went broke before the endeavor finally started to pay off.

Customer appreciation and great customer satisfaction was our primary mission and we were passionately committed to those ideals. We treated our regular customers like special friends and often sat down with them to enjoy an appetizer or a drink on the house. Soon, some became our strong advocates, proudly sharing their awesome dining experience at May Ling. In less than a year, weekend business was always packed with a long line. Building a good relationship with your customers is thus a great approach that can enable you to convert regular customers into advocates whose good word of mouth can be instrumental in helping you to build a successful business. When we sold the restaurant five years later with a nice profit, the thing we missed most were our friends – our customers.

It is also critical that you focus on that central point at which your employees actively interact with your customers. Some estimates suggest that two-thirds of customers who abandon a business do so as the result of negative interaction with employees. You can avoid that by recognizing the importance of both employees and customers and working to ensure that your team members understand their roles and know how to personify your company culture. That often involves emphasis on cross-training to reduce the likelihood of unforeseen mistakes and active support for teamwork so that your employees all work together to make every customer interaction as positive as possible.

There is a powerful correlation between brand loyalty and positive customer experiences that can lead to better customer retention and increased revenue growth. If you want to achieve true business success you will have to learn to focus like a laser on those customer interactions to ensure that you leave no stone unturned in your efforts to maximize the benefits that this critical business component offers.

Where customers are concerned, they can typically be classified as one of four basic levels: one-time buyers, occasional customers, those who frequent your business, and those who not only use your services but advocate on your behalf. To maximize customer relationships, you have to be focused on ensuring that your service is superior to anything else that these customers can encounter in the marketplace. That is the most effective way to not only encourage each customer to become a more regular consumer of your goods and services, but to even entice some to actively promote your company.

In essence, you want to ensure that the one-time buyer is so satisfied with your offerings that he or she returns in the future. When you can satisfy your occasional customers, you can encourage many of them to become regulars. And once they are regularly buying from you, their continued satisfaction can turn them into advocates and despite what some clever marketers might believe, positive word-of-mouth remains one of the most powerful and effective ways to get your marketing message out to a broader audience.

To maximize your customer relationships, it is important to identify them and get to know who they are and why they are buying from you. That entails gathering as much customer detail as you can, including information about what they buy from you, how often they purchase, and even certain demographic facts. Information such as customer occupation, interests, and expressed needs can provide valuable insight into which customers offer the best opportunity for long-term customer loyalty.

More importantly, that type of research can help you to remain on top of any changes in your customers' needs so that you can be proactive in meeting them. Remember too that today's customers want more than to just have their needs met; they have certain expectations about how those needs should be fulfilled as well. Different customers often have different expectations when it comes to things like customer service, and those expectations can vary among demographic populations and can even differ from location to location.

Efficient management of customer data, interactions, purchase history, and trend-lines are of significant value. Customer Relationship Management (CRM) software today is an indispensable enterprise-wide tool among larger companies. Most software providers offer a product line that is scalable to any size business. If your company already has an E-commerce presence you may already have been capturing some useful data worth analyzing on a regular basis to gain actionable customer insights. Examine and analyze the data often to spot developing trends so that you can proactively manage your business instead of reacting to it after the fact.

Always keep in mind that you are in business because of the customers. Your primary mission and purpose for being in business is to successfully provide for the customer's wants and needs with the greatest level of satisfaction and beyond what the customer can reasonably expect from your competitors. The customer is the most important among the four pillars of business success. Without sufficient customers to provide the minimum revenue to sustain your business, nothing else matters. Consequently, great customer satisfaction is the mother of all missions that must have top management support with overwhelming participation across the entire organization.

No matter how hard you work to avoid them, mistakes and customer dissatisfaction are inevitable occurrences. That makes proactive action to train a quick response team for these incidences a very prudent business investment. Remember, it is always cheaper to focus on retaining existing customers than it is to replace those you may lose due to poor customer service.

 With the right customer care program in place, well-executed by trained professionals, even the most damaging incident can be converted into a great customer experience. By minimizing negative word-of-mouth reports through prompt damage control efforts, you can often avoid costly consequences. Do more than your competitors would in every aspect of developing great customer satisfaction and a strong relationship with all your customers. No television, Internet, or print media advertisement can ever match the real benefits offered by overwhelmingly positive word-of-mouth. That is the best type of public relations available and a proven ticket to business success. After all, your business can only prosper if it has truly satisfied customers.

Alan Yong

Chapter 13 - Conclusion

I grew up in a family of two girls and six boys on a 50-acre coconut plantation located on the northern tip of the Borneo Island known as Kudat, in Sabah, East Malaysia. As is typically true for those living in farming communities, we learned the value of hard work from an early age. Though we were poor, we were all happy and content and there was never any fighting among the siblings. Much of the credit for that phenomenon must go to my mother whose team-building skills taught us from an early age to work together raising farm animals and produce to earn our pocket money. As we grew to adulthood, each of us had our own business at one time or another. Even today, all six of the boys still operate businesses.

I launched my first business some forty years ago - a Chinese restaurant - and have, since that time, seen my share of both success and failure. Each time that I decided to embark on another business venture, I found myself wishing that I was ten years younger. Looking back now, however, I understand that it was not age but the wisdom and knowledge I have gained over the years that would have made the difference for me. That is one of my greatest hopes for this book. For while I cannot ever be any younger, I can hopefully provide the benefits for the wisdom and knowledge that I have gained throughout my life and prove to be a source of insight that can help to inspire and guide you to early success in your own business endeavors.

The fact is that my work as a small business consultant has engendered many suggestions that I write a book like this. Since I do not consider writing to be one of my main areas of strength, however, I have avoided the idea. Writing is not really my passion and I have always been reluctant to engage in activities that fail to stir excitement within my being. That lack of passion has caused me to shelve the idea of a book until now - though I knew that my real passion would eventually bring me around to writing it.

You see, my true passion is focused on helping small business owners and those who are considering the launch of their own businesses. I have been blessed with knowledge, experience, and a strong conviction that it is possible to improve your odds of succeeding in business. It requires being passionate about what you are doing, committed to learning all that you can, and willing to do everything it takes to succeed in your business endeavor. This book is designed to help you in that process. If you can harness those things, you will be on the right path - a path that will take you as far as you want to go. While none of this is an exact science that offers certainty, I do strongly believe that you can improve your chances of achieving business success.

As you've no doubt surmised, the success formula - or theme, if you will - presented in this book is focused on a relentless commitment to be better in every respect than each of your competitors. It is about having as your ultimate goal the objective of being the best in class. That cannot be mere wishful thinking isolated in the mind of a business owner, but must instead be a mindset that originates from the top and reaches all the way down to the lowest level of the organization. It is about the top leadership's ability to inspire and empower followers throughout the organization by genuinely desiring that every team member have a successful career path laid out in front of them. It is about inspiring everyone to work toward the goal of ensuring that every customer is delighted to do business with your company.

It is ultimately about succeeding as a team and knowing that everything is interrelated and connected. Every aspect of your business, both internally and externally, ultimately impacts every other aspect. Always be mindful that any change can either help or hurt the related parties at some point in time. As a result of that interconnectedness, a happy, inspiring, respectful, and trustworthy environment that promotes mutual cooperation for the mutual benefit of everyone over the long term is ultimately more productive than one that fosters confrontation, negativity, and other destructive behavior for short term individual gain.

Everything starts with you in your role as the founder and top management leader of your company. You pick the players you believe are best for your team. Like a sports team, not everyone will make the cut. You are the coach, but at the same time, you are also the key player. You have one goal that really matters. That goal is to inspire, coach, and prepare your team to take home the championship. You all worked hard and are committed to great teamwork and flawless execution of strategies. Despite that effort, there will be good days and challenging ones. There will be great game calls and unfortunate mistakes made. But at the end of the season it is the final game played that will determine whether your team wins the championship. In business, that is the day when your vision is finally realized.

In many respects, business is similar to a team sport. It may be less intense and there are usually fewer injuries involved, but, in order to go home with the championship, you must have the right players to build the best team so that you can stay in the game. Pick your co founders and partners wisely. A winning team trumps a great business idea every time. Give high preference to someone you know well who shares your ideology and philosophy, and with whom you share great mutual trust and respect. There must be sufficient common ground to work together, but complementary skill-sets that can cover the deficiencies any one of you may be lacking. It is also important to have a high degree of mutual interest and a clear understanding that each of you will represent the other's best interest at all times. Your success in working well as a team is not likely due to how compatible the team members are, but by how well each of you can mesh together and make even your incompatible traits somehow compatible and complementary.

You must focus on hiring only those employees that hold forth the promise of being the best fit for your organization and be willing and able to end that relationship if it becomes apparent that continued employment is not in your or their interests. Your time is truly money. It is limited, and as a result it should be considered precious. No matter the job, a lack of passion makes for hard work - and that can make it difficult to even meet minimum requirements. That leaves career advancement a virtual impossibility. Because of those factors, you should quickly and decisively move to separate the company from employees who demonstrate that they have no real future in your organization.

The opposite also holds true, of course, for those employees who fit well within your company. You must work to take the best care of your employees that you can, inspire them daily, and empower them to share in and promote your grand vision as if it - and the company - were their own.

Obviously, it is in the interest of every individual, organization, state, and nation to practice self-protection. As an individual, you instinctively protect yourself and your loved ones before you concern yourself with others outside that circle of friends and family. Within your business you must learn to treat your employees as you treat your loved ones so that they will promote and protect your company's interests. Always focus on their positive contributions with prompt acknowledgment and appreciation. Positive reinforcement is the most powerful motivator of them all, and one of the best ways to correct weaknesses. You need all of your employees to be protecting and promoting your best interest at all times.

You must have a clear vision of where you want to take your company and be able to clearly articulate that vision to your followers and supporters. However, that vision is not much better than a dream or wishful thinking until you can back it up with strategic plans to fulfill the missions, goals, and objectives that can get you to your destination. There is a difference between projecting success and actually planning and positioning yourself to succeed.

You must plan and develop winning strategies. A truly effective strategic plan is one that enables you to channel all of your company resources, expertise, and organizational skills in a way that creates competitive advantages at every level of your enterprise, with a consistent focus on achieving quantifiable goals within a projected time.

Ideally, your goal is to create the type of company that is almost impossible for your competitors to fully replicate. However, you cannot do it alone. To be successful, you must learn to replicate yourself by transferring to your employees your own mindset, commitment, and enthusiasm. Since everything is interrelated, your company can enjoy greater inspiration at every level when mutual dependence, mutual cooperation, and mutual benefits are emphasized by all. The development of leadership skills throughout the enterprise can only enhance those benefits, enabling everyone on the team to think, communicate, and execute the company's plan in the same manner you would. When you inspire your followers to appreciate and develop great leadership skills within themselves they will gain a better understanding why you lead them to do certain things rather than just following you blindly.

Much of your focus must be on the effort to define your company's brand, values, vision, mission, and culture. These are tasks for leadership, and should not be left to others in your company or forces within the marketplace. When you fail to address these critical issues you will find that your company ends up being defined by others. That seldom ends well.

Work to differentiate your company from your rivals and create a valuable brand right from the start. Be certain that everyone associated with the company values the brand and promotes it. Use a smart public relation campaign to build awareness, brand recognition, and credibility. That is always a good investment even at the formative stage.

Use every opportunity to promote great customer experience and customer satisfaction. Remember always that no matter what service or product you are providing, the fundamental mission that empowers your business will always be the effort to satisfy the wants and needs of each one of your customers.

When you can accomplish these fundamental tasks, you will have set your pillars on the type of firm foundation you'll need to withstand the stormy weather you'll often encounter in the marketplace. When your four pillars are strong you will be providing your company with its best chances for achieving the sustained business success you seek.

Continuing Education:

Whether you are a young entrepreneur or a seasoned business owner, you should never stop working to improve your unique leadership skills. Knowledge is a powerful competitive edge for any entrepreneur, but one that must remain sharp at all times. An inspired and focused effort on continued self-improvement is the best investment of your time and money that you will ever make. That is why we are developing a membership site that will serve as a forum for those interested in further enhancement of their entrepreneurial skill sets.

Membership at The Four Pillars of Business Success site gives you exclusive access to information and materials that will expand on the concepts presented in this book. It will also provide you with access to Alan and his team - as well as a variety of useful and innovative tools designed to help your business succeed.

Chapter Summation - Key Takeaways

Introduction:

Conservative estimates suggest that more than 70% of new businesses fail within the first ten years, with 60% shutting down in the first five years. These statistics lead many people to believe that business is a gamble. However, there are clear differences between an activity like gambling that is almost entirely random in nature, and something like business ownership that has no greater randomness to it than most other areas of life. In business there are ways to effectively manage and control most situations. You can drastically improve your odds with a 70% success instead of failure.

Business success does not happen by accident or good fortune. It takes deep knowledge, passion, hard-work, focus, discipline, tenacity, and the right mind-sets to be successful. With passion and dedication, you can obtain the type of business mastery that will help you be the true architect of your company's success. This book covers the vital importance of developing a clear vision of where you envision your company's ultimate destination to be and how to build your teams to best succeed in achieving their missions, goals, and objectives to help your company get there. You gain the understanding and appreciation of all the critical components that must function well as a complete system or independently as a subsystem.

You learn to be the leader and mentor inspiring everyone within your reach to create a leadership culture of shared-vision. Together your team is unified in purpose, efficient, and capable of performing at optimal levels on a consistent basis. When you have a company that can achieve those standards, then you have a company that can achieve almost any goal. Ideally, your goal is to create the type of company that is almost impossible for your competitors to fully replicate. However, you cannot do that all by yourself. It all has to start with you, but at some point in time you will have to begin to rely on a team to help you achieve your vision.

You need to find the type of competent people who are capable of being inspired by your exceptional leadership style and strategic vision, as that is the only way to ensure that they are in turn capable of helping you to create the type of business culture that your enterprise needs for success. That culture should motivate everyone in the company to consistently deliver their highest level of commitment and performance, and thereby, contribute to the efforts to reach your business goals. Once you reached that point, you will have created a system that basically channels the mindset of its leader even when your attention is elsewhere. You will have designed a system for effectively cloning yourself.

No company ever becomes the best in class by accident. You have to position your business to achieve that status. The ability and discipline to focus on all of the things that matter, along with the passion to excel in every single department, function, and business activity, is absolutely critical for ensuring that you have the optimum opportunity for business success. You cannot afford to let yourself be blindsided by overconfidence due to a misguided faith in your ability to excel in just one or two skill sets - or hope that superiority in those areas will somehow mask your mediocrity in every other area.

When others on your team fail to bring their skill sets to bear in a way that helps you to excel in every area of your business, then you leave yourself open to failure. One or two areas of competency are not enough to succeed; the true measure of your competitive superiority can only be found in the total of all of your scores.

Just think about your favorite talent show or sports competition where winners are determined by a panel of judges, with the total scores from eight different criteria used to make that decision. A competitor who scores 10 out of 10 in two categories, but who has mediocre scores of 7 of 10 in the other six categories will ultimately lose out to the competitor who manages to score 8 of 10 across all eight categories.

And so it is with the world of business. Being the best in class in every category is always a winning strategy whenever it is tried. To be the best in class, you have to realize that everything matters. The most important of them all are the four pillars of business success; you, your great ideas, your employees, and your customers. Focus on them to improve your odds of business success.

Chapter 1:   Be: Equal to or Better than the Competition

Very few entrepreneurs start their businesses with ideas so revolutionary that they basically create their own industries. In most instances, you'll be entering an established market populated by established companies that will all be competing for the same customers and market share that you need for your own business success. To achieve your goals, you need to be at least equal to your rivals, and ultimately better than them. As your company's leader, the burden is on you to set the tone that will allow your business enterprise to become the best in class.

4. Focus on your own mindset, and direct your efforts toward being the best in every category that matters. If you believe that you cannot become the best in class, that mindset will become a self-fulfilling prophesy.

5. Focus your resources on those areas that promise the best return on your monetary, time, and labor investment. Look for ways to differentiate your offering from the competition, and then orient your company's messaging toward using those positive differences as selling points.

6. Remember these eight areas where you can strive to become the best in class:

1. Work to understand your customers.

2. Emphasize superior customer service.

3. Focus on differentiation.

4. Always look for ways to improve your branding efforts.

5. Invest in Public Relations early to build awareness and credibility.

6. Be aware of emerging trends and remain future-focused.

7. Pursue growth by identifying complementary offerings.

8. *Strive to become the best employer, to ensure that your employees are completely on board with the mission.*

7. *Understand yourself and your company, even as you work to gain deeper insight into the minds of your rivals.* Sun Tzu's philosophy is as relevant today as it was all those centuries ago.

Chapter 2: The Four Principal Components

Throughout the book, I emphasize four business components that I refer to as the pillars of success. These are introduced in a broad sense in the second chapter, and include:

6. You; as the leader of your company and chief architect of your business vision. Your vision is central to everything that your business does; leading to the formation of its culture, structure, mission, and strategies over time.

7. Your great idea; which manifests itself in the form of your company's marketable products and services. These ideas are the lifeblood of your enterprise, and the means by which you service your customers and provide for the needs of your employees. Innovation is important, but so too is the ability to communicate a unique selling proposition that entices customers to flock to your offerings, as well as the ability to target areas of the marketplace that offer long-term growth potential.

8. Your employees; who provide the team you need to replicate yourself and expand your own reach. The key to success in dealing with your team is to work diligently toward the goal of endowing each employee with your vision and drive to succeed. That makes effective hiring and training a priority for any company.

9. Your Customers; without which your company would have neither revenue nor reason to exist. Your customers are the real boss, since it is they who determine whether or not your company can be profitable enough to survive over the long-term. To successfully leverage the power of your customer base, you must learn about your customers and figure out how you can increase their value to your business enterprise.

Chapter 3: A System Approach – Designing Your Company

The systems approach to designing a business is one of the toughest things for many new entrepreneurs to grasp. Too often, they focus on the power of their ideas, and assume that their personalities are sufficient to create just the type of company they want. Misconceptions of this nature are the reasons that so many of today's companies are so dysfunctional. The reality is that your company is a system made up of many smaller systems, sub-systems, and individual components.

Each of those components must work in harmony with every other part of the business if the larger system is to function to its maximum potential. Everything within the system affects everything else, and it means that even seemingly minor problems in one area of the company can quickly ripple throughout the business and negatively impact other areas. Without a systems approach to problem-solving, these complications can quickly alter your corporate culture or otherwise cause broader dysfunction at every level of the organization.

Our systems approach analysis recommends that you emphasize active creation and definition of your business brand, vision, mission, values, and culture, and focus on that as a matter of course. By doing so, it helps to ensure that those fundamental aspects of your company are not changed by internal or external forces in a way that could ultimately harm your enterprise. The broader goal of all of this is to ensure that your team members have been properly empowered to implement your vision by maintaining your established business culture. Values must align with vision. Your culture must be in agreement with your mission. All of these components must be in sync to ensure that every system works in concert with every other system, together creating the broader system alignment every company needs to achieve its goals.

To accomplish this goal, you have to work to create excellence throughout your business, and in every category:

1. Leadership and Management

2. Strategy

3. Execution

4. Structure and Process

5. Delegation

6. Employees

7. Mutual Goals Review

8. Products

9. Customers

Chapter 4: Leadership and Management

Leadership and management are difficult concepts for many people to grasp. All too often, entrepreneurs confuse the two ideas, and that can lead many new business owners to assume that they are leaders just because they spend the bulk of their time managing operations and every other aspect of their companies. Nothing could be further from the truth.

The fact is that today's entrepreneurs are often followers. Rather than lead their enterprises and teams on missions that would carve out their own niche markets, many of these business owners are content to simply follow in the path created by their rivals and competitors. Many simply trust that they will get a lucky break that will help them to find the success they crave. The problem is that luck is one of those ingredients that are inherently unreliable. You can't count on it to happen to you. Instead, you have to create the conditions that can give your company the best opportunity to thrive. That is accomplished through excellent leadership and effective management. Though there is overlap between these two roles, they are very different in a broader sense.

- Leaders inspire people to follow them in pursuit of a broad vision and mission. They provide values and direction, and use persuasion to motivate others to follow them and join with them in their quest for some broader goal.

- Managers, on the other hand, do not have to necessarily inspire (though it can be helpful at times). Instead, they are given authority from their leaders, and use that authority to coordinate teams of employees to accomplish leadership's goals. They communicate inspiration that is derived from leadership, and channel company resources in an effort to complete the tasks that need to be performed to reach the ultimate objectives.

- Leadership is critical due to its role in providing ideas, focus, values, inspiration, and objectives for the team to meet. Management is critical due to its role in mobilizing the resources needed to make leadership's vision a reality. Followers look for certain traits in their leaders:

1. Passion

2. Far-sightedness

3. Wisdom

4. Trustworthiness

5. Generosity

   - While many small business owners are tasked with serving in both roles within their own companies, it is still important that they learn to identify the responsibilities of each to ensure that they are effective as possible.

   - Part of your company mission should involve the identification and cultivation of leadership traits within your team. That is part of building a leadership culture that can help to empower team members at every level of your organization and strengthen every system in your company.

Chapter 5: Strategy

Strategy is critical in all walks of life, for without a plan the odds of obtaining success are limited. Despite that obvious fact, a surprising number of entrepreneurs enter into business without taking the time to develop the type of strategic plan that can actually guide them to success. Many simply believe that their vision, coupled with a sound slate of products or services, will be all that they need to survive and prosper. True success, however, can never be realized without a well-conceived strategic plan that transforms your operational decisions over time.

Strategy is not just a broad concept used to guide your company towards its goals, but a necessary element for success at every level of your business. You must learn to think strategically, and do so in a multi-dimensional way that encompasses all of the systems, subsystems, and components that make up your company. Your strategic thinking must take into consideration the interrelated nature of everything within and outside of your business environment. Additionally, it must also take into consideration your goals, the company's core competencies, the available resources, existing leadership and management needs, and a viable timetable for implementation.

There are three stages involved in the formulation of any strategic plan:

- Create the strategy.

- Implement the strategy.

- Review the results and modify the strategy as needed.

As you develop your strategy, important factors must be taken into consideration throughout the process. You need to focus on customers, get to know them, and learn to engage them. You also need to take into consideration new technological trends such as mobile computing, blockchain technology, and other aspects of FinTech. In addition, plan to utilize effective content to ensure that messaging is handled properly. And you must make continuing team education a priority.

Chapter 6: Execution

There is a second component of strategy, and it involves execution. Strategies that never get implemented are nothing more than wasted words. And yet many companies seem to give little emphasis to successful execution – a fact that can lead to strategic drift over time. There are many reasons for this failure to execute, not the least of which is the simple fact that execution is seldom seen as exciting. Leaders love to plan, but far too few enjoy the follow-up necessary to ensure that their plans actually amount to something tangible.

A good execution plan should include a number of critical components:

- It must provide details that explain how the strategic plan is to be carried out at every stage of the process. Key decisions, needed processes, and other important factors should all be covered in detail.

- A good execution plan outlines responsibilities for decision-making, provides a blueprint for cooperation, and sets out standards for accountability.

- Finally, the best execution plans always include measurement standards that enable leadership to evaluate results, monitor overall progress toward the objectives, and inform any efforts to modify the strategy.

Failure in this area can be catastrophic for many businesses, and can rebound to leadership in a negative way. Leaders who fail to properly direct strategic execution often see employee confidence in the company's leadership drop precipitously. At the same time, the company can lose focus, the team can suffer a loss of cohesion, and customers eventually realize that something is amiss. Worse, such failures will prevent you from being the best in class.

To avoid such pitfall, be sure that your execution plan is one that is well-understood and capable of being translated into action. Never create an initiative without a plan for implementation. Communicate your goals, plans, and processes to your team. Finally, track results during the execution process, review them, and adjust as needed.

Chapter 7: Organizational Structure and Process

Organizational structure is not always given the emphasis that it deserves, and that can lead to serious consequences. The fact is that every organization has a structure, often times, both formal and informal. The only real question is whether that structure is created by design or develops organically in a less predictable manner. You need to design the structure yourself rather than waiting for employees or outside forces to organically create it over time. At times, you design project specific structure, define the process, and provide the necessary support and resources involving multiple teams and departments.

Most people limit their thinking of structure in a business to just the hierarchy of relationships within the organization. They look at how every member of the team relates to every other member, from top to bottom and side to side. While that is certainly one aspect of any formal organizational structure, it is by no means the be-all and end-all of this important concept. Dynamic and fast growth companies constantly create new structure and process, involving multiple departments, as they embark new projects. Beyond just the hierarchy organization chart, think of structure and process as part of a master logistic plan, involving command and control of communication as well as the allocation and deployment of resources. Structure and process can be created or modified as deemed necessary to best accomplish the mission involved.

The right structural choices are essential for a systems approach to business, since your structure will be necessary to ensure that each component and subsystem properly complements and interacts with every other part of the company. In this, a structural diagram can be invaluable for outlining priorities, detailing assignments, responsibilities, and accountability, and helping to channel the entire team's efforts toward the common pursuit of company goals. Good structural design also provides safeguards to facilitate progress, while reducing duplicative efforts.

Strategy and structure are inexorably linked, since structure is essential to strategic execution. Even the best strategies will never succeed if there is no effective structure in place to carry out the plan. Worse, strategies often succumb to the gravitational pull of structure, as misalignment of strategy and structure results in your plans being broken by the very systems and subsystems you've put into place. That typically ends with the strategy being essentially rewritten by the demands of your company structure. To prevent that, remember:

3. Directives from on high are not enough to overcome misalignments between strategic plans and structural imperatives.

4. As a result, changes in strategy often necessitate modifications in your structure to create alignment.

5. Strategy and structure are so closely linked that you cannot effectively alter one without altering the other.

6. Your role as leader is to develop plans, and ensure that the right structure is in place to execute your directives. As you do so, you must consider the impact on employees, processes, and other strategies within the company.

7. Structural deficiencies must be addressed promptly. Where change is not possible, strategies need to be modified to reduce structural tension. All structural and strategic changes need to be continually revisited to track progress and evaluate progress.

Remember, structure should be defined by need. When process, employee, and strategic needs are all taken into consideration at every level of your organization, the structure you ultimately settle on should provide you with the ideal environment to execute your plans.

Chapter 8: Delegation

The act of delegating responsibility or tasks seems so simple that most leaders and managers just assume that they know how to do it properly. Sadly, that is simply not the case. Far too many managers operate under the assumption that the best way to make themselves indispensable is to ensure that no one else knows how to do their jobs. Others simply don't trust subordinates to handle certain tasks. There are even managers who do things on their own because they believe that delegation would take longer.

Successful companies, however, make delegation a priority, even going so far as to look for delegation skills during the hiring process. For your business to be successful, team members must know how to do other employees' jobs. That cross-training can be one of the best ways to ensure that every employee understands and appreciates his team's contributions, which in turn promotes the unity you need within your company culture. At the same time, a culture that values delegation can reduce productivity losses due to illness, injury, or employees leaving the organization.

As the leader, it is your task to create a culture of delegation by leading from the top. You should train managers to perform many of your tasks, empowering them to learn everything they can about the company. You then encourage them to do the same with their own subordinates. In this way, you elevate each member of your team to be the best they can be. And remember, effective delegation involves delegation of responsibility, authority, and accountability.

Chapter 9: Employees: A Pillar of Business Success

Though many modern business owners perceive their employees as cost burden that must be managed, there was a time when almost every employer understood the value of his people. You can benefit from modeling your company after those savvy entrepreneurs, by recognizing that employees truly are your best asset. To get the most out of your business relationship with each employee, you need to begin with a culture that fosters appreciation for each member of the team.

It is true that employees can be a source for dysfunction, but in most instances those problems are the result of poor leadership, poor management, or both. Inferior recruiting processes sometimes lead to inappropriate hiring decisions. Many entrepreneurs hire family and friends who are not committed to the company's success. Expectations for employees are sometimes left unclear. In other instances, there is no mutual respect, which can lead to poor morale. In many of the worst company cultures, managers stand by as a confrontational environment develops over time.

The good news for you is that you can achieve a different and better result. Recognize that your employees are your best non-binding partner, and they have a vested interest in their own career advancement and job security. When you focus on hiring and training the right candidates for your company, and then work to ensure that they are placed in the right positions within your organization, you will be creating a dedicated team that focuses like a laser on achieving your company goals. And when you give priority to helping them increase their own value as employees, you will unlock the true potential of your company's most valuable asset.

Chapter 10: Beyond Employee Performance Review – Mutual Goals Review

If you're like most leaders, you've probably dealt with managers who absolutely dread employee performance reviews. To be fair, there is something inherently distasteful about any process that practically begs evaluators to search for even the slightest flaws in their employees' performance over any given period of time. For that reason and many others, these periodic reviews have fallen out of favor in the halls and offices of many companies around the world.

That lack of interest in these reviews does not mean that they have no value, however. You need some way to ascertain an employee's progress, focus on his accomplishments, identify areas where improvement could be made, and determine future rewards. The key is to avoid the most negative aspects of traditional performance reviews – like using them to emphasize any areas in which the employee has failed to excel, or relying on untrained managers who often despise the very process of evaluating their subordinates to exercise their own judgment.

"Mutual Goals Review" that I am introducing is significantly more rewarding and collaborative in promoting employees' career advancement than the subjective grading of employees' weaknesses. It serves the mutual interest of both the company and the employees with a unified purpose of fulfilling the company's goals, missions, and the ultimate vision.

It differs from traditional methods, however, by focusing more on the future than the past or present. That's why I call it a Mutual Goals Review. It should be conducted a minimum of four times over the course of each year, and can use a formal or informal process in a one-on-one or even group setting.

Rather than focusing on how poorly an employee has performed during the previous year, the conference should be an inspirational and productive gathering designed to strengthen the relationship between employer and employee. It should thus be designed to fulfill the distinct needs of both parties, and provide an opportunity to chart that employee's continuing career path.

Chapter 11: Products - A Pillar of Business Success

Products and services are the lifeblood of any business, and are essential for any effort to become the best in class. Your goal should always be to create that sense of amazement in every customer you encounter, with product offerings that exceed expectations on a consistent basis. To develop products that can achieve those goals, you need to focus on the essentials.

That means gathering knowledge about the marketplace and your rivals. You must always remember that your ability to grab market share does not occur within a vacuum. Instead, you are almost always going to find yourself in direct or indirect competition with other companies who want your customers for themselves. Your ability to research your marketplace and your rivals will have a direct impact on how successful you can be in differentiating your offerings and earning customer loyalty.

You'll have to do more than just bring your great ideas to life. In addition, you have to identify your unique selling proposition and communicate that information to potential customers. Furthermore, you have to ensure that you are targeting markets that offer the potential for sustained growth over time, and work to position your company and brand in a way that offers you the best opportunity to capitalize on what you do better than anyone else.

Chapter 12: Customers – A Pillar of Business Success

When it comes right down to it, there is no escaping the simple fact that every business owner has a boss – many bosses, in fact. Every person who buys your products or pays for your services is your boss, in the purest sense of the word. Because of that undeniable truth, your primary mission is always to find the most effective and efficient way to cater to those customers' wants and needs. If you cannot do that, then nothing else will matter. Your company will have no revenue, and it will perish.

Your company structure, processes, and culture must be directed toward achieving the greatest amount of customer satisfaction on a daily basis. While much of that involves the quest for excellence in product development and manufacture, customer service can be even more critical. You must have plans in place to manage problems as they occur. The good news is that even bad customer experiences can be turned to your benefit if your customer service and problem resolution strategies are effective.

Customer satisfaction surveys should also be integrated into your systems. These surveys provide invaluable feedback that you can utilize to fine-tune your customer service protocols, and serve as beneficial tools for employee training. A well-designed survey, limited to no more than ten questions, can help you to identify potential problems early enough to institute needed changes. By properly utilizing these surveys and other information gathered from customer interactions, you can work to develop the type of customer brand loyalty that can dramatically increase overall customer retention and turn your most loyal customers into your most ardent promoters.

Chapter 13: Conclusion

I have a strong conviction that it is possible to significantly improve your odds of succeeding in business. It requires being passionate about what you are doing, committed to learning all that you can, and willing to do everything it takes to succeed in your business endeavor

What it takes is a relentless commitment to be better in every respect than each of your competitors. It is about having as your ultimate goal the objective of being the best in class with a mindset that originates from the top and reaches all the way down to the lowest level of the organization. It is about the top leadership's ability to inspire and empower followers throughout the organization by genuinely desiring that every team member have a successful career path laid out in front of them. It is about inspiring everyone to work toward the goal of ensuring that every customer is delighted to do business with your company.

Above all, it is about succeeding as a team and knowing that everything is interrelated and connected. Every aspect of your business, both internally and externally, ultimately impacts every other aspect.

Always focus on their positive contributions with prompt acknowledgment and appreciation. Positive reinforcement is the most powerful motivator of them all, and one of the best ways to correct weaknesses. You need all of your employees to be protecting and promoting your best interest at all times.

Chapter 14 - Smokeys Daylily Gardens – A Tale of Hard Work, Clear Vision, Strategic Execution, Tenacity, and Team Work

Smokeys is a case in point about a typical hard working small business owner with the tenacity to hang on for over two decades, never giving up hope that success was right around corner. There was good team work and strong support from family and friends, but that was not enough to cross over the chasm to the promised land of true business success. This is a story about starting over after a long struggle for success since 1981, in a different business. It is about designing a new company from the ground up with a clear vision and a relentless commitment to be the best in class coupled with a fundamental mission and purpose of providing great customer experience and satisfaction.

Smokey's original product was stoves, fireplaces, and chimney sweeping. The business was getting by but after many years it became clear that it had no opportunity to get ahead. Each year was a struggle. Since stoves are largely a seasonal (winter) product, Kevin, the owner, believed that an additional product was needed as a supplement during the off-season (summer). I was consulted about what that additional product might be.

Kevin still remembers the day he agreed to give my seemingly outlandish suggestion a try.

"Here we were, owning a fireplace shop for over twenty-five years, had fifteen to twenty employees, and you WANTED TO SELL FLOWERS? I thought you were nuts! We had no equipment, no knowledge of the business, AND no daylilies! I still remember the day I "got it". You took me out to the warehouse, and pointed to a woodstove sitting on a rack. You said, what if you bought that stove, and had a choice.... you could sell it now, and have no more stoves on the rack. OR....you could leave it on the shelf, and in one year, there would be two to five stoves sitting on the shelf!! Then, I could sell two or three of them, and have five or ten stoves sitting there the next year. The light bulb went off. If I paid a thousand dollars for a stove, I usually sold it for about fourteen hundred dollars. If I bought a thousand dollars' worth of daylilies, I could sell that daylily FOREVER, and never buy that particular cultivar again! I got it right away.......forty percent gross profit VS ninety-nine percent gross profit. That is what really sold me on it."

A successful business starts with a great idea of a product or service, often reflecting a unique opportunity based on a better solution to an existing problem, fulfilling an unserved need or a drastic improvement in efficiency. To give you a better understanding of the thought process that led to the selection of the new business almost nine years ago, here is a brief background of the daylily industry.

Daylilies are among the top perennial plants, but are yet to be discovered by most gardeners, a fact that would weigh heavily in Smokeys Gardens' decision to grow them. Their stunning beauty has attracted a large number of breeders or hybridizers with a passion to create their own flowers. They are often registered and named after loved ones and sold as newly registered cultivars online for as much as $100 for a single plant.

According to the American Hemerocallis Society (AHS) founded in 1946, there are 81,972 registered cultivars of daylily as of February 2016. Popularity of daylilies spread rapidly as breeders discovered how rewarding and easy it is to create unlimited variations of colors, forms, substance, texture, styles, bud counts, heights, and blooms. With some planning and garden design skills, daylilies, supplemented with a small investment in annual flowers, are the most cost effective means to showoff gorgeous gardens with dazzling colors.

The scientific name for daylily is Hemerocallis and it is derived from two Greek words meaning "beauty" and "day". Each flower only lasts a day, but is replaced by many new flower buds opening each day for a period of two to three weeks. Depending on the characteristics, the cultivar may be considered as a re-bloomer, with more than one bloom cycle each season. Daylilies are among the hardiest perennial plants and propagate to form a clump of ten or more fans, each of which can start a few whole new plants in a couple of years. They are able to survive with very little care in wide ranging climates. Daylilies are also drought resistant, and for the most part, free from plant disease or insect attack. They are very adaptable to almost any soil conditions except very dry rocky environments.

Daylilies are commonly used for commercial landscapes, generating large orders with requirements of several thousand plants per order. Many highway departments in the United States are beginning to use daylilies to prevent soil erosion and to serve as fire control barriers while providing great beauty during the bloom season.

Stella de Oro is by far America's most popular daylily and almost always used in landscape projects with any daylily selections. It is highly valued as a compact, most reliable re-bloomer, with preference for full sun yet excellent tolerance for shade and dry conditions, making it a hardy plant that requires little maintenance. *Stella de Oro* is Smokeys Gardens best seller. Being one of the largest growers, with over three million plants in inventory, it positioned Smokeys Gardens to offer their customers the best prices around for small or very large orders.

Smokeys Daylily Gardens, now one of the largest daylily growers in the world, became a success story by exploiting a void in the daylily industry. In reality, the daylily industry was quite fragmented back in 2007 when Kevin and I were discussing the reproductive capabilities of stoves vs. live plants. It was a patchwork of hundreds of backyard gardeners selling daylily plants online as a hobby. There were also a few wholesalers who carried daylilies along with many other types of plants. What was lacking was any kind of specialization, as in a grower dedicated to the production of daylilies. Smokeys Gardens decided to fill that void. They made an initial investment of just $500 and have never looked back.

Kevin recalls that first purchase very well.

"Alan convinced me to spend five-hundred dollars to buy some daylilies from a local Mom and Pop daylily "farm" located about twenty minutes from our store. I say 'farm' because it was only about a half acre of flowers. It seemed like a lot at the time."

This initial purchase was supplemented with daylilies from my own gardens, which ended up completely taking over what was supposed to be a vegetable garden for Kevin's wife, as Kevin recalls:

"Alan started bringing his daylilies from his house. He had been a big fan of daylilies since moving to the United States. He ended up bringing thousands of flowers and planting them in our "vegetable garden." That fall we ended up buying all the daylilies and some old equipment from the Mom and Pop farm."

After acquiring those initial flowers, Kevin and his employees had to figure out how to plant, harvest, and clean them more efficiently. Kevin recalls buying and modifying a vegetable harvester from a farm in Illinois.

"The folks there had a "vegetable harvester" that was made in Canada by a specialty shop catering to the vegetable industry. I made a deal to buy that machine for five-hundred bucks the first time I saw it being used. We contacted the manufacturer, and they helped me design improvements into the machine to make it more durable. We still use this machine today."

The modified harvester immediately gave Smokeys Gardens an advantage over their competitors, as Kevin explains further:

"The way 99 percent of our competitors harvest daylilies, is to send two strong, young guys out there to dig. If I were to have them dig a row of mature clumps in a wholesale field, these two strong guys would take at least eight man-hours to complete the job. Using the tractor and digger, two men can dig and collect one row in less than thirty minutes. So, one row would take eight man hours to do by hand compare to one man-hour with machinery."

The next improvement was with the way daylilies are planted. The industry standard up to that point had been to hand plant the flower fans. Kevin bought a strawberry planter from a neighbor and then took it to its original manufacturer who modified it so that it could effectively plant daylilies. This modified strawberry planter could plant up to ten times as many plants as could be hand planted in the same amount of time, as Kevin explains:

"As an example of the difference this machine makes, to hand plant flowers, it would take a person at least two hours to plant a row of 200 flowers. Now, with the planter, we can plant 2000 to 3000 plants per hour, using a 3-man crew. So now, instead of costing one hour of labor to plant 100 plants, one hour of labor will plant 660 to 1000 plants."

Next came modifying the washing process, which has to be done, in order to satisfy laws that prohibit shipping any soil across state lines. Daylily hobby farmers typically hand washed the plants they wanted to ship with a garden hose. Kevin located a manufacturer in Canada who had already designed an automatic washer he thought would work. He bought the washer on the spot and it paid for itself within one month.

Kevin remembered that, "We used to have six full time people washing plants. Now one person can wash for four hours a day and keep up very easily. So now, instead of being able to wash about 100 plants per man hour, we can wash well over 1000 plants per man hour."

Smokeys Gardens seized the opportunity to turn a popular hobby into a business with a commitment to be the best in class. By reinvesting its earnings in acquisitions, equipment, and well refined processes, Smokeys has reached the scale of efficiently planting, harvesting, and shipping more plants in a week than most of the competitors in an entire season. The company is positioned for high growth for many years to come. Once established the plants multiply quickly with nearly zero cost of goods sold. With more than 3,000 cultivars and over three million plants in a single 38-acre farm, Smokeys Gardens is now the lowest cost producer with the largest selections of popular to premium daylilies.

A new business starts out with an idea of a product or a service. It may be a proverbial "better mouse trap" or an improved product or a solution to an existing problem. In the case of Smokeys, it identified an opportunity to solve an inefficiency problem inherent in highly fragmented industries. Initial research suggested that other than a few large commercial growers that supply a limited selection of daylilies as one among hundreds of other annual and perennial plants, no one else specialized in large scale production of daylilies. Smokeys decided to be an exclusive grower of daylilies. To make the opportunity even sweeter, initial research concluded that despite many beneficial features, daylilies are virtually undiscovered by most gardeners, giving Smokeys a huge potential for future growth.

Once the idea evolved to become a serious business investment consideration, the initial vague vision was given significant thought and refinement to become a clear vision of where the venture needed to be in ten years. Smokeys' vision was to become the lowest cost producer with the largest selections of popular to high value daylilies sold at attractive profit margins coupled with sustainable growth. To this end they divided the market into four basic segments: the casual or backyard gardener, the wholesale or reseller market, the collector market, and the seed market, and strove to most effectively meet the needs of each one.

With a clear vision of where Smokeys needed to be in ten years, the next step was to determine its missions, goals and objectives that needed to be accomplished to make the vision a reality. At the same time, it had to examine its strengths and weaknesses as well as opportunities and threats (SWOT). Early on Kevin realized that they needed a better way to control inventory having unintentionally sold out of a few cultivars and some other plants which should have been held back for reproduction during the first two years. The goal of inventory control was to know in real time how many plants were truly available for sale.

As Kevin pointed out, "Inventory Control is CRITICAL. The worst thing you can do to a customer is to sell them a flower we don't have. The worst thing you can do to me is NOT LIST a flower for sale that I can sell. If it is not listed, we can't sell it."

He turned to a computer savvy friend and employed technology, as Kevin explains:

"This is where Joe came in and played Superman. He developed an Admin Panel that tracks inventory of each flower in real time. It also tracks all the websites in real time (we sell on several of our own websites, E-Bay and Amazon). This Admin Panel automatically pulls a flower off the market when inventory levels fall below a certain level. It also puts up flowers for sale, and offers them in "wholesale lots" when inventory gets above certain levels. It tracks where each sale originates, average sale, running sales information, and MUCH MORE!!"

With the various existing resources retooled for the daylily venture and the process of making each stage of the growing and harvesting season more efficient well underway, it did not take long for the excitement to build. Despite the long hours and hard work the employees are highly motivated with a mission to be the best in class with the goal of exceeding customer's expectation. Though most employees are only hired for the season, they are well trained, highly motivated, and worked very well in any team they are assigned to. Since many are high school and college students, most of them are returning employees for many seasons. Kevin explains:

"Wealways share ourvision of becoming the largest and the best daylily grower with our employees and consistentlypromote team work while doing a lot of extras our competitors would not do. Our work force is always excited and committed because we lead by example. In addition to standard employee benefits, all our employees are well rewarded with a significant amount of DNotes the company purchased for the employees' retirement savings. They areimportant DNotes stakeholders and supporters. They are among Alan's biggest fans."

A highly motivated work force is crucial to accomplishing the company's mission to be the best in class. Management made the commitment of sharing the company's vision with the employees, always stressing the vital importance of great customer satisfaction. The mantra that "We will do things that others won't do, so that one day we can do things others can't do" was often heard. Many of the employees got to experience how the farm evolved from every plant being hand planted, hand harvested and hand washed to the modified equipment making those jobs easier and less labor intensive. Even during the most labor intensive time, every phone call is immediately answered or promptly followed up with a polite callback. Phone calls are still picked up beyond midnight. All sales come with a 100% satisfaction guarantee with full a refund including shipping and handling charges.

Smokeys Gardens went on to acquire five daylily growers within the first five years and ended up with ten separate gardens totaling over 30 acres within a three-mile radius in Ashley, Indiana. As it gained the economy of scale, it lost significant efficiency until it sold the fireplace business and moved to a single 38-acre location in Coldwater, Michigan. The relocation and consolidation took two years. The consolidation into a single location allowed for the entire planting and harvesting process to take full advantage of heavy farm equipment, with drastic improvement in efficiency. It also greatly sped up the fulfillment process to the point that orders are now shipped within 24 hours from the time of order, a touch match for the competitors.

This is a true story of a typical small American farm business. With the right leadership and inspiration many are willing to work tirelessly when their hard work is appreciated as they contribute towards the attainment of common goals. It is not the pay scale, status, education, or intelligence that inspired people to contribute their maximum efforts, but the genuine ownership of shared vision, missions, goals and objectives.

Looking back, I am still in awe as to what Smokeys has accomplished with so little. This is truly a tale of hard work, clear vision, great strategic execution, tenacity and great team work. This is a story of a great American dream come true.

Chapter 15 - The DNotes Story – An Unfolding Big Bold Idea of Global Scale

Introduction:

This is the true story of how DNotes founder Alan Yong's vision, leadership, and winning strategies positioned the organization to best compete in a crowded and chaotic industry at its formative stage. The decentralized, "Wild West" nature of the industry is unforgiving - the lack of regulation, and the inability of centralized authorities to govern the cryptocurrency industry, makes it strategically vital to protect the business against unpredictable market movements. The DNotes story is unique in that a similar situation has not previously existed where so many challenges and uncertainties coincide with a new business startup in a nascent industry.

This chapter will showcase the development and execution of multiple business strategies and principles outlined in this publication. This is the story of a startup that began with a bold global ambition to revolutionize the controversial and well publicized cryptocurrency industry made famous by "Bitcoin"; possibly the greatest technological revolution since the internet.

The intention is to explain why digital currencies matter in the world's rapidly changing economic environment in plain language. It is told by Tim Goggin, ("TeeGee" in the DNotes online community), Community Outreach Director at DNotes, against a backdrop of concern over mounting national debts and the threat of widespread financial crises that have led to growing skepticism of centrally controlled economies and top-down power structures. Cryptocurrencies are a direct response to this social change at a time when people are increasingly connected thanks to widely accessible computing and mobile devices.

Digital currencies, and the "blockchain" technology which underpins them, are perhaps the most effective innovation aimed at promoting equitability of economic growth and opportunity and improved access to essential services globally. It is estimated that more than 2.5 billion people live without basic banking and financial services: digital currencies render the traditional banking mechanisms – which underserve these people – obsolete, bringing financial services within reach of the underbanked and disenfranchised.

The global financial crisis of 2008 was the worst global economic shock since the Great Depression (1929-1939). The unavoidable loss of economic wealth on the heels of a relatively prosperous period led to widespread mistrust of the modern banking system. Many relied on assistance from the US government and were rewarded with the Dodd-Frank Wall Street Reform and Consumer Protection Act (2010), while others increasingly began to view governmental intervention as a band-aid, plastering over years of state policies that enabled and propagated the banking crisis in the first place. If one were to believe the restricted debate in mainstream media, it would seem the crisis was caused by a lack of regulation in the financial sector. I suggest that the mortgage collapse in the lead up to the financial crisis was merely a symptom of government policy, and design flaws inherent to fiat (i.e. government-backed) money creation. Wall Street was the conduit through which these failures were realized. While the detailed causes of the crisis are beyond the scope of this chapter, the debasement of the fiat money supply was a contributing factor that provides some context to what follows.

For the better part of a century, US government fiscal policy and central bankers had been given academic justification by the writings of John Maynard Keynes (1883-1946). Keynes popularized the idea that governments could regulate economic performance with political decisions that would influence consumer demand (spending). By lowering interest rates below the market price, the Federal Reserve was only able to accomplish this "better" economic performance by inflating the money supply. These policy decisions distorted rational consumer behavior and investment decisions. Consumers responded to the policy's incentives by purchasing houses and other commodities that they otherwise would have been unable to afford.

Increasing the money supply and higher government spending are both highly effective ways to boost economic growth indicators in the short term until economic reality forces corrections, known as recessions. It is similar to how hangovers are the inevitable result of drinking; the only variable in outcome is the severity. Continuing to drink may postpone the hangover for a short time, but eventually you must stop drinking and endure the discomfort of recovery.

Global financial models have relied on this 'drunkenness' among the public encouraging them (with low interest rates) to continue borrowing, thus spending more. In this way, governments spurred on economic growth and staved off recession, allowing politicians to claim that the economy remained healthy under their stewardship. But this was merely an illusion; in reality, financial wisdom was traded off for political capital. As with a game of musical chairs, everybody has a great time dancing until the music stops and the last person to sit loses.

Unfortunately, the people who lost the most were the ordinary working and middle classes who only responded rationally to the incentives put before them by decision makers in government and bankers who mostly remained unaffected (or worse, were bailed out using the public purse). The crisis demonstrated that Joe and Jane Six-pack had little control over their financial destiny; in response, a man pseudonymously named "Satoshi Nakamoto" drew the proverbial straw.

"The Times 03/Jan/2009, Chancellor on brink of second bailout for banks." - Satoshi Nakamoto, inventor of Bitcoin.

These words, included and processed in the first transaction by Satoshi Nakamoto via his pioneering payment protocol called "Bitcoin" is where it all began. It is a rhetorical, but polite statement in line with the widespread public mistrust of the modern banking/monetary system and general disapproval of bailouts of those responsible using taxpayer money.

It is said that "necessity is the mother of innovation". Satoshi, convinced that fiat currency was no longer the optimal monetary system, wrote a white paper that would result in the first modern decentralized currency. His 2008 paper "Bitcoin: A Peer-to-Peer Electronic Cash System" made a compelling case for implementing digital currency as a new payment system that would allow any two parties to send payments directly to one another and securely store money without the need for banks or financial services. This innovation opened up the future potential for people to be their own bank, and neither hand over the security of their money to any third party, or pay fees for the privilege. Bitcoin was a proof of concept and it works.

Satoshi's invention was built with maximum security in mind. The Bitcoin network is currently considered "unbreakable", and this gives Bitcoin a significant advantage over credit cards and other forms of electronic funds transfer for payment processing and the movement of money or digital assets.

Not only are digital currency transactions essentially free compared to the merchant and banking fees in the range of 2-4%, but digital currencies do not require their users to send their personal data over the internet. It is commonplace for credit cards to be stolen and unauthorized purchases made online. With digital currencies you can be certain that the payment came from the money's legitimate owner - your identity is protected online. Also there are no risks to businesses of chargebacks which account for, on average, one-percent of all payments made in the USA.

Digital currency enables efficiency, reduces cost, and increases profit margins for small businesses. It should not come as any surprise that Alan Yong and I believe that digital currencies are crucial to improving small business bottom line and survival rates. The cost savings and other benefits, including gaining a competitive edge, are significant.

Perhaps the greatest benefit of Satoshi's creation is the algorithmic money creation process. The predetermined increase in a digital currency's money supply controlled by the network itself can protect users' savings by preventing inflation by any third party – (government or bank) – which uses discretional tools such as "Quantitative Easing" to affect money available for loans. The decentralized nature of the network meant that money was no longer held in the hands of a few large banks, nullifying the ability of central banks to influence the demand for money by manipulating interest rates.

While the market does operate cyclically, and market movements will naturally sometimes overvalue assets, the severity of any potential bubbles will not be fueled by monetary stimulus nor backstopped by governments that destroy the incentive for due diligence by financial institutions. Digital currency's algorithmic money creation process is the solution to the fiat money creation problem.

Contingent to this is the invention of the blockchain, the verification technology which underpins Bitcoin and perhaps the most important technical innovation. The Blockchain, a series of immutable transaction records ('blocks') associated with a particular 'coin' which must bear a very specific mathematical relationship with the previous 'block', even has utility far beyond capital transfer. This technology has massive implications for any field in which the verification of transactions plays a role, and has already led to numerous viable business opportunities and innovations.

Bitcoin was the first of many peer-to-peer digital currencies that would allow the transfer of capital directly between two people. The fact that it can do so instantly, for anybody, anywhere in the world at nearly zero cost makes it an incredibly valuable asset for the benefit of humanity. This caught attention of the DNotes founder Alan Yong, and by late 2013, when the value of the Bitcoin network exceeded US$10 billion at one time the rest of the world took notice as well.

Bitcoin's dramatic rise in value inspired a proliferation of copycat currencies which essentially reinvented the wheel, with, at best, marginal improvements enabling their creators to also get in on ground level investments. Over time, the industry's unprecedented earning potential and relative immunity from interference by governments struggling to catch up, caught the attention of bad actors.

The digital currency industry quickly became littered with scam currencies and predatory speculators manipulating the attractiveness of currencies in elaborate pump-and-dump schemes (the so-called "whales"). It became difficult to sort out legitimate investments from get-rich-quick schemes causing confusion for serious investors and concern for regulators. This resulted in negative headlines for the industry in the mainstream media, which naively failed to recognize the far-reaching societal and economic potential of what they were reporting on.

Blockchain has many potential applications where immutably time-stamped bookkeeping of any activity or asset transfer is of great value for verification, publicly or privately. Essentially, blockchain provides an undisputable audit trail of irreversible records. This poses serious threats to various industries faced with the need to innovate or else decline and has already stimulated the creation of many new startups with viable business models.

Digital currency is a once in a generation opportunity that will catalyze a multitude of new jobs and wealth over the next several decades. Many startups will have the chance to participate, but few will succeed without a clear vision and sound strategic plans that are successfully executed over a sustained period. However, being a social-economic movement, rather than a typical business, it also requires strong leadership to inspire and build communities of passionate supporters dedicated to long-term organizational objectives aligned to be mutually beneficial to everyone.

This leads us to the introduction of DNotes.

Following several months of meticulous analysis, the DNotes founding team concluded that the incipient digital currency phenomena would likely be the beginning of the next greatest technology revolution since the internet. Their forecast was that the decentralized payments technology would be the ultimate disruptor to banking and financial services systems worldwide. The lack of business expertise and experience in bringing forward new technology to the mainstream present in the industry did not escape their notice. Convinced they had a massive competitive advantage in mapping out and effectively executing crucial winning strategies, DNotes was launched on February 18, 2014.

DNotes is a Bitcoin alternative digital currency, built from the ground up to succeed where Bitcoin has been struggling. It is designed to exploit the strengths of Bitcoin and overcome the baggage that has discouraged Bitcoin's popular mass acceptance. The DNotes vision is to build DNotes as a trusted global digital currency to supplement national fiat currencies in global commerce by simplifying its use so that anybody in the world can participate. In order to minimize industry threats and be in the best position to succeed, DNotes has been created within and alongside its own business ecosystem.

As Alan Yong recalled he had just completed a seven-year project to help Smokeys Daylily Gardens from its beginning to become one of the largest daylily growers in the world:

"I was looking forward to enjoying retirement and spending more time with my family. Initially, I was very skeptical if I would even invest my 'lunch money' in an industry that seemed to be dominated by bad actors, fraud, and hostile communities. As a favor to an old friend, Joe, who had worked very hard with me at Smokeys, I agreed to take a serious look at Bitcoin and any potential business opportunities with a commitment to at least give him some advice.

It took me a while to catch on - but it became clear to me that digital currency had fundamentally transformed every aspect of money with built-in capabilities to be far superior to fiat currency. It is much like a precious rough diamond left to be recognized and treasured.

There will be many challenges to overcome. I thrive on big challenges; big bold ideas or problems that demand exceptional strategic thinking and execution. That was how I got hooked. In order to come up with a clear vision, I must first gain a very deep knowledge of the industry so that we can be in the position to develop winning strategies and build an organization that others can not replicate."

In any major emerging industry or technology, pioneers and early adopters are always confronted with significant challenges. These obstacles may include a variety of unknowns, unproven technologies, untested assumptions, and commercial hostility. Furthermore, technologies always evolve over a period of time. While there are first-mover advantages such as name recognition and network effects, being a true pioneer in any industry can also come with the excessive and unpredictable costs of navigating unknown territory.

Bitcoin is a truly decentralized and leaderless system. There are no centralized controllers or coordinators. Some have referred to the Bitcoin snag as a new experiment with some level of frustration and struggle being unavoidable, having more than the normal growing pains typical of other new technologies.

In essence, a fledgling and leaderless industry has emerged and now seeks to challenge the most powerful incumbents in the world's monetary power structures. It is fair to assume that there will be forceful pushback and multiple attempts to slow the impending threat. This has already been observed in anti-cryptocurrency regulations, banks refusing services to cryptocurrency firms, and even creating their own blockchain technology.

This problem is further compounded by competing parties promoting different agendas, making this the most controversial and well-publicized technology revolution in recent memory. In any case, it can take up to decades for new technologies to gain mass acceptance by the general population. There are many examples; such as personal computers, the Internet, online banking, and more recently, mobile devices.

There will remain resistance, reluctance, and doubt for many years. And the costs of mistakes to first-movers are significant. Consequently, strategic positioning is wiser than simply jumping in to join the party with costly attempts to develop speculative applications without viable commercial use cases. Instead, the DNotes team and its communities have focused on creating strategic units as the foundation of its own ecosystem while building a trusted brand.

Naturally, the main incumbents who face the most disruption from this new technology - banks, credit and debit card processors, and providers of other financial services - were instinctively dismissive of the early growing threat of digital currency. Fast forward a few years and these players have back-pedaled to pursue their own version of the blockchain technology – "permissioned blockchain" - a reduced and stripped down version that provides only a few of the advantages that unrestricted digital currency offers. Permissioned blockchain preserves incumbent revenue streams only possible with centralized monetary systems by blocking the advancement of more efficient and cheaper systems.

Although permissioned blockchain does not take full advantage of all the original features, the DNotes team has recognized that this development should not be underestimated. We believe that the better strategy is for DNotes to offer a full array of financial services in cooperation with partner banks worldwide, than to work against them. Global collaboration for mutual benefit is the key to progress.

It is vital to gain an up-to-date and clear understanding of the complexities and the dynamics of an industry at its formative stage. As the vision is refined, sound knowledge is of paramount importance for the formulation of great strategies in its pursuit. Alan went on to explain:

"In reality, one can only start with a general vision at such an early stage. Many issues are unsettled, with constantly moving targets. Nonetheless, it is important to be able to

articulate your sense of direction or vision as to where you want to lead your organization with the benefits of new information."

Instead of joining an increasingly crowded industry as a "me too", DNotes decided to take a very different route, creating a long-term vision that could take decades to accomplish in its entirety. The decision to develop and deploy all the ecosystems necessary to achieve DNotes' core goals and objectives of building a globally accepted digital currency is one such example.

The team made the strategic decision to remain lean and nimble by self funding our projects during the formative years: an agile development method often not possible once others' money has been taken to grow. Carefully thought out strategic positioning, using highly scalable building blocks, is incorporated as a part of our tool kit. We build each component of our infrastructure block by block, analyze where we're at, adjust if necessary, and continue building.

"I strongly believe that success in fast-paced industries like ours comes to the swift, to the agile, to those able to respond to the industry's ever-changing demands, and the relentless pursuit of innovation. As you can imagine this approach combined with some hefty goals can only be accomplished with dedicated commitment over a long period of time." - Alan Yong

I have observed, supported, and acquired DNotes since its launch in February 2014. Throughout this time, I have read every post at the forum. I have listened to, and absorbed Alan's consistent message about what the goal is, where we're at, and where we are heading next. One by one I watched those plans come to fruition in his favored "block-by-block" manner.

Alan is a leader who toils to ensure his team and the communities are onboard with his vision, values, and philosophy with consistent communication; he reminds us of the meaning and purpose of what we are working for. Alan has taken DNotes in a different strategic direction from the "me-too" in the industry. When analytical pioneering entrepreneurs like Alan look at a sea of opportunities, they look to the future when payoff potential is not patently clear. Market conditions are not constant phenomena, and Alan is building business strategies that will flourish under a likely different set of environmental factors. For Alan, DNotes is to lead, and not to follow others.

What has impressed me the most is how DNotes differentiates itself from the rest of the industry.

Looking around at the cryptocurrency industry, DNotes' competitors seem to behave in an impractical and idealistic universe of their own. They are trapped in the belief that enhancing the technical aspects of their currency is key, rather than improving the 'usefulness' of the currency as money itself. With a background in economics this approach was obvious to me as meaningless and cosmetic - like the government releasing banknotes in a new color. It might look new, but it doesn't improve money in any meaningful way (in fact, the inflation from printing it would probably even slightly devalue it). Bitcoin and the blockchain are revolutionary because they improve the durability, portability, fungibility, scarcity, and divisibility of money.

DNotes recognizes these improvements in the characteristics of money; however, we contend that focusing on upgrades to our currency beyond these characteristics is not an efficient use of our resources at the formative stage. We are focused on bringing digital currency to the mainstream. To do this, digital currency must first meet all of the key functions of money - to be a unit of account, a store of value, and a medium of exchange.

Digital currencies are excellent mediums of exchange, and will make for a great unit of account for mainstream use. They remain, however, volatile due to low market liquidity. Until digital currency better acts as a safe store of value, people won't want to hold onto it for fear of devaluation. Technological advancements that neither improve the characteristics or functions of money should therefore be considered a secondary concern to the creation of a currency with ongoing relevance in the future as anything more than a trading instrument for speculators.

DNotes' leadership has always been very respectful and appreciative of the community's suggestions and contributions. Together our community actively identified and recommended solutions to industry challenges and problems. The best of these ideas were promptly responded to with the creation of community projects. I specifically recall one member highlighting the industry's divide in gender participation - with males outnumbering females ten-to-one in what will be one of the biggest markets for future wealth creation. A few weeks later CryptoMoms was launched as a community to help women get in at the ground level.

In late 2014 team member Cindy Williamson ("Chase" in the DNotes online community) proposed trust accounts for children in cryptocurrency. This idea allowed people to save and use cryptocurrency as "money", and a key component of encouraging adoption is to enable participants to use their money in the same ways that they have always been accustomed to previously. With the usefulness of our currency, and the future in mind, we released an offering of CRISPs (Cryptocurrency Investment Savings Plans) including trust funds, retirement plans, charity accounts, student services and employee benefits.

There is something special about DNotes. It is built with a clear vision and passionately supported by a community committed to building a new world with better financial inclusion and opportunities for all to advance up the socio-economic ladder. This extends all the way to developing nations, where a low-cost decentralized payment network utilizing mobile phones and DNotes can service the billions of unbanked worldwide in countries where establishment banks are largely only patronized by the local elites.

What has DNotes been doing differently?

1. Culture

In consideration of the fragmented, chaotic, and insular nature of our industry, where users often prefer anonymity that often resulted in aggressive online disagreements, DNotes began bycreating a culture of mutual respect and cooperation. This resulted in a productive and rewarding community atmosphere that many characterized as "refreshing". Every new member is promptly welcomed and all questions are respectfully answered. DNotes is respected as a mature community, and a currency with a purpose. This team-work made it possible for DNotes to establish the beginnings of its ecosystem system without outside funding. It is quite a remarkable accomplishment for anyone who knows what it takes.

2. A Trusted Brand

With a great sense of direction, coupled with a well defined mission, and a clear vision early, DNotes has built a trusted brand by being engaging, appreciative, and respectful. We highly value the support and confidence of our communities as well as that of our stakeholders and supporters. Our commitments have always been to follow through with all our stated plans and goals. We have built a proven track record of doing so. Trust is invaluable in financial services, which will account for a significant part of DNotes' future growth.

DNotes' leadership has always been responsive, transparent, and trustworthy; committed to building a purposeful currency focusing on educating and benefiting the largest population possible. Outside of Bitcoin, DNotes is among the most publicized digital currencies in the industry.

3. **Dedicated Long Term Commitment**

The DNotes team and many of its stakeholders are long term investors. The vast majority of them are net buyers investing for the long term. Our goal is to make DNotes the first currency to fulfill money's requirement as a store of value. Unfortunately, trading bots including a few likely operated by some exchanges [market operators] are making price stability nearly impossible to achieve in the short-term. That said, high volatilities are not a great concern until we start promoting DNotes as a medium of exchange. By then, we believe that other mechanisms will be in place to address the issue.

4. **Women's Full Participation - CryptoMoms**

DNotes is committed to encourage and assist women's participation in the digital currency space. According to Forbes magazine, women account for 70 to 80% of household spending and half the population. However, the female population todayrepresents just one in ten of the industry participants. We created CryptoMoms as a community to help remedy this underwhelming participation. CryptoMoms has been well received, reaching more than 20,000 registered members in its first two years. A lot more will be done to assist female participation in the market and women's small businesses using DNotes.

5. **Saving for the Future – CRISP**

"It is not how big the project is at launch, but how well positioned it is for global expansion at the appropriate time." Alan often reminded us.

Our family of CRISPs for children, students, employees and retirees is designed to fulfill our mission to make DNotes' ecosystem available for everyone worldwide to participate. We believe that disciplined long term savings, done on a regular basis, is a good thing for everyone. Our job is to provide for the convenience, safety, and long term appreciating value of DNotes. Consequently, DNotes is managed as a business, but not controlled as one. The CRISP plans have been launched as pilot programs for second stage development that can be scaled up quickly.

6. **DNotesVault**

DNotesVault is a significant accomplishment that is difficult for its competitors to replicate. It demonstrates the mantra of DNotes' willingness to go the extra mile of *"doing things that others will not do, so that one day it gains the advantage to do things that others can not do."* (Alan Yong)

DNotesVault is one of the major steps to positioning the digital currency as money. While it does not sell or trade DNotes, the vault is set up like a bank with comparable convenience and ease of use. It is easier to set up an account at the DNotesVault than it is to set up a bank account. DNotes can be conveniently sent to an email or a DNotes deposit address. Account holders also have the option of scheduled payments or "timed released" over a user defined period of time with specified amounts.

As the industry first, it also serves as the home of "CRISPs" a family of digital currency savings plans for children, students, employees, and others interested in saving for their retirement. Above all, the deposits are securely stored off-line and backed by 100% verifiable matching funds stored in other locations.

DNotesVault is a prime example of the incorporation of multiple viable solutions to overcome known problems typical of an emerging industry. We strongly believe that to gain mass acceptance of digital currency it must meet or exceed the full functions of money along with providing ease of use and secure storage solutions. It must also be conveniently available for everyone worldwide to participate, without barriers, for small savers. Above all, it must earn the privilege of a trusted brand.

7. DCEBrief

The latest addition to our ecosystem - DCEBrief was created in response to digital currencies biased and misunderstood reporting in mainstream media. The site provides objective and unbiased news on the latest developments in our industry with articles written by journalists who specialize in blockchain and digital currency. The target markets are busy executives, business owners, philanthropists, regulators, and other decision-makers to help them understand the digital currency environment. Due to the busy nature of the website's readership, all articles are packaged into "executive summary" format without fluff or filler.

8. A Book for Small Business Owners and Startups

Alan has always been very passionate about helping struggling small business owners having lent his business expertise to many entrepreneurs in the capacity as a small business consultant for more than a decade. As a community, we are often inspired with respect for his business experience and strong leadership as reflected in the management of DNotes.

Consequently, we have often encouraged him to write a book one day.

This book is a key foundation block to our ecosystem. It will serve as a launching pad for funding upcoming projects and further development. Equally important is the opportunity for DNotes to connect with small business owners and their employees. I believe that this book will be of great inspiration and help to entrepreneurs.

Furthermore, I trust that this book will also help to promote our CRISP for Retirement and Employee Incentive Benefit programs which will greatly benefit business owners and their employees. Additionally, this chapter will help spread the word and recognition about DNotes, piquing the interest of potential stakeholders. We are proud to have assisted Alan in an editing capacity and in the writing of the DNotes story.

9. Integrated Private Company

Although DNotes is managed as a business, it is not controlled like one. Being a decentralized autonomous organization, the DNotes currency is owned by its entire group of stakeholders on an "at will" basis. Any stakeholder can change ownership at will without notice. We have taken this ownership structure one step further by owning up to a 25% stake of the equity in the privately held for-profit company, DNotes Global, Inc., incorporated in the State of Delaware, USA. By extension, all of DNotes stakeholders have an ownership stake in DNotes Global, Inc.

This company does not control the currency itself. However, among others plans, the company will help to develop and fund our growing ecosystem and projects that are going to be essential in taking DNotes to the next level; to become the dominant digital currency leading to mass global acceptance. Extending the company equity to currency holders is expected to provide significant fundamental and intrinsic value to the currency as the company expands.

Leaderless organizations can be a big hurdle to ongoing development. This has been witnessed in Bitcoin's community in solving the issue concerning the maximum number of transactions its network can handle simultaneously. We see the potential of chaos and impotence as an inherent weakness of decentralized systems that forego leadership. This risk can be minimized with the presence of a group of developing stakeholders who have sufficient self-interest to help protect and promote the organization.

Alan Yong

Digital currency and the blockchain are the best opportunity in a generation to invest in the future from the ground floor. The next several years will be pivotal to DNotes' rise to preeminence in the financial technology industry. Upon release of this book, Alan and the team will switch into the next phase from planning to execution of technology development. The last two and a half years have been spent carefully analyzing market and consumer behavior, working on our value proposition, building critical infrastructures, and waiting to spring forward at the most opportune moment. We are confident that we will dominate the industry swiftly when we are ready. This book serves to throw the gauntlet in our self-imposed challenge.

Arnold H. Glasow probably said it best when he said *"Success is simple. Do what's right, the right way, at the right time."* DNotes is focused on exploiting its competitive advantages at the most opportune time.

Made in the USA
Columbia, SC
12 February 2018